THOSE WHO SAW THE SUN:

AFRICAN AMERICAN
ORAL HISTORIES
FROM THE
JIM CROW SOUTH

THOSE WHO SAW THE SUN:

African American Oral Histories from the Jim Crow South

JAHA NAILAH AVERY

Montclair | Amsterdam | Hoboken

This is an Arthur A. Levine book
Published by Levine Querido

www.levinequerido.com · info@levinequerido.com
Levine Querido is distributed by Chronicle Books, LLC
Copyright © 2023 by Jaha Nailah Avery

Library of Congress Control Number: 2022945161

ISBN 978-1-64614-244-6
Printed and bound in India

Published in June 2023
First Printing

To my grandparents, Reverend Nilous McKinley and Mrs. Christine Watson Avery,
who taught me about life, love, and literature.
Y'all will always be my heroes. I'll see you in the morning.

TABLE OF CONTENTS

INTRODUCTION

"When an elder dies, a library burns."

African proverb

I was born in Asheville, North Carolina, and was raised primarily by my grandparents. This meant that my world was full of things loved by Southern African American elders. For over two decades, I accompanied my grandparents to country buffets all over the South, watching them pour packets of sugar into white ceramic cups of steaming coffee—the kinds of cups that those lovely little places are known for.

We'd meet up with Deacon and Mrs. Splawn from church, and share a meal at Shoney's. Or, we'd head to J&S Cafeteria for Sunday dinner, where half of Black Asheville would stop by our table to extend their greetings to Reverend and Mrs. Avery (and me). When Aunt Elsie and Uncle Curt would come to town, Bojangles was the preferred fare, eating inside next to the window so we could observe the comings and goings of the town before us. And always, I was there: my grandparents' tiny companion. I knew better than to get into "grown folks business," so as they talked, I would busy myself with coloring, reading, or, later, my cell phone. But I was always listening.

I listened to my grandparents and their friends tell stories of their youth, stories of festivals and parties long since past, stories of what had happened at church on a given day decades prior, and various others. Some stories were steeped in humor, some tinged with disbelief, others told solemnly. There were many that I could relate to, like the stories my grandmother told about growing up on a farm, and playing outdoors with her siblings. I didn't know what the words *sharecropping* or *debt* meant at the time, but I definitely understood "hide and seek."

My granddaddy loved telling the story of how nervous he had been to go to my grandmother's father and ask for her hand in marriage. I could just see the two of them, young and in love, graduates of Shaw University in Raleigh, NC, excited about building their lives together. Whenever he would talk about those days, my granddaddy would beam and laugh, and he'd have the whole room smiling along with him.

Then, there were the stories that I couldn't understand. They were stories about a world that no longer existed, a world that was hard for me to even imagine. It was ruled by somebody named Jim Crow. In these stories, my grandparents had to jump off the sidewalk when a white person walked by. In these stories, when my grandmother visited the Ambassador Theater in Raleigh as a college student, she had to sit in the balcony because Black folks weren't allowed on the ground level. These stories saw my family placed under police protection in the sixties because of their work in the Civil Rights Movement, while evil people placed bombs under their cars to stop them from protesting.

I couldn't imagine anyone seeing my grandparents as something other than what I knew them to be: kind, generous, exceedingly intelligent, brave, highly capable people. Racism, at its core, is nonsensical. And so, as a young girl, I struggled to make sense of the senseless. Why had my grandparents been treated that way?

My grandmother passed away in 2011. It occurred to me then that, if my family hadn't been listening to her stories and her life advice, it would have been gone forever. I realized then the importance of documenting the things that seem ordinary to us, because one day, our "ordinary" will be "history" to someone else. Someone yet to be born will look back and wonder, "What was it like?"

This is especially true for African Americans, because for centuries in this country, we were not able to document and preserve our own stories. Our ancestors were brought to America in chains, torn from their native land, languages, and communities. Forbidden from learning to read or write, they did what they had to do to survive American slavery. I realized how privileged I was to be living in a time where I can read and write, seek higher education, and speak the truth about my own experiences. So, I decided to use that privilege to do what so many generations of African Americans could not: tell the truth about history.

Following my grandmother's death, I interviewed my granddaddy and several of my elderly family members. I interviewed people from church. I interviewed elders that I knew in the community. I interviewed for no other reason than to collect and preserve the wisdom of the elders. I'd do interviews here and there, nothing too structured or scheduled. It was something I did in my spare time, and I enjoyed hearing people talk about their lives. I started out asking the same questions of everyone to start, and I'd modify the questions asked later in the interviews, depending on what they said.

Years later, when I connected with Nick Thomas at Levine Querido and started working on this book in earnest, I realized something very peculiar that I had only half-understood earlier: a lot of African American elders didn't want to talk about the past. I had heard of similar sentiments before—from elders whose grandparents or great-grandparents simply refused to discuss what their lives were like during slavery.

In my search for people to speak with for this book, many potential interviewees told me that they'd rather not bring history up. A 95-year-old elder in South Carolina said, "It's best not to drum up the past. Let it lay." An 87-year-old elder in Louisiana told me to "leave those old days alone." I had many people agree to the interview at first, then call me back days later to withdraw. One person, an 81-year-old in Georgia, actually stopped me mid-interview, right after I'd asked the question: "Did you know anyone who was lynched?" Apologetically, she told me that she wouldn't be going forward with her participation. "Turns out, this is all just too much for this old girl," she remarked, before hanging up. For many African American elders, the past is just too painful to revisit.

But here are two major lessons that this process taught me as a writer and oral history curator:

One, don't interview anyone who isn't excited to participate and eager to share their story.

Two, the right people will come. And when they do, their contributions will be more extraordinary than anyone could have ever imagined.

I met Mr. Walt Carr at Inkwell Beach on Martha's Vineyard and I just sensed that he had an incredible story to tell. Ms. Johnnie Booker and I are both members of Delta Sigma Theta Sorority, Inc., and we were introduced by our Soror, Muriel Buck-Evans. Her confident, commanding presence told me instantly that she would make a compelling interviewee. I met Ms. Florence Hayes while visiting Fisk University with my family. (Whenever we travel, we visit local HBCUs and support the campus bookstore by buying school apparel.) I stopped her to ask for directions to the bookstore, and her warmth was a signal to me that she would be a wonderful person to interview. While working on a project about African American land ownership in the Black Belt of Alabama, I met Mrs. Leola Joe. When I spoke with her about my efforts for this book, she said, "Oh, you need to talk to my pastor!" And that's how I met the bold, self-assured Reverend John Kennard. These are just a few examples of how all the right people came!

We all know Dr. King, Rosa Parks, Angela Davis, and many others whose names have gone down in history. But there are people walking among us who were leaders, too . . . heroes, too. It took an abundance of courage to survive Jim Crow, and even more to actively participate in the Civil Rights Movement and other efforts to secure rights and opportunities for African American people. This book uplifts the lives and experiences of people that we haven't yet heard about. And there are countless more out there.

Who are the people that you're walking alongside every day? They have stories, too. If not documented, those stories will be lost. I encourage you, dear reader, to start interviewing your family members, community members, teachers, mentors, and everyone in between. Preserve their experiences, because there's nothing like hearing somebody's story in their own words. Don't wait for others to tell it.

The title of this book comes from the Bible verse, Ecclesiastes 7:11 (NIV): "Wisdom, like an inheritance, is a good thing, and benefits those who see the sun." The people who have entrusted all of us with these stories have given us something very valuable: their wisdom, knowledge, and life lessons.

Most of the photos included with each interview come from each elder's personal collection, and a few are drawn from archival materials to illustrate some of the interview themes. The appendix at the back of the book offers more detail on various topics, and can be used as a starting point for further research.

Since 1619, people of African descent in this country have suffered some of the most horrifying abuses known to mankind. But the African American story is ultimately one of beauty and joy, and the fact that we are still here—living, loving, *thriving*—is nothing short of miraculous. The memories held within these pages are a testament to that miracle. I hope you are as empowered by these accounts as I am.

A young Clotie (center) with her sisters, brother, and uncle.

INTERVIEW NO. 1

CLOTIE GRAVES

W*here were you born and what was your home/community like?*

I was born right in the spot where I'm living now, Clinton, Mississippi. On the same land. Ten miles west of Jackson.

We live in the country. We lived on my grandparents' property that they bought in 1908. It was called the Mount Hood community. My dad had built a house. His part of the house was a two-bedroom shotgun-type house. There was a bedroom and kitchen, and that was it. And then he later added on two more bedrooms, a larger kitchen, and dining area. A woodframe house with a roof and siding on it.

Mom and Dad had eight children. Two boys and six girls. I fell in the middle, I'm the middle child. My family is a unique family situation because my father married this lady. She was a young lady named Rose Daggers. They had one daughter named Virginia. My older sister, Virginia. And Rose died when Virginia was three years old, of cancer.

My mother was married. This guy, she married a man named Excel Russell. Excel got killed in a truck accident around the time my father's wife died of cancer. And Mama was left with. . . . Excel had a son named Tony. And she was pregnant with Excel Junior when her husband got killed in the truck accident. He was riding on the back of a truck, and the truck turned over. And he was killed. So that left my mother pregnant with one child and she already had one child.

That one, the child that she was pregnant with, lived to be two years old, and then he died from pneumonia. And so when my mom and dad got together, Mama had one son, Tony, and Daddy had the one daughter. So that's the first two sets of children. And then they got married. They were married—Daddy said four years—and then they had my sister Gladys and then my sister Amy. And then I came. I'm the third child, but I'm really the fourth girl. And then my sister Edith and my sister Ann. That's six girls. And then they finally had another boy. Mama and Daddy had five girls and then they had one boy. And the other two kids that they brought into the marriage made eight of us.

Both of my parents' spouses died young. They were in their twenties. They died young, but if they hadn't, we wouldn't have come on this earth.

What did your parents do?

My father was a farmer and worked at O. R. Johnson Milling Company in Clinton. That's a company that made cornmeal. They also made horse and cow food from the corn, and that kind of stuff. My daddy ran one of those machines, that's all I know. I have heard him say he would have to hold the sack as the mill or the feed would come out of the processing machine; he would hold it and fill it up, then put it under the machine where it was sewed up and closed. That was full-time. Eight hours a day at the mill. He would get up in the morning time and go to the field too. We had three acres of cotton. Two acres was on the white folks' land that he'd lease, and then we had one acre on our land. We had 10 acres of land that my grandparents had bought. So he'd get up and work in the field in the morning before he'd go to work, then come back in the evening time and go back to the field and work. And he did that five days a week.

We had what he called a truck patch. A truck patch is something larger than a garden. It's like a whole field of vegetables that he raised. And so on Friday night, we would have to pick all the vegetables, then on Saturday mornings, we'd shell the peas and butter beans and measure them out so we could sell them by the quart. Then we would go to Jackson and he would walk the streets selling vegetables to the white people. And, of course, we always had to go to the back door, you couldn't go to the front door. We always had to go to the back in those days. Blacks could not go to the front door of anybody's house. And he would sell those vegetables, and the amazing part about that, he would make more money selling those vegetables on Saturdays than he would make working eight hours a day for five days at the milling company. Sure would.

He worked every day to take care of all of us. On Sundays, he was like the Uber driver. A lot of people didn't have cars. He always had a car. And on Sundays, he would carry people to visit family members up in the Delta, up to the prison system, wherever. He'd drive people to church. . . . He just worked nonstop.

My mom was a housekeeper and raised all of us. She had this one white lady, that she knew as she was growing up, I think, that would come maybe once a month and get her to go work for her for about two hours, and then she'd ride her back home. Other than that, her job was to raise us. Daddy didn't want her to have to do anything but raise all of us.

You said that your grandparents were able to purchase 10 acres of land that y'all lived on? Do you know how they were able to purchase that land?

Yes. My daddy . . . this was my daddy's parents. William Robinson and Avis Dar-rages. They had a son named Rafe, and he married Julia. And these are my grand-parents, now. They're the ones that bought the property. My grandmother, they said, ironed clothes for all of the white folk. That's what she did, ironed clothes. And my granddaddy was a farmer. And once he got the land, that's what he was doing. I don't know how they saved the money. But they said my grandmother Julia paid most of that money to buy this land. And the land was what they call landlocked, when you don't have no frontage at all. And it was 10 acres. And so the white people sold it to her because it was landlocked and they figured it would never be worth anything. And that's how they bought it. She ironed clothes: washing and ironing for the white families to raise the money to buy this land.

Y'all had the 10 acres but then your dad also worked on white people's land as well. But y'all lived on your land right?

My dad leased two acres of land from the man that owned the milling company, and raised cotton. We never had over three acres of cotton.

I'm wondering why he would go and lease land from people when y'all had 10 acres yourselves.

That's what I don't know. I don't know why he did that. But like I said, he was farming it, our land, he was using it to raise the vegetables on. And you know back in those days, cotton was just a going thing. I guess he just wanted to have some cotton. But after some time, he realized that there was more money in the vegetables than in the cotton. Because see, with three acres of land, he might would get three bales of cotton. The first acre of cotton that we got went to the man for leasing the two acres. It went to the white guy, Mr. Johnson. Anything else that the land produced went to him [my father]. It was a business arrangement.

Most of the time, he would get about a bale per acre. So he would clear two acres of cotton, two bales of cotton. Do you know what bales of cotton look like? Big old things.

We really weren't sharecropping in the traditional sense. Everybody else around here was sharecropping, living on the white man's place. And they never were able to work out of debt with those white people. Because they made sure they kept them year after year, not being able to pay off their debt. We were the ones that were not doing it like that.

I was speaking to somebody else. She was actually raised in Alabama. And like y'all, they also own their land. And she was telling me that, in school, she would be one of the only people that would be able to stay in school the whole year, because the sharecroppers' kids had to leave school to bring in the harvest. Was it the same for your classmates?

They would, that's true. And then, see, this is the thing. The cotton gets ready in the fall. We would all stay out of school, sharecropping or not, maybe the first two months that school would start back. Because we would have to pick the cotton and get the cotton from those three acres that we had. But we would always get back to school, though, before the kids that were in a sharecropping situation because they had more cotton to pick than we did. So, we would miss school because we were trying to get it in before the rain started.

September and October were the months that we would be out. Only time that we would go to school during those months is when it would rain. Because it would be too wet to pick. The sharecropping kids, everybody. Okay. And we'd miss the first part of school, but we would always catch up.

It's interesting that your lives revolved around cotton in a way.

It did. Mmhmm. Even though we weren't living on a white man's place, cotton was a way for us to make money.

What was school like for you? Did you enjoy it?

Loved it! I loved it until my fourth grade year, when I had a new teacher. My first grade year, in the community, we had a Rosenwald School. Rosenwald schools were started by—you heard of Sears and Roebuck, right? Well, Booker T. Washington and the Sears and Roebuck guy, with his money, set up what they called Rosenwald schools within the community. The school that I went to was called Mount Hood. It was a church building that they put the school in. Black folks, we didn't have schools built specifically for us at that time. I was born in '46, and I guess I started school in '51. So it wasn't that long ago.

It was grades one through eight in the same room, but at different tables. So it was a community school, and we had one teacher that taught grades one through eight. I only went to that school for one year. By my second grade year, they closed the church school down and moved us to the public school in the city of Clinton named Sumner Hill. And that was first through tenth grade.

Why did the school close?

Rosenwald schools were put in the churches. The county, or the state I guess, was putting some money into [public] schools for educational purposes, to educate Blacks. But we didn't have the nice schools and stuff like the whites did. So they decided they would consolidate schools in this area and put us all in one school. That's when they moved us to Sumner Hill.

What was your favorite subject in school?

History. It was history and science!

Were you and all of your siblings able to finish school?

Yes. My mom and dad, they had one goal: every last one of us had to finish high school. And all of us did. And all of us went to college, except three. The three older ones didn't go to college, but they were able to get training in special fields.

Were your parents able to finish school?

My dad finished sixth grade. And my mom finished eighth grade. And see, back during that time, if you had an eighth grade education, you could teach school. So my mom taught school for a while until she had all of us. Then she started just raising us.

After all of us were out of high school, Mama went back to get her GED, and then her high school diploma. And she was so proud! And we were proud of her, too.

As a little kid, were you aware of any unwritten rules that governed race relations in your area?

Oh, yeah. You had to be. You knew it was strictly separate and not equal, in everything. Some rules were written, but they were all taught to you. And your parents made sure you understood. Like, if a white person was coming through the door and you were getting ready to go through the door, you had to back back and let them go. I remember once, my mom was in line in a department store in Jackson, getting ready to pay. We had been standing on the line, and she was the next person on the line to pay. And this white person just walked up there, and she had to step back and let the white person pay. And I couldn't understand that. I said, "Mama why you back up?" And she said, "Just be quiet." So then, when we got to the car, she told me that she had to do it and why.

I remember once, I asked my daddy, I said "Daddy, why?" You know, I got to the point when I was about 14 or 15, after I'd heard about Emmett Till and a lot of other things, I couldn't figure out why everything we did, the white man decided for us. If it was something going on in the world, in the city, the white man's going to do this, the white man's going to do that. So I said, "Daddy, why is it that the white man makes all the decisions for us?" And he said, "That's just the way it is, Clo. And we just have to deal with it." And that's what he said. So I left it alone. But I couldn't figure that out.

Then, I realized the issue was we couldn't vote. They could not vote. We didn't have the right to vote.

So when you were a kid, Black people couldn't vote at all?

Oh no, no. My goodness! Didn't get the right to vote until . . . whew . . . Medgar Evers came on the scene and started registering people to vote, then the Voting Rights Act passed, Lyndon Johnson . . . President Johnson. . . . I was out of high school by then.

Did people talk about wanting to vote or show interest in wanting to vote then?

They wanted to, but if you went down there and voted, see they had these unspoken rules for you. First of all, you had to pay what they called a poll tax just to try to get a chance to vote. And then, when you tried to vote, they'd ask you these awful questions. Now, they wouldn't do it to the whites, just the Blacks. Like, "How far do you have to walk before you strike a sweat?" Now, you know don't nobody know the answer to that. Or, "How many bubbles are in a bar of soap?" That's how they disqualified us to vote. It was just old crazy stuff like that.

Did people try? Do you remember people trying to go and vote?

They tried. They would try, but they would make sure they failed every time. And wouldn't let them vote. I don't remember my parents trying to vote, but I know my grandfather did. He was voting in 1871 after Reconstruction. After the Civil War, during the Reconstruction era. They literally, him and his brother, were voting right here in Hinds County. They had been slaves, but during Reconstruction they were voting, able to vote. And then, of course, they put Jim Crow laws in place to take away our voting rights and all that.

But yeah, my grandfather was voting. We have proof that he voted in two elections. They had senators, and we have not been able to get a Black senator in Hinds County since. Well, in Hinds County, we had this Black senator, and my grandfather voted in the election that elected him to the Senate seat. And then, white people, they had a riot here in Clinton. It was 1877 or something like that [author's note: The year was 1875, and the senator was Charles Caldwell]. The state had elected this Black guy here in Hinds County, in the state of Mississippi. And the white people had a picnic; that's what they called it officially. They wanted to kill the Blacks because they were making progress during Reconstruction.

So here in Clinton, they invited them to have something like a political rally, and they told them they were going to have food and all, and told them to come. But it was a setup to kill the Blacks here in the city. Well, the Blacks did go, but they took their guns, too. Well, history shows that 50 Blacks were killed, and the Blacks killed five of them. But looking at how they twist things, I don't believe those numbers are true.

Okay. So they had the "riot," and that was after the election of the senator. So this happened in September. And then this Black guy that was elected senator from this area, they invited him on Christmas Eve or Christmas Day, telling him to come to the market—to the store—saying they wanted to talk to him. So he went, and they assassinated him. They killed our Black senator. And now, we have two markers here in Clinton to commemorate him. But the point is, my grandfather and his brothers voted in that election. So the answer to your question, did Blacks try to vote, yes they did, until Jim Crow was put in place to stop us.

Was your grandfather a part of the "riot"?

I'm sure he was. Because he was living during that time. But he didn't get killed. Now, I'm told that when they started shooting and killing, people ran everywhere. And they came north of Clinton. Well, one lady had her baby. And she was running. And she found a tree that had a hollow in it. And she put her baby up in the hollow of that tree until she could get back.

In the cemetery where my grandparents are buried, some of the people that were killed in the "riot" are buried up here in this cemetery. I've been working so hard trying to get it set aside as a historical place. They stopped the Blacks from burying in it, but the markers are still there. But you know how they don't want us to preserve any of our history. So that's what I've been battling here lately. But I'm not going to give up. God will work it out.

That history is not that far away. Some people think that it happened so long ago, but it really wasn't that long ago, when you think about it.

It wasn't. I lived it. I'm 76 years old now. The Jim Crow laws went up until the Voting Rights Act was passed. And Medgar Evers was working to get people registered to vote. I was not old enough then. But that's when my mom, dad, and every Black person that we know went and registered to vote. And they voted. And they did not miss one election. I don't care what it was. They were going to vote.

Those of us that lived through it, we know. Because the *right* to vote is the thing. I have my company, the African American Heritage Tours, and I speak to young people who say, "Well, they don't count my vote anyway." That's probably true, but the point is, you're exercising your vote because people *died* for us to have just the *right* to vote. Stop worrying about whether it's counted; exercise your right. Don't stay at home just because you *think* they won't count it!

So aside from having to allow white people to go first and not being able to vote and these things that you started to see as a kid, what other rules became apparent to you?

Everything we got was used. Like our books would have four or five names in them, of the white kids who had already used them. We always got used books, we never got new books. They would call a Black adult by their first name, but we had to address them by Mister or Missus. But Black people couldn't be called that. That was a rule.

When integration came and all the Jim Crow laws were swept under the rug, rather than call us Mister and Missus, they started calling everybody by their first name. That was so obvious to me. And then, public transportation; although we didn't travel that much on public transportation, I knew that we had to move to the back. Black people had to sit in the back. That was an obvious thing.

The injustice of police brutality was right in our faces because my brother got beat up by the police. They said he was resisting arrest. They beat him so bad that when my mom and dad went and got him the next day out of jail, we didn't even hardly know him. His head and face was so swollen and big.

What did he say happened?

He said that he was in Jackson in my daddy's car, and the people that saw it happen, they later told my mama and daddy that he wasn't doing anything. They were picking on him because Daddy always had a car, we lived on our own place, and we just think he was singled out. Their attitude was, "You think you somebody," and all this kind of stuff. But he said that they said he resisted arrest. And everybody that saw it said he did not resist arrest. But that was what they said.

When they got him in the car and took him to the jail—they hadn't put their hands on him then, he said. But when they got him in the elevator, where couldn't nobody see him, that's when they beat him up. And they would knock him down and tell him to get up. And he got up the first time. The second time, when they told him to get up, he got up. And he said they knocked him back down. And that's when he realized, "They're gonna kill me if I keep getting up." So he stayed on the floor, and laid there. And there were three or four of them in there just beating him with those sticks and knocking him down. He was like double his size when Mama and Daddy picked him up.

So after that, Mama and Daddy sent him to California. He was already out of high school and working with my dad at the milling company then. And Mama sent him to California.

So she sent him to California because she was concerned about his safety going forward?

That's correct.

What would have happened if he stayed?

You know, he could have been killed. Lynched. Anything could have happened.

Did you know or hear of anybody in your family or neighborhood that had been lynched?

I knew a lady. This was when I was about 10 years old or so. This lady went to church with my mom, a Methodist church here in Clinton. And I remember seeing her once or twice at church. Her name was Miss Jane. I don't know her last name.

I remember Daddy coming home from work and telling my mom that they hung Miss Jane. They found her hanging in her outhouse one morning. She lived here in Clinton. I never will forget it. I talked with one of my cousins and asked him about it earlier, to be sure I remembered this right. Miss Jane was working for this white lady. And the white lady was fussing and arguing at her and hit her. And she hit the woman back. And that night, the white woman's sons came and drug her out of her house and hung her outside in her outhouse. And nothing was ever done about that lady's death. I never will forget that.

There were two lynchings that stood out in my mind growing up. Miss Jane and Emmett Till. And I couldn't deal with it. I wasn't able to reckon with it until later, when I was grown. Emmett Till and Miss Jane's hanging.

Did she have a family?

All I know was that she had a brother. I think she lived by herself. There was a road here in Clinton at the time called Sand Road. She lived down on Sand Road. But now, they never arrested anybody. Back then in those times, if somebody killed a Black person, they weren't going to do anything about it anyway. But this white woman's two sons came to that house that night. Somebody saw them go. And they hung that lady. I think my mom went to her funeral.

I wonder what they would have written on her death certificate. They always had some trumped-up reason.

They probably said self-inflicted suicide. They might not have even put anything on there. But she was lynched.

Did you hear of any other racially motivated violence that took place in your community?

This guy that lived right up the hill from us. But he was . . . he was kind of a disorderly person.

He got in trouble a lot, okay? I remember he went to prison, but I can't remember what they sent this boy to prison for. I can't remember, but he would be considered a bad child in the neighborhood, right? So he wound up going to prison. And somehow he escaped. And in the process of him escaping up in the Delta area, where the prison is, they claimed he broke in this white woman's house, and that he raped this white woman. Of course they got him and they put him back in prison, and they electrocuted him. Now, I remember that.

I'm surprised that a mob or something didn't come to the prison and get him out.

I know. No, they electrocuted him. His mom and dad lived about a mile from where we stayed.

And then, I remember my uncle, my mom's sister's husband. He was on this bus. He got on the bus in Jackson going to Columbia, Mississippi, which is down in south

Mississippi. And when they got to some town, the police got on the bus. My uncle had a cap on, and he was at the back of the bus. And they said, "You, the one with the cap! You come on off the bus."

Some lady up in Greenwood, Mississippi—which is north Mississippi, about 100 miles from where he got on the bus in Jackson—said that some Black guy had touched her hand, or some old crazy mess like that. The police was looking for him. They got my uncle off this bus, brought him all the way back from Brookhaven, I think was the name of the town, and carried him all the way up to the Delta, which is about 70 miles north of Jackson. And by the time they got up there he said it was about three o'clock in the morning. They go take him to this white man's house, knock on the door, she come out and they say, "Is this the one that touched your hand?"

And she looked at him. And she said, "No, that's not the one." Now, all she had to do was say yes—if she had said yes, they would have killed him right then and there. After she said he wasn't the one, they carried him back to the bus station up there instead of bringing him back to Jackson where he got on. He didn't have the money for another ticket, and he said, "Ain't y'all gonna take me back to Jackson?" And they said, "No, you got to get back the best way you can." They were just lowdown and evil.

It makes me also wonder what was going through his mind, you know, the whole time. That had to be so scary.

It took them three hours to get there, he said. He said all he could think of was: "They're gonna kill me and my family will never know what happened to me." But God blessed him and they didn't kill him.

If she would have said yes. . . . It's so crazy how just one word could have changed everything.

Could've changed it all, that's true. That's true. But God was in the plan that she didn't say he was the one. Because they were so sure they had him. They thought they had them somebody to hang and kill that night.

One thing that is hard for me as a millennial, and as somebody who never experienced slavery, Jim Crow, the Black Codes, none of it, it's hard for me to understand what it was like to live in an environment where anything could happen. And you could be beaten or killed at any time, just based on whether a white person was having a bad day. A lot of people that read this are going to be like me—like, we can't imagine a world like this. Can you comment on that?

All it took was somebody to lie on you and you were gone. For me, it was the feeling of—and I don't know if I ever heard anybody really tell us this, but it was the fear of thinking that I'm the dumbest person. God created me and I'm dumb, and these other people are superior to me. And I will never be able to accomplish things and get to where they are. But that was the mind job they were doing on us because, you know, they owned everything and they had everything. Everything you saw on TV was white.

I didn't really worry about them killing me. But then, when they beat my brother up, that kind of made it full circle. We would feel insecure and not safe, because you were Black. The only thing that ever happened to me that really made me really afraid for myself was in fall of '65 when the Civil Rights Movement was really going, and I was down in Vicksburg, in nursing school. We had all been out that night and we were walking home and these white kids just came by and just pelted us with raw eggs. They threw raw eggs all over us. And it's that kind of stuff that makes you afraid because you don't know what they're going to do.

The same man I told you about—my uncle who married my mama's sister—when I got out of high school, they paid all my money to go to college. They lived in California and that's the same family that my mom sent my brother to after he got beat up by the police. When I got out of high school, they said, "Clo, if you want to go to college, we'll pay your money." They paid every penny. I never had to pay one penny to go to college. And so, the fear of messing up when they were spending money on me kept me going.

When Johnson signed the Civil Rights bill, I was working at a hospital where I was doing my clinical work. They had a colored cafeteria and a white cafeteria. We had to eat separately. We worked on the floors together, but we'd eat separately. The superintendent of the hospital came in one day, and, I guess it wasn't a fear, but I felt like I let my race down at that point, because the day came when they had to take the Colored and White signs down. The superintendent came and said, "The federal government says I have to take these signs down. But if I catch any of you over there in the white side eating, I'm going to kick you out of school and I'm going to call you a rabble-rouser, and fix it to where you'll never be able to get into nursing school again."

I felt like I couldn't mess up my aunt and uncle spending all this money on me. The next day, the nurses and all the Black people working there got together and said, "We going to the white side." About two or three of us, including me, didn't go. I felt guilty and beat up on myself for not going, because they went on over there and ate in the white cafeteria, and they didn't mess with them! So, the next day, we all went over there and ate. And they didn't do nothing to us. They didn't want to lose that money, see. He was playing with our minds.

And what school was this?

My college was Mississippi Valley State University. And then, in the last nine months, we had to do clinical work on the floor at the hospital. And it was at Kuhn Memorial Hospital in Vicksburg, Mississippi.

What was that experience like being in that environment?

When we left Mississippi Valley, that was a historical Black college. I was valedictorian of my class, and all my instructors were Black then. My teacher called me in and she said, "Robinson, you going there, and I want you to know that they're going to pick at you because all your teachers are going to be white there. Because you had your good grades, they're going to pick at you."

We had orientation the first week we were there. The white instructors told us that the first week we were on the floor, we would be shadowing a senior student. They would assign us a senior student. My senior student was this white girl, and I was shadowing her. That's all I was supposed to be doing. Okay? So, the first day I was on the floor, we had a patient who was on complete bed rest. We go in the room to take care of this patient, and the white girl, the senior student, I was supposed do what she said, right? Okay, the patient was on complete bed rest. That means she doesn't get to use the bathroom, she ain't supposed to get up out this bed. The white girl said, "Let's get her up and put her in the chair to make up the bed." I said, "Oh no, we're not supposed to do that." She said, "I know what I'm doing, you have to get this woman out the bed and we're going to put her in the chair." And I've got to do what she say, right?

The minute we put that lady in the chair and start making up the bed, here come our teacher. She walked in that door and saw that woman sitting in that chair, and she didn't call nobody but me. She said, "Nurse Robinson, come to my office!" Now, this is my first day on the floor. I went in there. Now, one thing my mom taught all of us was to never hold your head down, and look people in the eye. She would never let us hold our heads down.

I go in that office, and she said, "Did you look at the patient's orders?" I said, "Yes ma'am, I did." "What did those orders say?" I said, "They said she is on complete bed rest." See, she thought I was going to lie. But that was the first thing I told her. Complete bed rest. She said, "What does that mean?" I told her, "It means she wasn't supposed to get up out the bed for anything." She said, "Well, why did you get her up?" I said, "I didn't get her up. You told me to do what the senior student said to do, and the senior student told me to get her up. That's why we got her up out the bed." She jumped up out of her chair and told me to go on back. And from that day forward, I didn't have trouble out of none of my instructors.

Isn't that something that she called you though and didn't call the other girl.

She didn't call the white girl at all. And she was ready to kick me out of class, right then and there. And, because of that one run-in. . . . See, we had to do six weeks in OB. And then, six weeks in the nursery. I hated it because I hated seeing the premature babies. So, she asked me one day how did I like working with the premature babies? I said, "I hate it." So she made me stay another six weeks down there with those babies.

But actually, I grew to like that old white lady because she became somewhat like a mother to us. After we got to know her, she would look out for us, bring snacks and stuff to school. She was really a nice old white woman at the end of it all.

How did your parents feel about you being in this environment and them not being able to protect you?

Well, my mom's thing was, "Always follow the rules." That was the first thing. See, I'm in nursing school when there's very few Blacks going to nursing school. And they said, "Clo, if it gets too rough, you can always come home." But you know, God is always good, and He works things out for you, so I was able to make it through. And once I got out of school, then they started putting school nurses in the school system. And so I was one of the first nurses in the state of Mississippi. I came home and I thought I was going to take it easy for a while. You know when you're young you say, "I'm going to take a break, I'm not fixing to go to work right away." But I got a job three weeks after I got out.

Were you in a white school?

No, it was a Black school. Public school. It was a high school in Ackerman, Mississippi. It was one of the poverty-stricken areas. And it was during that time, you know Headstart? It was a three-year program where they put nurses in these poverty-stricken areas. One of the things they don't teach you in nursing school, because most of your training in nursing is to work in hospitals, is how to work in schools. The person who hired me—this man had never seen me, but he wanted a Black nurse. My mom and dad were friends with the . . . they called them Jeanes supervisors. These were Black people that were over the Black school system. So, the Jeanes supervisor, Louise White, told this principal in Ackerman about me, and he called me and said, "Well, if you want the job, you can have it." This man had never seen me, and hired me just like that!

And so I went there to Ackerman not knowing what to do. I was 21 years old. They had all these things that they wanted me to do, and I said Lord I don't know where to start. Something told me to get up and go to the local health department. I went to the health department in Ackerman, and of course they had colored and white, so I went to the colored side. Told the woman who I was and what I was doing, and of course they were all white too, so she said okay, but didn't try to help. I was wanting to order supplies through them like eye charts to test the kids' eyes, and most of them had never had vaccines, and things I needed to do. I had to get them to help me.

From there, I was supposed to set up an agreement with the medical doctor in the community, so if the kids got sick at school, I could take them to the doctor. And then a medical agreement with the dentist for dental work and all that stuff. So, I went to the medical doctor first. And I walked in there with my white dress on, and they were looking at me like they had never seen a Black nurse before. I remember them. They were real cold. I told them I needed to talk to the doctor. Finally, the doctor—an old white guy—came down. And he was acting funny. But after I told him how much money I had available to spend on the medical treatments for these kids, his whole attitude changed. They realized I had all this money!

So then I went to the dentist and told him the same thing. Now, the dentist was a younger guy. He was more receptive to me than any of the other ones. He worked real good with me. It was all such a learning experience. I realized that community health and school, working with children in school, was what I wanted to spend the rest of my life doing. So that's what I wound up doing mostly, working with children and teenagers.

When the public schools integrated, did that affect your job since you were in the school system?

I was there on a program that had a three-year grant, and the schools were integrated the year after I left. They closed the school where I was working. It was 1st–12th grade. They made it an elementary school, and then the high school, they moved the Black kids to the white high school. I was gone by the time they integrated.

What did you do for fun as a young person?

Okay, up until I finished high school, the fun was Friday night football games, school dances, and going to the movies. Clinton was a small town, so we didn't have a colored theater and a white theater. They had the white folks on the bottom floor, and the Blacks had to go upstairs in the balcony to watch the movie. We all went to the same theater. There was this old crazy boy named Dave. I ain't going to say his last name. Up in the balcony, we didn't have a bathroom to go to, right? Dave went to a movie one day and had to use the bathroom, so he decided to take his thing out and pee down on the white folks. So that was the end of our moviegoing in Clinton! Black people couldn't go back to that theater anymore. No more Blacks could come to the movies.

So he ruined it for everybody! But that's what they get for making y'all sit in the balcony. That's funny!

Very funny. So then, we had to go to Jackson if we wanted to go to the movies. And in Jackson, we had separate theaters. We had two movie theaters for Blacks in Jackson: the Ebony and the Alamo.

Did y'all ever want to sneak and do something like, for instance, drink out of the whites only water fountain?

I didn't, but they used to have these restrooms at the Greyhound bus station. The waiting rooms were all separate. They had two doors at the Greyhound bus station,

Clotie's great-grandparents, Frank and Edith Woods, her Aunt Gladys, and her mother, Exie.

colored and white. Everything was separate, you couldn't really do anything. But my sister did something, I can't remember what she did. She went in the whites bathroom or water fountain or something, and we said, "Mama is going to have a fit!"

I remember you used to have to put 10 cents to use it, and maybe she crawled up under the door and just used it.

Did you have a good relationship with your grandparents?

I never knew any of my grandparents. My mom's dad died when I was five years old, so I remember him. But her mother died when my mom was eight and her sister was 10. And her grandparents raised them. Then my father's father and mother were both dead when I was born, so I didn't get to really know any of my grandparents.

Did you have a lot of extended family members?

Oh, yes. And this was the unusual part about my mother. Because her mother had died, we only knew her mother's side of the family. One lived in Atlanta: Uncle Scott, her mother's brother. We would go see him once a year. And the other was in South Mississippi. But the unusual part about it, my mom's dad who died when I was five years old? She used to tell us all the time, she used to say, "I'm sorry, I cannot tell you all anything about your ancestors, your grandparents, because my daddy left Florida, ran away when he was a young man, and never went back because he and his brother got in trouble."

She used to tell us this all the time. They went into this town and these white people were acting like they'd never seen Black people before. Calling them monkeys and all this kind of stuff. And in the process, they got in a fight. In the process of the fight . . . now, remember, in Jim Crow, you weren't supposed to be fighting white people. So they got into this fight, and my grandfather's brother ended up killing one of the white guys that was messing with them.

And so, my grandfather ran. The two of them left Florida, and never went back. They left their family, their grandmother, and their mother, which would have been my great-grandmother; she never knew what happened to her two sons. Now, they ran from Florida. Later, we got letters from my cousin who had saved the letters from my grandfather. My grandfather stopped in Mississippi, and his brother continued on to Louisiana. They split up so they wouldn't be caught, you know. But they survived killing a white man under the Jim Crow law.

So what happened was, from the late 1800s until around 1980, the families on my mom's dad's side—the Florida family—knew. Their mother always told them that she had two brothers that had just disappeared and she never knew what happened to them. And then, *our* mother, and my aunt in California, always told us that their dad said, "Well, we have sisters and brothers in Florida, but we never went back to check on them after that trouble." So my sister Edith, my sister Amy, and myself went to California, and my cousin, the son of the brother that went on to Louisiana, he had these letters. When we went to California, we met him for the first time. He showed us these letters where my grandfather wrote him.

He wrote my grandfather wanting to know why the two brothers had different last names. So my grandfather took the time, wrote this letter back in 1937, telling him that his daddy changed his name because of the trouble that he got into. He changed his name from Jackson to Hall. He was really a Jackson, but he changed his name.

Have y'all been able to connect with the Florida family?

Yes. When we went to California and we read those letters, it was like the spirit of my grandfather and his brother . . . their presence was in that room as we read that letter. And my grandfather was saying that he wanted to go back to Florida. He was up in age when he was writing that and begging his brother's son to come get him and take him to Florida. And I told my sister that we had to find the family so our grandfather could rest at ease. We set out and started looking. All we knew was that his last name was Jackson. We didn't really know where to start.

This was in 1975. We knew they were in Tallahassee, Florida. And this lady I was working with was going to visit Tallahassee. I asked her to bring me a phone book back so I could see if I could find some last names of my family. So, when she brought it back to us, my sisters Edith, Amy, and I drafted a letter and just started sending it out to every person with the last name of Jackson. And we also knew that one of my grandfather's sisters had married a Wynns. So we sent these letters to every church, people with the last name of Jackson, and people with the last name of Wynns in Tallahassee. We sent out the first batch of letters, waited for about two months, and we didn't hear anything. We sent out the second batch of letters—and see, we were prepared to send out letters until we found somebody. But we sent out that second batch of letters, and one of the letters went to the church that their mother, which was my great-grandmother, was a member. She had died at that church on New Year's Eve; they say she was praying on her knees. She never knew what had happened to her two children.

And so, when the preacher got the letter, he knew one of our relatives. He told them that we were looking for our family. So the person he showed it to carried it to Jacksonville and showed it to one of her first cousins in Jacksonville. So, they debated on what to do next. But they remembered that their mother had always said that she had some brothers somewhere.

So finally, one Sunday morning, I never will forget it. My husband was sick that morning. I went to church and he stayed at home. And he called me at church and told me to come on home. He said "Clo, I think y'all have found your family. A lady called here and left her phone number. They got your letter and she wants you to call." So I got home and I called. And you talking about some crying? We cried and we cried. We were separated for over a hundred years.

And we finally got back together.

Clotie's grandfather, Tony Calvin Jackson, who escaped from Florida along with his brother, Louis Jackson Hall.

So we went to Slidell, Louisiana, and met the Slidell family. And finally, we connected to the family in Florida. It was so amazing because the two brothers had told their children about their sisters and brothers and Florida, and then the siblings in Florida had told their children about their missing brothers. And we could put the pieces together finally. And we finally had a reunion. God brought us back together.

That's a beautiful and amazing story. But it's also a hurtful story because these two young guys had to leave their entire families and were never able to go back home again.

Never. And their mother never knew what happened to her two children. And my granddaddy told my mom that they had a mob after them, a lynch mob, when they ran. And what they did, the way they survived, was that they came up on a creek, and the creek had an embankment up under it. They could hear the bloodhounds barking, they were right on their trails. So they jumped off into the creek and got up under the embankment where the dogs couldn't smell them. The mob went all up and down the creek and never did find them, but they were right there. Somehow or another, the dogs lost the scent of them. And they stayed there until the sun came up, and they got out from under there.

Mama said my granddaddy said that they would travel at night. Then my grand-daddy stopped in Mississippi. His name was Tony Calvin Jackson. And his brother was Lucius Jackson. And Lucius went on to Louisiana and changed his name to Louis Hall. But that just goes to show that Black folks, we have always been able to survive.

I wish there would have at least been a way that they could have told their parents what happened.

I tell you what else they say happened. Until those boys came up missing, she and her husband, my great-grandfather, they were still married. They were living together. But they wound up separating after all this happened. I guess the stress and the pres-sure of losing the boys and all that. . . . He ended up leaving her, and she ultimately lost her husband and her two boys.

In a world like that, I'm sure both of them were thinking, you know, there're just so many things that could have happened to them. I wish that they would have been able to reach out, but I know that it would have been too dangerous for them to do that.

Exactly. It would've been. They didn't have telephones. And they couldn't write back because the letter could have been traced. It just would have been too dangerous. Neither one of them ever went back to Florida. They say she died one New Year's Eve at a Watch Night service, on her knees praying.

Goodness. I do thank God that it's come full circle. And God has brought the family back together even though it took 100 years. But it's yet another element of racism and white people's laws ripping families apart. It reminds me of people being sold away, on the auction block, and never being able to see their family again, not knowing what happened to their family members.

Exactly. It's the same thing. That's exactly right. I think about that. Crossing the Atlantic on the slave ships; it's all the same thing. I make sure my kids and young people in my family know about all of this.

In my family, I am the second generation away from slavery. My kids are the third generation away from slavery. And my sisters and I are passing the torch to the younger members of the family. Because we had written and documented all of our family history on the Jackson side and the Robinson side. And I tell the young people, it's time for you guys to step up to the plate and just document stuff. Because when you're gone, and we're already gone, all this stuff can be lost. You've got to document.

Black folk, we've always preserved things through the oral tradition.

That's right. Because we didn't have anything else. White folks get a joy out of telling our history. I don't like that. They don't know nothing about our history. Talking about how we lived as slaves and how happy we were. One of the things that the white man tried to do was break our spirits. They don't understand how all of the stuff they inflicted on us. . . . Sure, we were singing. Sure, we were dancing. Sure, we were laughing. That doesn't mean it didn't affect us. They thought that because we were doing that despite all they did to us, that we didn't have the ability to love. But that wasn't it. It's the fact that we are so heartstrong. We are heartstrong.

And I tell my kids that the mere fact that you are alive here today tells you that your ancestors survived coming across the Atlantic. You've got to think about that. That's a serious thing. If your ancestors hadn't made it, you wouldn't be here today. And the willpower that they had is what you need to maintain.

As African Americans, our existence alone is a miracle. And existing with our spirits intact.

It's all about maintaining power.

Were you involved in the Civil Rights Movement at all?

I didn't march because my parents were so protective of me after my brother got beat up. But my sister Amy, when she went to college, she marched with Medgar Evers. She was involved with the Movement. And we did some integration stuff on our own. My dad would always do things. For instance, when Billy Graham came to Mississippi in the '50s, he told the white folks that if Blacks couldn't come to hear him preach, he wasn't coming. So they advertised it. Daddy and Mama got us ready, they said, "We going." And they carried us all over there. It was outside on a hill, you know; you could sit outside, everybody was on their blankets and all. So, we would always do things like that. We integrated on the ground like that.

They made sure to expose us to what was going on, but they didn't let us get out there and march. But Amy did when she left and went to college and stuff. My cousin, Dr. Amos Brown, he was the youth president of the NAACP, when Medgar Evers was living. Amos went to jail because of his work with the Movement. He's my first cousin, and they have a record of him in the Smithsonian.

Do you believe that Dr. King's dream is possible in America?

Oh, yes! It is definitely possible. But we have to get back focused. You know, when Dr. King was alive and Medgar Evers was alive, and the churches were united and we were organized, with God's help, yes. The dream is coming true. It's already coming true, and I believe that.

It's swinging toward justice for us. I truly believe this country has to be turned around, because you can't have this prejudice and discrimination embedded in your laws. It's in the laws. A lot has happened, but that has to change. But I choose to believe it's possible.

It's just so interesting that despite all that you've been through, you have this optimism about where this country could be.

I just think we are headed to that "more perfect union." And that's why defending democracy is so important. And that's why some people in this country don't actually want democracy. But your perfect union will come about with democracy. But see, when they penned those words, they weren't thinking about the perfect union including us. Black people. That's what's powerful about Dr. King. He said I'm ready for them to pay me. They owe me. Because you put it in your Constitution, you wrote it in your rules, you wrote it in everything. I just want you to give me what is in that. When they wrote all men were created equal, they didn't include us. They wasn't talking about us. They need to stick to the Constitution that they wrote.

If you remember when David was getting ready to go fight Goliath, God told David this battle is not yours, it's mine. It's really the Lord's battle.

I watch a lot of documentaries. This lady asked this old white guy something in an old clip, and he said, "The Blacks should've been content when they were slaves. We were good to them. They didn't have to worry about paying bills, we were good to them. They should've just been content." And the newslady asked, "When you brought the slaves over, did you really think that they would stay your slaves forever? For the rest of eternity?" And you know what he said? "We didn't make it that far with the plan. We never even thought about them wanting to be free."

Remember when they fought President Obama for eight years over Obamacare? And then when Trump got in and asked them what they wanted to do about it, they didn't have a plan? That's the point I'm making now. They ain't have no plan! They never have a plan. They never thought when they brought us over here that we would be free. They didn't plan it out. And their only thought now is to tear up democracy. Just like the Civil War—they wanted to tear it up, but they didn't have a plan. They're still mad they lost the Civil War, that's all that is.

What would you say to an African American person a hundred years from now?

I think the message would be to remember your ancestors. Always know your history, your family history, and the history of your country. And the most important thing is: never, never allow anybody to put your race down. Know within yourself your value, and your self worth. And if you do that, no matter what's happening, you will survive, and will carry the rest of your generation and family along with you. Always lift your head. That's what my mama and my daddy taught us. They preached that to us day in and day out. Never let anybody take your self worth away from you. God and your ancestors are calling you and pushing you to do what you need to do. When our ancestors came over on the slave ships, they survived, and they want us to keep it going. Take it another notch forward.

I remembered I wanted to tell you, going back to being involved in the Civil Rights Movement. My neighbor was Alice Walker, the poet and the writer Alice Walker. Alice came here to Mississippi during the Civil Rights Movement, and she and this white guy, Leventhal, got married. So, they tested the laws of Mississippi that there couldn't be interracial marriages.

Alice and I got to be the best of friends. We lived right next door to each other. One of my major parts of the Civil Rights Movement was my husband and I watched their house for them. We lived in danger because they tried to bomb houses and all. Alice's husband was the civil rights attorney that integrated the public schools here in Mississippi. So, everybody had a role. Big or small, we all had our roles.

INTERVIEW NO. 2

ELEANOR
BOSWELL-RAINE

*C*an you tell me about your childhood home and neighborhood?

Yes, I was born in Los Angeles, California, in 1945. And my family moved to San Francisco in 1947, when I was two years old. And we grew up in a predominantly white neighborhood, two neighborhoods, actually, both of which were predominantly white. My father was a United Methodist pastor, who had a large church in what was called the Fillmore District, which was the area where most Blacks lived in San Francisco during that time.

So it was kind of like, you know, two different worlds: the white world that we grew up in, and went to school in, and then on Sundays, we were exposed more to Black folks. So for example, in my elementary school, I don't think there were any more than maybe seven or eight of us who were Black. And my junior high school was a little larger—I would say, you know, maybe 25 Blacks, a larger school than in elementary school. And then, high school, again, we were a real minority, under 5 percent. So most of my younger days were very much influenced by that kind of exposure to people in my neighborhood. It was a middle- to middle-upper-class neighborhood, made up primarily of Europeans. Professional Jewish people, really. But there were a lot of European people in general, from Russians, to Greeks, to Italians, and the accompanying synagogues and Greek Orthodox churches. So I mean, it was really broad European, but I would say more predominantly Jewish.

And so, that was reflected in the schools. For example, when I became a Girl Scout, the meeting place was always the synagogue. So many of the friends I grew up with were Jewish, until I went to high school, which is when things changed. My Jewish friends then went off to private schools, and I continued on in a public school. So, you know, there was that point where it was very clear that the families did not want their children to get too mixed up with diversity. So, that was a little bit different. In the meantime, there were the social experiences I had growing up in a Black church that was in a white institution—the United Methodist Church is still part of the white institution. But they had Black churches, because, of course, they did not want Black pastors in white churches.

So my father took a church in San Francisco very purposefully because he knew he would be able to stay there for 30 years. They weren't going to move him around. And that gave him an opportunity to do a lot in terms of civil rights and getting involved in the government. He was a housing commissioner for 10 years, built the first Black credit union, the first Black senior housing, helped promote many of our congregants to become involved. The first Black judge and even the mayor of San Francisco was one of my father's protégés.

So I lived a very split screen life until I was 17, when our parents sent us off to Fisk University. And that also was a very determined move, because both of my parents had grown up in the West, attended elementary, middle schools, and high schools that were predominantly white, went to white universities like UC Berkeley and USC, and had terrible experiences because of race. And so my mother, for example, after having gone to the University of Oregon, having a bad experience, and then UC Berkeley—where she couldn't even live on campus . . . the Fisk Jubilee Singers had come through Portland, and convinced her family that she needed to go to a Historically Black College or University. And so that's how my mother got to Fisk.

My father, who had grown up in Los Angeles under pretty much the same circumstances, got very involved with the Hollywood scene in Los Angeles. And his parents were none too happy about the direction his life was going in. And so he was sent to Wiley College, which was a Historically Black College in Marshall, Texas, where his father's people had gone since Reconstruction.

A young Eleanor, her parents, and her sister.

So you said that your mother wasn't allowed to live on campus at UC Berkeley? Can you talk a little more about that?

Well, at that time, they would not allow Blacks to live on campus. So, she had to live off campus. And as a matter of fact, she had a close relationship with a Jewish fellow, and he actually gave her his fraternity pin. Well, his parents showed up on campus, reported it to the college administrators, and my mother was really ostracized because of it. And that's why she left UC Berkeley.

What did you do for fun when you were growing up, especially during your teenage years?

I was very involved in music. I was a violinist and a violist. I played in the San Francisco Junior Symphony Orchestra. I loved languages. I thought I was going to be an ice skater for a long time. We did a lot of different things in terms of keeping busy. Our parents put us in tap, ballet, and acrobat school. And then, every summer we would spend one month in Portland, Oregon, and one month in Los Angeles so we could get to know our extended families, because we had no family in San Francisco.

And so I had an opportunity to get outside of the city setting and to the family farm for a month. And help out. Pick all kinds of vegetables and stuff. And I loved that. Although my sister—who was a book addict—couldn't stand that life. She would sit in the house and read books. And then in Los Angeles, we had a pretty active life. My father's people were mostly educators in Los Angeles. His family had originally moved to Los Angeles in 1889, and then moved back to the South. Texas. And then moved back again around 1919. So most of what we knew was that whole, you know, Pacific West Coast life, where you were always in the minority. It was much more subtle from the standpoint of racism.

For example, my first experience head-on with racism that I recall is when I was in elementary school, and was asked to write an essay about a famous person. Well, I chose my great-grandfather. He was born in 1864, and managed to get a medical degree and move to Los Angeles, where he was the first medical person to pass the exam. And he was also a civil rights person. He was an editor. He lived many different places, and really made his mark. And so as far as I was concerned, he was famous. He'd written a book called *Noted Negro Women: Their Triumphs and Activities*, and I thought, oh, this is great. Well, I was given an F on my essay. Much to my shock and amazement, my teacher said that the problem with me was, I wasn't following directions. And she had said, "I asked you to write about a famous person, and you wrote about somebody who could hardly be called famous." That really hurt.

Naturally, I went home and told my parents, who showed up the next day to help this white teacher understand that what she was doing was very detrimental to my development, and how I thought about myself. And, as far as our family was concerned, my great grandfather *was* famous within the Black race.

So, even when I graduated high school, we had a young British musician who had written a musical about Huckleberry Finn. And because I played in the orchestra and sang in the choir, I wanted to try out for a speaking part in the play, only to be told that I couldn't have a speaking part, that I could only be one of the slaves with a handkerchief on my head and sing.

So there again, I went home; I was really upset. And actually, what happened was many of us boycotted our senior play. Blacks and some whites. It was televised, and it didn't give the school the kind of publicity they were looking for.

Were there any other incidents that really showed you that there were some underlying things going on when it came to race relations?

Only when we traveled. I had the privilege of knowing my great-grandfather, who lived to be 96. He was born in 1868. We have longevity in our family. My grandfather died at 101. And so, all my life, I had heard stories. I knew my Black history. I got it from my own people. I didn't know a lot of people that knew Black history. I just had a different experience. It's probably because, especially on my father's side, the education level, even then, was very high. They had all gone to HBCUs or white universities, even when Blacks weren't supposed to go. So, we always had that connection, even though we were in Los Angeles.

In terms of other things that I can remember, as I say, it's mostly when we traveled to the South. And for the first time, I saw a sign over a water fountain that said, "For coloreds only," or "For whites only," and the bathroom situation, and all that. So it really wasn't until I went to Nashville to school as a freshman at 17 that I experienced the full obvious manifestation of racism in what I call the raw. And, of

The medical degree of Monroe Alpheus Majors, Eleanor's great-grandfather.

course, I was there. I started in 1962, which was exactly the right time to be there. Because Martin Luther King, actually—I remember very well, him coming to our gym and recruiting us, so I began marching downtown. I experienced a cigarette being pushed down my blouse. I remember the hatred, and the yelling of the crowds and the children and being called "nigger." I recall how scary it was to be marching.

And they kept these Jane and John Doe warrants that they would pass out, so you never knew, you know, if you were gonna get one. And I'll never forget the image of my classmates being hauled into paddy wagons. So it was really the South that helped me better understand from firsthand experience what we were really dealing with.

When you traveled did y'all use the Green Book at all?

No, I don't recall that. It seemed as if we always knew somebody. And when I say travel, we did a lot of traveling up and down the coast, right? Because my mother's people were in Washington State and Oregon. And my father's people were in Los Angeles and San Diego. And we used the trains. Many of my mother's people were Pullman porters. So, my parents used to literally put us on trains and get us over to the Pullman porters when we were little girls, and they would take care of us.

And traveling across country, we took trains as well. I remember the shock of transferring in Chicago, to the train that would take us down to Nashville, and going from a very comfortable car and seeing these Jim Crow cars that were wooden. You know, it was very clear that they were made to make you feel uncomfortable. And the bathrooms were always in disarray. And they were nasty. I remember that. But when we used to drive across country, my father would always plan it so that wherever we stopped, most of the time, especially when we entered the Southern area of the country, we had someone we knew who we would stay with.

So you're preparing to go to Fisk, you're going halfway across the country and you're going into a different environment. Were you excited, nervous?

I was scared to death. You see, when I told my counselor in my high school that I was going to Fisk University, they panicked. Because they were under the assumption that all Black universities and colleges were substandard. And my friends were going to Stanford and UC Berkeley. And, I remember my parents coming to meet with the counselor. And she stated that she was very concerned about why they would want to, you know, send me to a substandard school.

But she was talking to the wrong people. Because my parents helped them understand that, you know, my mother, she went to Fisk, and then went on to graduate school in San Francisco, and never lost credit. My father, who went to Wiley College, then went to the University of Southern California, never missed a credit. And my parents explained that they just were ignorant of the standing of some of the Historically Black Colleges. So, it was really the lack of knowledge, the ignorance of counselors in dealing with African Americans that had parents with those experiences.

Now, I saw my friends who may not have had that kind of experience or background, in terms of their family situations, who were very much misled in terms of what their opportunities were. I mean, we had to fight to help these teachers and counselors understand that we were interested in academics. I was not interested in home economics; I was not interested. And the Black boys were really pointed toward shop or mechanics or whatever, but really dissuaded from seeking academic achievement. It was obvious. It was blatant.

And even to this day, there are studies that come out every year that demonstrate how Black students who go to undergrad at HBCUs do better professionally. Does that surprise you?

Yeah, I mean, it's true. I mean, even when I was at Fisk, a number of my friends went on to Harvard. That was a myth that was kept alive through ignorance, especially in the West, where you could get away with it. We didn't have any Historically Black Colleges in the West.

Why do you think it is that Black students do better having gone to an HBCU than going to a PWI for college?

Because you have the full opportunity to be accepted as a whole person. Now, it was terrifying to me at first, because I'd never had a Black teacher in my life. I had never been in a classroom full of Black students. I didn't know how acceptable I would be. I was very sure of myself in a white environment, and less sure of myself in a Black environment in the beginning. Also, the things that were emphasized in the Black schools from a social standpoint, I've never, ever experienced in white schools. It was just a fuller experience that I think helps the development of not only the mind and the body, but the spirit. And once you have that under your belt, I think perhaps that gives you a leg up as you go further into some of these graduate schools.

What did you major in at Fisk?

At Fisk, it was social psychology. I only went my first two years there. And that was the requirement, that I go at least two years. And then, I moved to Chicago. And then I moved back to San Francisco. And everywhere I went, I got into college, but I was always moving. So Chicago to San Francisco to Los Angeles. Each time, I would get into a state school. And then Washington, DC. And then Japan—I lived in Asia. And then came back and finished at California State University, Hayward. Finished my undergrad there.

So can you go more into detail about the day when Dr. King came to campus and he was trying to recruit you all?

In 1962, we were absolutely in the middle of the Civil Rights Movement, and Nashville was a hub. Right? I mean, John Lewis was in my class, actually. And there are other notables who were focused on Nashville, Tennessee, as a place that was kind of a hub for the sit-ins and so forth. And so as a freshman, we learned that he was coming to our campus. And so all of us went and crammed into the gym. And there he was. Now, I knew that my father knew him. And I was so impressed with him, because I come from what I consider a civil rights family of generations—because it didn't start with King, right.

It was a natural thing that I knew I had to be involved. And so, I participated as a result. I mean, it was wonderful to see him and the way he presented the whole thing. But even before he got there, many Fisk students had already been involved in the Movement. In fact, my family in Nashville, many who were professionals, actually put their pennies together to get Fisk students out of jail. And that was happening even before I arrived at Fisk University. So there was a lot of activity going on.

My sister decided she didn't want to be involved, but I was game. Because at the same time I was doing that, my father was leading marches down Market Street in San Francisco.

Was your sister at Fisk also?

Yes, she went. Both of us had to go. We had to go. From our parents, it was: "You are going. We're not going to let what happened to us happen to you."

How frequently would you all march?

Well, '62 and '63, sometimes it would be two or three times a week. But we had to be careful because we were getting arrested and it was interfering with college. And so people like John Lewis just kind of gave up the college thing. He'd already been in Nashville attending another college before he entered Fisk. So I mean, you just had a lot of activity going on, and some people were more involved than others. And of course, what used to be called Tennessee A&I—an agricultural and industrial school—had a huge campus, a Black school. They were very involved as well.

So where would y'all go? Where would y'all actually march?

One of the places I remember was across the street from Vanderbilt. We would go into lunch counters. I can remember sitting at a lunch counter—I think it was, gosh, what would you call it . . . a Woolworth's or some kind of dime store. Where they had a lunch counter. And that's where the man put a cigarette down my back. I know that sometimes we would just be marching wherever the retail store areas were.

How did it all work? Okay, so y'all signed up and said I want to be a part of this. Did you all have trainings?

There were definitely trainings. Because see, the whole point was nonviolence. And you gotta be trained not to be violent, when you have people shouting at you and jeering you and throwing things at you. The trainings were needed in trying to help people not get so overheated, so that it wouldn't end up in fights. That was really rough. And so, the training was necessary in order to be able to pull it off.

We learned techniques; there were people who literally were teaching. We even had a white student who would play the role of the white jeerer to try to antagonize the students, to make it as realistic as possible. So that when they were confronting this horrific scene, they knew what they were doing. I know when the cigarette got pushed down my back, I was sitting next to my college boyfriend, who was not known to have a lot of patience. And I mean, I was really afraid that he would erupt. But he didn't. He was from Chicago.

So when you all go, how long would you stay out there?

We had to do it around our classes. Right? Because I mean, our parents had sent us there to go to school. Although there were some people like Lewis, who are a lot more focused on the Movement. And I wish I could remember some of the other names that are now known in history, who were there. In fact, just recently, I know one of our Fisk students—who was very well known—was just presented with a presidential award. I wish I could remember her name. [author's note: It's Diane Nash; President Biden awarded her with the Presidential Medal of Freedom.]

But these things were going on, you know . . . definitely Nashville was a hub, but I know it was going on at other campuses as well. I used to listen to my father talk about what they were doing at Wiley College when he was there in the 1930s. He was one of the Great Debaters of Wiley College. And in fact, James Farmer, who founded the Congress of Racial Equality, they did things like banning the Greeks [the Black Greek Letter Organizations], so that they could come together to be able to demonstrate downtown. Marshall is a real tiny town. They got tired of having to sit up in the balcony in the movie theater. You know, this was in the '30s. So nonviolence, while definitely King absolutely perfected it, there were others who were always seeking social improvements, as far back as Emancipation.

Were you ever arrested when you were protesting?

No, I was lucky. I mean, my heart was in my mouth. Because it's really something. You're walking, and they didn't care who they gave it to. And that's why they called them Jane and John Doe warrants. It was arbitrary. We would be walking around. We were always moving so we wouldn't be thought of as loitering. We were always moving. And then, when they got tired of it, the police would come, and they had these warrants, and they would just hand them out arbitrarily. So, you know, if you got one, you got one.

It was just something that I felt I needed to participate in if I wanted to contribute to a better life for all of us. And of course, as I say, my father was very involved in civil rights in the West. And in fact, when King would come to San Francisco, it would often be my father's responsibility to make sure he would be safe. My father also was very involved in raising money for the SCLC. And he and Abernathy became close friends. There are some wonderful letters that I still have. Yeah.

There was no logic to it. It was just exercising power. And they could drag anyone into jail that they wanted to. We had attorneys as well, who would come in, you know. They would have to bail them out. Because they were considered a public nuisance, or any other trumped-up charge that could be thought of to justify their actions. But generally speaking, nobody cared. It was a very different world then.

The Nashville that I encountered when I first went there in '62 was not the Nashville that I left just two short years later. Because, by that time, you literally were able to go into these places that had been trying to keep you out. I think they just got tired of us and gave in, you know; it was disruptive to business. I think some of them said, "Oh, just let them in. We're losing money here."

And then, when it got national—remember now, the South had never been exposed the way it was when the TV cameras started rolling. And so, I mean, there was the embarrassment factor as well. The world now knows how we treat these Negroes. And we call ourselves such a free society and so forth. And it's so ironic as to be almost comical, if it wasn't so horrific. See, when my father was going to school in Wiley, and traveling with the Great Debaters across country and so forth, they were witnessing lynchings. It was very dangerous, which is one of the reasons my father would send me telegrams, so afraid that I might really get myself in trouble.

From left, Eleanor's great-grandmother, Georgia Anna Green-Majors; her great-great-grandfather, Strother Green; and her grandmother, Grace Louise Majors-Boswell.

I had family there, and they would ask them to try and make sure I wasn't out there too much. And of course, I had a sister who was a tattletale. So every time I'd go, you know, she'd call Mom and Dad and say, "Ellie's back down there!"

See, in the West, as I've told you, our experience was different in its manifestation. But racism was still there. After the Civil War, there were whites who took their slaves with them to California to work in the gold mines, and even Oregon, I think one of the reasons it was so prejudiced had a lot to do with the political power that the former Confederates had. So it's everywhere, not just the South. But because our history books are so weak, and full of distorted information, this stuff gets lost. We have to preserve it.

They knew more than anyone about the dangers associated with you marching.

And theirs was more traumatic, because they were much closer to it. Having been born in 1914 and 1916, having known their parents who were very close to slavery—and their grandparents who definitely were enslaved people—you can just imagine. The reason they were in California to begin with was because of racism.

On my mother's side, her family moved to the Northwest because her mother—who was part of a family of 16; 12 girls. . . . Her father, my great-grandfather, who lived in

Weatherford, Texas, during the turn of the 20th century, told his oldest son to get his kids out of Texas because there was so much lynching and stealing of land and property, and so forth, and so on. And so my mother came from a family who systematically moved 14 out of the 16 children to Washington State, from around 1906 until the last ones arrived. And it was because of racism.

The reason my father's people moved was also because of racism. And I have all kinds of stories that have to do with the Ku Klux Klan, have to do with properties that were taken. That's why it's important to really know some of these stories—as well as to contribute to information of daily life. You know, it wasn't all running away from racists, the lives that they led. In spite of everything that was going around them, they were building their lives. And even though they suffered terribly, and, it seemed, the more success they managed to get, the steeper the fall. . . . You know, their hearts were broken, but they managed somehow to be able to stand up again and persevere. And that's something that I think it's important for all of us to know. You never give up. You keep going. And in order to do that, you need to be kind to each other. We have so much more ground to cover in our relationships with each other, such that we can, together, manage what we need to be whole in this country.

The other thing I would say also is: ignorance is something that is rampant in America, I don't care what color you are. History is mythical. Knowing the Constitution, and really appreciating that the words may say one thing, but the circumstances upon which they were written were very different. So when you have this kind of rose-colored view of the Constitution and the preamble, you have to understand who was writing it, and what their real objective was. And where were their heads then. And remembering that they were slaveholders then. And remembering that, even though Lincoln freed the slaves, he was not interested in freeing our people from a social perspective.

And you see, those things aren't taught, right? And so we get all mixed up, and we get angry. Because we, you know, we read the Bill of Rights, and we say, "Well, why is it that we can't achieve that?" And what I'm saying is we were never meant to achieve. Although it was a wonderful idea, which I pray at some point will come to fruition, let's be real about it. And let's not set ourselves up. Right?

Well, I do want to go back and talk about social life and campus life at Fisk!

Oh, my God, it was wonderful! I got there, and all of a sudden, for the first time, I had a social life with people I went to school with! And then they made me Miss Freshman, which blew me away. You know, we didn't have anything like that in the West. Kappa Court and the idea of seeing a marching band like Tennessee A&I and Florida A&M and all of that! I mean, we didn't have anything like that in the West. You know, so it was a wonderful experience. They celebrated all that, but at the same time, they celebrated academics.

And, believe it or not, even though it only makes up two years of my whole college education, I am very close to the same students that I met when I was 17, who went to Fisk. We visit each other all over the country, and we're getting together in Las Vegas at the end of the month, six of us. We've known each other for over 55 years. They are the closest friendships I've ever had.

Even when we had to stop traveling because of the Covid, every Sunday we started to Zoom. We've been Zooming almost three years now, every Sunday. And so we're gonna stick our heads down and go to Vegas and pray we don't get the Covid!

That's amazing. So that ended up being a very definitive period of your life, it sounds like.

Well, you know what, it absolutely changed my life and my outlook. That whole experience. My parents knew exactly what they were doing, because that's what happened for them. See, they understood the deficit that Black folks—at least during that period when I came around—had, because there were so few of us. And you know, we didn't have the appreciation for the richness of our own social and academic and political perspectives.

Did you have a favorite professor or class there?

Señorita Warfield. When I first went to Fisk, I was majoring in languages. And she was my language teacher. I was crazy about her. But the other teachers were dynamic, too. The history teacher, whose name I can't remember, he was amazing. In fact, he was there when my mother was there. He made history interesting. He was very dynamic. I felt like the teachers loved us, you know?

Going back to talking about . . . about racial violence. Did you ever know anyone person-ally who had been beaten or lynched for being Black?

Thankfully, no. But I heard so many stories. For example, my great-grandfather used to tell the story of Brennan, Texas. When he started a practice there, I think it was around 1887, it was one of his first practices. He had been kicked out of so many towns because he was such a radical. But what had happened was, the amendment so the Black men could vote had passed. And he was very involved with the Republi-can Party. There was some kind of a problem in that there was a Democrat, a white Democrat, who came to the polling place with the idea of stealing the voting box. And one of the Black Republicans shot him. Killed him. Because people didn't know who had actually killed him, they arrested a number of Black Republicans and put them in jail. And of course, it's the same old story. A huge crowd came, took three of the Black men out of the jail, and hung them. Okay.

When my father and Tolson and some of the other Great Debaters were—I don't know exactly where they were, I think it may have been Oklahoma—but a man was being hung. And because of my father's color, Tolson told everybody else to get down on the floor of the car, and my father drove. And he said almost up until the day that he died, he said he would never get over the horror of it. And to see whole families with children there, you know, taking souvenirs off of his body . . . he said that cruelty is something he just never would ever get over. It was a good interview; he was interviewed for the *New York Times* when the movie came out.

I remember that scene in the movie.

Yeah. So to answer your question, thankfully God has spared me in that regard.

Can you speak more on your family's issues with the KKK?

That's a big reason why we came to the West. My father's family on his mother's side owned a lot of property in a place called Huntsville, Texas, where the penitentiary is. That area was my great-great-grandfather's land. He was born before the Emancipation, but after the Emancipation, he and three or four other men actually ran the penitentiary. There's a book by Joshua Houston, who was a slave of Samuel Houston. He talks about it. He was one of the members [author's note: staffers] along with my great-great-grandfather who ran the penitentiary. Over time, my father's parents moved to that land.

They had been living in Dallas, Texas. My father's father was the superintendent of the colored schools for Dallas. He was also a violinist. And he hit the white superintendent of schools for Dallas over the head with his violin. And so, my father's family had to go into hiding. And my father's grandmother, who had this land that she had inherited in Huntsville, where the penitentiary was, she gave them land so that they could farm. And they did a halfway decent job, although both of them were ill-equipped to be farmers, because one was a violinist and the other one was a concert pianist who had gone to Boston University School of Music. And they had things going pretty well. But then, when my grandfather would take his bacon and other things from the farm into town, the townfolks started stealing his product. And then the Klan got busy. And he got notice from a neighbor who said that my family was on the target list for the Klan to burn their property down. So my grandfather had to go into hiding. My grandmother took her, by then, three, children and went to Los Angeles. So that was around 1920 or thereabouts. So the Klan ran them out.

My great-grandfather, Monroe Majors, Dr. Majors, was always being pursued by the Klan. He went from Brennan to Dallas to Calvert, Texas, and then escaped to

California. Same thing on my mother's side of the family. The Klan forced family on both her father's side and her mother's side to move West. So yeah, the Klan has had a profound impact on my family. Which is why when I, you know, even think about it, and that whole Charlottesville thing, and where we are right now, who would dream we'd be going back to this craziness?

On my father's side, my grandfather was born right after Emancipation. So I mean, he lived in Reconstruction. And he lived in a situation that was very abnormal, because his mother died in childbirth. He was maybe the fourth child, and she lost the next child. And then his father got into some kind of altercation with a white person, and ended up killing this person. And he was mulatto, so his white half brothers were able to ship him out of Weatherford in a barrel to Georgia, where the Boswell family really comes from, plantation wise.

And so, my grandfather and his siblings were split up among the brothers. My grandfather was reared at the age of one by his half uncle and aunt, and the census will show him there listed as a servant. But what they did, which was interesting, was they educated all of them. But it was so traumatic for my grandfather that he never wanted his children to know the story. It's only been through research that I've been piecing this big puzzle together for so many years. And I've even written a letter to Dr. Gates [Henry Louis Gates] asking if he would help me, because he had written a little bit about one of my relatives.

It's so interesting because that's actually what I want to focus my next big project on. The fact that there is so much land that has been stolen. I keep telling myself that I'm going to delve into that through the lens of a couple of families who had their land taken because of racial violence and were never compensated for it.

Or they would give you a pittance, with a threat. Even the land on my father's side, my great-great-grandfather's land. . . . I know my father said, even growing up in Los Angeles, there was always someone coming out trying to get more and more of the land. Until my great-grandmother, and my grandmother, finally sold it—but they tried to maintain the mineral rights. And then that became a big issue, the mineral rights.

And lest we forget, that is the way in which the United States developed. So, this was not new. I mean, the Native Americans will tell you! Look at the whole story. You know, this did not come out of nowhere. The way that people are treated, there are patterns here. And that is what is so sad. The fact that so many of us do not know our history. We fall prey to the repetition.

These patterns that have been going on forever. I mean, all you have to do is look at the major cities and look at urban renewal and look at redevelopment projects. I mean, it happens in every major city, where minorities lose their property. Eminent domain is declared, people have to move out. This evidence is there. All you have to do is look at it.

And when you look at our political discourse, oh my God. You know, you look at our, unfortunately, ill-functioning government, where one body of our legislature just absolutely refuses to move forward, and is only moving backward, and we have a Supreme Court that is making judgments based on laws that are not appropriate in this day and age . . . you gotta step back and say, what the heck?

You knew your great-grandfather, right?

Yeah. Big Dad. His name is Monroe Alpheus Majors. A lot of people have written about him. Wikipedia has done a decent job of it. I knew him. And through him, I learned about his father and mother, who were born as enslaved people. His father was Andrew Jackson Majors from Tennessee. You know, I can only think that they were probably part of that whole President Jackson Tennessee plantation. But he moved to Waco, Texas, before Emancipation. They were so determined that their children would get an education. My great-great-grandfather had a rig in Austin, Texas. He moved from Waco to Austin because he thought his children might be educated there. And he was very political, from the standpoint of trying to get Black men to vote. He drove a rig. He used to drive the legislators back and forth. And he would listen to their conversations, and then inform the Black community.

So that is the way that my great-grandfather got interested as a very young boy. He became kind of an intern in the legislature. He would do things for politicians in the Capitol. Probably went and got them lunch or whatever, but he was very young. He got interested in politics as a very young man. He had a good relationship with Frederick Douglass. By that time, Frederick Douglass was much older. But being able to sit down and talk to him as a young person was great. He was a writer, a poet, a physician, and a newspaper editor. He said that when he wrote the book, *Noted Negro Women,* he sent it to Frederick Douglass. Douglas didn't like his title. Originally, he had called it *Famous Negro Women.* And so we have this letter from Douglass that says basically there are no famous Negro Women. There are Negro women of note. But be careful, be true to the language. You should not push the paddles of time when the Negro man has yet to prove himself. He was basically saying, "Don't be talking about all these Negro women! We've got to get these Black men out there first!" (Laughing)

How were y'all connected to Paul Laurence Dunbar or knew him?

Big Dad. Dr. Majors. They were very good friends. So that's the connection. See, this was right in the middle of the Black Renaissance. So he knew everybody. And he was living in Chicago, which really was the second hub, second only to New York in terms of the Black Renaissance. So he knew Zora Neale. Langston Hughes of course came along a little bit later, but he was also very close to our family. It's a long history.

His [Big Dad's] daughter was Margaret Bonds, who was my grandmother's sister, who was a classical composer of some renown. In fact, her music is now being played all over the world . . . I went to New York to see her music being played at the Met, you know? So, there are just so many Black people who are not written about that were doing things that were just amazing. But nobody talks about it, right? Because we have been taught to think that our accomplishments don't mean much. And tha is the sadness of the whole thing.

When my great-grandmother and great-grandfather were in school, in college, those connections between Black folks were going on. They were the most mobile, con nected, extended group in their interests and their absolute belief that they could raise our race up. And that we could be accepted. W. E. B. Du Bois was another one of my family's acquaintances. And he absolutely believed that. And even when I read the preamble to my great-great-grandfather's book, you can feel that excitement, the excitement of a bright future.

You just introduced me to Margaret Bonds, because I'm ashamed to say that I haven' heard of her as a composer.

I'm not surprised. To me, she was Aunt Margaret. My grandmother had gone to Boston Institute of Music, and she [Margaret]—who was much younger, through another marriage—she and her mother were really into music. She put Langston Hughes's poetry to music. So if you've ever heard *Ballad of the Brown King*, it's by Margaret Bonds. I went to New York to hear it at the Met, and the week before it was at Carnegie Hall. And now it's all over the world. And in fact, just recently we were trying to get the rights to some of our music because some of it has been discovered. And, unfortunately, it seems like everything is cannibalized. You know even my great-grandfather's book. Someone has taken it and changed the name of it—although it gives him credit for having written it. And the same thing with Aunt Margaret's music. It's being cannibalized.

Like you said, same old story.

Same old story. There's a harpist who did her dissertation on Margaret. She gradu- ated from Juilliard, and she said that there aren't a whole lot of Black harpists. Okay. And she said it was Aunt Margaret's music and determination that kept her going. Since then, I've met two other women whose dissertations are on Aunt Margaret.

*A book inscribed by Langston Hughes to a young
Eleanor.*

The other thing a lot of people don't understand is that Black folks have been in classical music so much longer than people ever dreamed. I was looking up Frederick Douglass III—he used to be my mother's fiancé. And he. . . . His father, Joseph Douglass, was an acclaimed violinist. And his wife was also a classical musician. So, you know, people just don't know that we've been on every front.

I realized that my family has fought in every war since the Revolutionary War—every single war. And the big thing was education, education, education . . . even if you had to hide to do it. And we have done so much to try to be accepted. But look what's happening right now. It's just absolutely mind-boggling. You know, when I moved back to the South, I didn't really think about it. I didn't think about it because I really did believe in the New South. And I haven't had any problems, I live in a wonderful place. My neighbors are wonderful people. But I go to the Y to Silver Sneakers, and some of the conversations I overhear. . . . My goodness.

Are there any stories that were passed down from your enslaved family members that you can recall?

So often, the stories that I remember were passed down by those who may have missed slavery by a year or something. They were stories about their folks, right. But no one would talk about slavery. And I think it's because it was so painful. I think they just didn't want to tell us about it. And because my sister and I didn't—nor did my parents—grow up in the South, they were far enough away from it that even *they* weren't told that much about slavery. Because their parents who were born right at Emancipation, and knew a lot, probably, I'm assuming, because some of their parents were still living who had been enslaved. . . . You didn't talk about it.

And that's the unfortunate story of the Great Migration, especially the West that has its own history of Black arrivals, even in the 1700s. But after World War II, when the Great Migration came, people were further cut off from their roots and they have no connection to the past. And I don't know about your folks, but some of my folks just didn't want to talk about slavery. They didn't want you to know. It was so brutal, they just didn't want us to know.

And then, I come from a family that was very mixed up from the standpoint of intermixing. Right. And there was a lot of confusion in families like that, because of the way our minds were shaped. And it's really funny because now, in my mid-seventies, I'm crying over it. See, I didn't think about it before—what my ancestors went through. And the reason I look the way I look, you know, I didn't personalize it. I do a lot of genealogy. And you know, my DNA is there. And there are a whole lot of people that are not Black that are related to me. I'm African and European. So England and Scotland are on the European side. And then my African side is Ghana, Benin, and Togo.

I was always considered the darker part of the family, although I'm not that dark. But see, there was a time when there was something called the mulatto race. And the idea was to keep it mulatto. And what some families did was to say, "Okay, you stay within the race." Right? And then when Jim Crow came along, and it no longer benefited Blacks, politically—when the vote was also something to be considered—they didn't want a mulatto race. In fact, I can't remember which census it was, but there was actually a column called mulatto. And then that changed. And people like my family, who were so mixed, they had to make a decision. Am I going to live white? Or am I going to live Black? Those who had color had no choice. And there were many who looked white but said, "To heck with that, I'm Black." So it's just another part of the sad tale of chattel slavery, and the different ways that were conceived in order to keep us separated.

Only to find that, hey, there's the one-eighth rule, right? There's that case called Plessy. The guy was only one-eighth Black and he still couldn't sit in the car.

What did you do after you graduated?

I worked for the IBM Corporation in marketing, sales, and management. I did that and got credit for 30 years, even though I took an eight-year bridge. So I was able to retire when I was 48. And then I, along with other retired IBMers, started a company called Power Learning Systems. And our objective was to lift African Americans to a position of equal status in the American society. And we lasted about eight or nine years. And what we did was, we split up the country and formed groups in different geographic areas, and presented a curriculum that would have as its goal to have Black people be able to show economic presence in major SIC codes. And so that was a rough, rough, rough time.

I had everything from Denver west. So I organized groups in Washington, Oregon, California, Colorado. My other IBM friends who had retired, who were all male, and had all been in marketing, took the rest of the country. And we had a pretty good run for a while. But part of the sadness of it all was our utter distrust of each other. And you saw the Willie Lynch syndrome come to life. It just didn't work out, from a social, economic, experiential, and even breaking-the-slave-mentality perspective. It didn't work out. We learned a lot of good lessons, but it took a high toll. So I got out of that, recuperated, and then I went into the newspaper business. I was copublisher of a local newspaper in the Bay Area. It was called *The Globe*. It was a Black newspaper that was serving Oakland, Richmond, Berkeley, and San Francisco. It was quite an experience. I think the reason I got into it in the first place was purely romantic—just the nostalgia of thinking about my great-grandfather, who had edited all these different newspapers in Chicago and all over the place. And I got way deeper into it, more than I had planned. But it was a good experience.

You know, everything I've done has been a wonderful experience, really. I got into politics, I ran campaigns for city council people and one mayor. I won every one of them. I almost went into politics, changed my mind. And then, I decided that I'd go back to school. Enrolled in John F. Kennedy University, and got a master's in psychology. I graduated in 2014! I was always the oldest one in my class, but I loved it because I was with all these young people! And they liked me, which I thought was interesting. I learned so much from them, and I guess they learned a little bit from me. And then I said, you know, I'm getting out of the Bay Area. So I moved South. It's full circle. We all have roots in the South, of course, that's where we all came from.

Do you believe Dr. King's dream is possible in this country?

I think anything is possible. I like his method better than the let's-shoot-and-kill-everybody mentality. I am definitely a nonviolent person. I really thought, though, given my age and everything, that we would almost be there by now. And so I'm deeply disappointed in terms of . . . of where we are in this country. So I want to say yes, I believe it's possible. But I would also have to say that I doubt seriously that it will be in my lifetime.

Well, at this point, I don't even know if it's gonna be in mine either.

But you always have to remember that you must persevere. Because if you give up then it will be a self-fulfilling prophecy. That's it. And so, I think we should always work toward the goal. You have to have a destination, or any route will do.

You have to have a destination, you have to be able to dream about what you want. And you have to be able to see yourself in that dream. Because if you can't see yourself in that dream, you are doomed. I'm not saying we're not crying. I mean, I'm very distressed. But I'm not giving up. And the thing is, I'm not going to be out there marching anymore. My girlfriends and I talk about it all the time. You know? When Black Lives Matter was happening, I was on the phone with my girlfriends, and I joked with them, "Hey, I thought you were gonna be out there in the streets!" And they said, "Wait, hold the phone. My marching days are over!"

I'd be happy to help and give as much wisdom as I can. But this is a young person's time. They've got to be the foot soldiers now. My generation has gotta know when to sit down. So we won't be out there in the streets, but we certainly are people who can be there to pick up young people and give them as much hope as possible. You know, we didn't have a whole lot of hope in the beginning of the Civil Rights Movement. But in any revolution, you have to see the dream.

I just thought about it. With you being from California, did you know any Black Panthers?

Yes. In fact, Huey and I were very good friends.

Oh my gosh, you know everybody!

No, I don't! But I mean, I have some books upstairs, he had written little notes to me. He really loved my dad. And when I came back from Asia, I had a friend who knew Huey well, and they picked me up from the airport. And so, from that moment on, Huey and I used to love to talk. He was writing a book and I was trying to help him

Eleanor's father, uncles, and grandfather.

a little bit. But you know, he always wanted to keep me away from some of the stuff that was going on. We had a very good friendship.

Did you ever consider getting involved with the Black Panthers?

No. No.

They were a little more radical than you?

It wasn't that, it was just at that time, what was going on, it just wasn't compatible with where my head was. And . . . I was not accepted that well. At least on the Oakland scene. It might have been different maybe in Chicago or New York. But, you know, I was considered bourgeois. And I was fine with that. And the last time I saw Huey, it was a very sad occasion. But he and his bodyguard—Big Man, I think they called him—never wanted me around potentially dangerous places.

They had a lot of good ideas. They were visionaries, too.

They were. They were visionaries. They were set up in so many ways. Purposefully. Hoover did a lot to them. Huey really was very intellectual. I think, though, there were people who really led him astray, especially when it came to the drugs. Way too many drugs around. And Huey had a temper, no question about it. I've seen it. It's not pretty. And there was a lot of rivalry within the Panther party.

Even SNCC, they kind of lost their way. Stokely lost his way. But I'm not hard on those brothers because I know what they went through. I know what *I* went through growing up, you know—we lived in a household where we would get threatening calls all the time. If you talk to my sister, you would swear that she grew up in a house of fear. To me, it was always kind of exciting. Because of my father's activism, it was nothing for us to get calls all the time saying they were gonna kill us. At one point, my sister and I were being followed. Members of the church would sit out in front of our house when the threats became really tough. My father, I can see him now, sitting in the window with a gun in San Francisco. He was also the chaplain of the police department. And boy, did a bunch of the police hate that!

What my dad used to say was, you know, don't get upset, because when someone announces they're going to do something to you, 9 times out of 10, they're not going to do anything. It's the ones that don't announce. So you always have to know where you are, what you're doing, and who's around you. And I never forgot that, which is another reason I wasn't real comfortable in the presence of the Panthers, and I did not become a Panther. All right. I did not socialize with the Panthers. I knew some of them.

What did your dad think about the Panthers?

He and Huey liked each other. My father at one point said, and this was way before they—really, Huey—lost his way, my father said, "You know what? I think if I had grown up around you this time, I might be doing the same thing Huey's doing." My mother was very upset, and so were other people, because of the relationship that we had. But my father really wasn't that taken aback. I'm very much like him. And he knew that.

Now, we have the opportunity to tell our own stories.

You're right. And I mean, we have to be depicted beyond our suffering. People should understand our humanity. We get up in the morning and brush our teeth. It's like some white people don't even think about us in that way. So I believe that one of the ways to get to—hopefully—where we want to go, is by finding that common ground. Well, how do you find that common ground? If Blacks and whites can't even relate to each other, and they are still listening to these ridiculous, mythical characterizations of us, we continue to be objectified.

You know, this reminded me of something else. I'd heard this story about my great-grandfather in Brennan, Texas, all my life from him. And something dawned on me . . . I said, let me Google "Brennan, Texas hangings." Boom, here came the articles. I think there were three of them. One was by a white paper. And two were by Black papers. It was as if they were two separate incidents. I mean, just totally different. When we don't have an opportunity to testify and be able to tell the whole story, it's just a partial account. And we're supposed to be satisfied with it.

In my files, I have a piece that was written by my grandfather, who was born in 1868. He wasn't a writer, now. And guess what? It's not a story about slavery. It's actually a story about these characters that he made up that were ogres living under a bridge. And the reason I find the story so interesting is because of his perspective. You know, sometimes when people aren't talking about anything serious, you can still glean from their writing a bit about who they are.

Florence and her daughters.

INTERVIEW NO. 3

FLORENCE HAYES

Okay, my maiden name is Florence Louvinia Morbley, and my name now is Florence Hayes. And I was born on March 2, 1951, in Lexington, Kentucky. My birth certificate is so old that where it says "race," mine has the word *colored*.

Well, in Lexington, Kentucky, my dad, he was somebody that bathed the horses and took care of them. So I figure we lived for free from his services of taking care of the horses. The horses he took care of were the horses that went to different races like the Kentucky Derby and other horse-racing activities. Then, we moved to Nashville. We came on a train down at the L&N train station on Union or Broad or wherever it is. But that was a real train station. And we came on the train and moved to Nashville. And I went to Wharton School and Pearl High School. I went to kindergarten also in Nashville. So pretty much all my schooling was in Nashville.

You know, I didn't realize I had actually moved somewhere probably until I wasn't where I grew up. I don't know why we moved. Everywhere I lived, there was no indoor plumbing. So, interestingly enough, when I got in the 11th grade, we moved into a house that had indoor bathtubs and hot running water.

What did your parents do for work when they got to Nashville?

My dad, he worked at the stockyard. It used to be a place down in Nashville where people bought and sold their candles and goods. And it was called a stockyard. But it's probably updated now, there's probably some nice restaurants or something there now. It was down on First Avenue in Nashville.

And then, when I was probably seven, my dad hung himself. That happened in Gallatin, Tennessee, because we were visiting my mom's brother and his wife. So he hung himself, and that was when I was probably in first grade.

I grew up in an era where you really didn't ask a lot of questions. You kind of just went with the flow. And I didn't know to ask questions. And probably knew *not* to ask questions. My mom became a single parent. She did pretty well, but during that time I thought she was really strict for no reason. But she became a single parent all of a sudden, so everything changed.

My uncle found my dad hanging. Back then, when a meal is fixed, you don't eat until everybody comes to the table. So we were waiting on him to come to breakfast. Bacon and eggs and biscuits and homemade jelly was sitting in the house, and we was waiting on him to come in to say the blessing. And of course, back then, the bathrooms were outside, also. So after he didn't return for a while, my uncle went out. Interestingly enough, there's a college called Vol State in Gallatin. And part of that university is built on that property where my dad hung himself.

They expanded it because the people that owned the property, they were very wealthy people in Gallatin, and that's who my uncle worked for. He took care of his sheep and blueberries and blackberries . . . he did that type of work. I think my dad went there maybe to look for work or something. I don't know exactly why we went to visit, but we went to visit them. We rode the Greyhound bus down there and I don't know how we got back. After my dad died, I don't remember a lot of what happened in between, you know?

My dad. . . . I always knew every Friday that he would bring home some bananas. Every Friday like clockwork. I would sit on the porch and wait for him to turn that corner. And he always had bananas with him. And when it was real cold and my mom wanted to dress me one way, but if I didn't want to wear that, when my mom would already be gone to work, I would talk my dad into letting me wear what I wanted to wear. And I remember one time after that, she always got me ready before she left, because I guess it was cold and maybe he just let me wear something that could be some summertime thing. I know he didn't have any choice in helping me get dressed anymore after that!

It was just me and my mom after he died. My mom and my dad apparently never got married. I don't know why. I don't have any siblings. I used to ask my mom if I had sisters and brothers, and she would say, "Sure, you do," but she never gave me any names or a way of trying to find them. So, to my knowledge, I don't have any sisters and brothers.

When we returned to Nashville, she did day work. That's like when you clean people's houses and they pay you every day. She had certain houses that she did maybe twice a week or whatever. And we lived with her other sister until my mom found somewhere for us to live alone. That was the first place that didn't have indoor plumbing. And then we moved to another place that didn't have plumbing, but it was much nicer than the first place. Finally, we moved to a house with the indoor plumbing. And that was how I knew about it—I'd go to my friends' houses and see that they had bathrooms. But I didn't worry about that because I was always fed and was never hungry.

I still have one friend that, even when I didn't have what she had, her parents would make sure they bought me Easter outfits and things like that to help my mom, and help me not be without. So we always ended up in a circle of good people. So I guess I didn't feel so deprived. If they took their daughter out to dinner, they took me too, so it was like, I didn't pay the price because I moved around just as much as everybody else did. Maybe a different fashion.

My mom never really talked about my dad's death. We had to survive and make it without him. That's not what she said, but that was in her actions. Even when I got older, she never really mentioned him. And neither did I.

In the back of my mind, I've always felt that my dad was lynched. When they took me outside that day, see, there was a bucket that you would sit on when you were milking a cow. And he was hanging above that, and the bucket was kicked over. When you hang yourself, apparently once you hang, you kind of unwind and go back the other way. But your head is still in the noose. And he was actually going back the other way. I still remember seeing that bucket. I saw his body. He was hanging there. I don't ever remember anybody asking me any questions. Nobody.

There are a lot of things about this that aren't panning out. There was a time, when I found out they were going to build Vol State on some of that property, I wanted to contact an attorney to see if there was something like abuse of a corpse or whatever to look into it more.

So, I don't know. Maybe he was lynched. Maybe he actually killed himself. Maybe my mom learned to shut it out and shut down. Maybe she knew why he did it and never wanted to tell me, or maybe she knew things were going on. Maybe he couldn't find a job or feel like he could be the provider. Maybe he left a note that she never showed me. I have no clue. Either way, the South killed him.

Now, I do know that one of the ladies that she worked for helped her dig into it and got her some money. She dug into it and got his Social Security money after he had been dead for years. She's the one that got my birth certificate because my mom didn't really have a birth certificate. So she got the birth certificate and then got my mom the money. And she's actually the one that got my mom a telephone at our house. So, as far as having prejudice, I'm not prejudiced because I know that a lot of white people helped my mom. Even if I'm in an unpleasant or toxic situation, I can deal with them until I can move on. And I've learned to do that, and I guess that's it.

I didn't know my grandparents on either side. I have no idea. I never met them. Now, some of my mom's family, I know names, but I don't know them. And they're just names that you heard growing up. Because my mom was originally from Pulaski and Columbia down further South. And I don't know at what age she came to Nashville, or if Nashville was her first stop before she met my dad.

In our neighborhood, everything was pretty much within walking distance. You'd walk to school, walk to the little corner store. My mom's sister had a garden where she grew vegetables, and I actually grew up about a half a mile away from Fisk

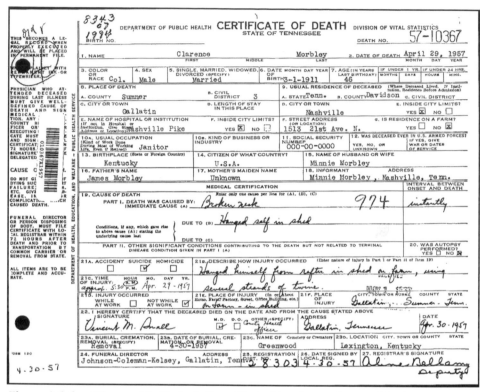

Florence's father, Clarence Morbley's, death certificate. Note the stated cause of death.

University. I grew up in that neighborhood. In fact, we used to trespass and cut through Fisk to get to our high school over by the railroad tracks. But, you know, we didn't worry about trespassing. That was a shortcut. And we didn't really pay that sign a whole bunch of attention because we were going to high school and we thought we knew everything.

When I went to elementary school—which the name has changed now, but it was called Wharton—I lived across the street from the school, so that was easy. There weren't any school buses that were in our neighborhood. Public transportation, the MTA . . . if you were Negro, you sat at the back of the bus. And the little burger place, Krystal's, you couldn't eat in Krystal's or Woolworth's. Krystal's would sell you food to-go and Woolworth's had an old-fashioned counter, but you couldn't sit there. There were water fountains in all of the public places downtown, and they were labeled *colored* and *white*. It appeared to be the same water.

I had my daughter at 18, so I became a single parent at a young age. My mom and I still lived together because I was still in high school. And I had a baby and dropped out. I did get my GED years later. And when my daughter was three, my mom lost her eyesight due to diabetes. I do know that diabetes and cancer both run in my family on my mom's side. That's about all the history I know about that side.

That's kind of where my life started with bad marriages, bad choices, and everything else. However, I'm still thankful that I have what health I have and the strength to still work—some by choice because I enjoy it, and some out of necessity because I need the funds.

At age 71, I was just very thankful to have found a company that is hiring seniors, because a lot of companies. . . . I mean, I have a couple of friends younger than me, and they have lots of skills, but most of it is technology stuff. And some of them are still having to work temp services because of the job market. So I have a full-time job with benefits, and that makes me feel happy each day when I wake up, because there are a lot of people that don't have that. The offices I clean at Fisk, they really treat me like a human.

As a young girl, I guess I didn't know the rules of segregation. One day, I went into Krystal's on a cold, snowy day. And there was a stool at the counter. Being young, how young I don't know, I went and sat on that stool. But before my bottom could hit the stool real good, my mom kind of picked me up by the hood of my coat. She said, "You can't sit there, we got to get our food to-go." I remember getting the Krystal's, and her explaining to me that we couldn't sit in there.

I wasn't a part of the sit-ins and protests because during that time, my mom and her sister tried to keep us away from that type of stuff. We didn't get to like ride the bus and go downtown and protest or anything, during the time that everybody was standing up for our race. And I remember one time around Christmas, the organizers wanted the Black people to not spend their money downtown at the store that wouldn't let us sit down and eat. They were standing in front of the stores to make sure that other Black people didn't support them. And I remember my mom telling me, "Christmas gonna be a little different this year because we can't shop downtown. They boycotting." So we didn't support the white stores.

When my mom would clean white folks' houses, I would go, but most of the time when I went I had to sit in a set seat. And I had my coloring books and my paper dolls. But when I got maybe like 14 or 15, there were things she would let me do, but they were very limited. You know, she might say, "You can run the vacuum in this room here." She would limit it to protect me.

Most of the time when my mom cleaned their houses, she cleaned in the daytime and they weren't there. I remember one of the families had dogs, and they were mean dogs. They would bite. I remember she said that when she found out that the dogs were scared of the vacuum, she would turn the vacuum on when she first got there, and that kept them quiet and away from her.

Some of them got very picky. Some of the work she got was from running ads in the paper: "Day work wanted." And people would look in the paper and call her. You could run an ad in the *Tennessean*, and that was how she got some of the jobs. She would try to get regular clients, and we would always get a better place to move to when she secured regulars. Occasionally, somebody that she met knew somebody that had a better place than where we were staying. So, it was always associated with her job because we would upgrade from where we were.

There was a lady in the neighborhood that kept the kids. She had nine children herself and was a stay-at-home mom. She was at home all the time. So that was where I would go before and after school. And then anybody in the neighborhood whose parents weren't at home, that needed to stay there, could. Many times, my mom and I, we spent the night there. My mom got out late at night, so we would just stay. If you needed her, she was at home.

SERIAL NUMBER	1. NAME (Print)			ORDER NUMBER
466	JAMES (First)	MORBLEY (Middle) (Last)		2004

2. ADDRESS (Print)
466 BreckinRidgeSt LEXINGTON FAyETTE Ky
(Number and street or R. F. D. number) (Town) (County) (State)

3. TELEPHONE	4. AGE IN YEARS	5. PLACE OF BIRTH	6. COUNTRY OF CITIZENSHIP
	22	LEXINGTON (Town or county)	
	DATE OF BIRTH		
	10 - 5 - 18	KENTuckY	U.S.
(Exchange) (Number)	(Mo.) (Day) (Yr.)	(State or country)	

7. NAME OF PERSON WHO WILL ALWAYS KNOW YOUR ADDRESS
KatHERINE JACKSON
(Mr., Mrs., Miss) (First) (Middle) (Last)

8. RELATIONSHIP OF THAT PERSON
MOTHER

9. ADDRESS OF THAT PERSON
466 BRECKINRIDGESt. LEXINGTON FAyETTE Ky
(Number and street or R. F. D. number) (Town) (County) (State)

10. EMPLOYER'S NAME
HuBBARD and CuRRY

11. PLACE OF EMPLOYMENT OR BUSINESS
SHOLT and LiME LEXINGTON FAyETTE Ky
(Number and street or R. F. D. number) (Town) (County) (State)

I AFFIRM THAT I HAVE VERIFIED ABOVE ANSWERS AND THAT THEY ARE TRUE.

REGISTRATION CARD
D. S. S. Form 1 (over) 16—17105
James Morbley
(Registrant's signature)

Florence's uncle's draft registration card.

It was a very close neighborhood, and people really did look out for each other. The generations before them always paid it forward. If people had a garden in their back-yard and they needed tomatoes, the neighbors could come over and get tomatoes. Somebody else may have green beans, and they'd say you can come over and get your green bean. They always kind of shared with each other.

When did you realize that you were Black?

Well, the first time I realized I was Black. . . . In Nashville, there is a public housing area called Cheatham Place. At the time, it was 100 percent white. My mom and I were walking through the neighborhood, going to the Dairy Dip to get some ice cream, and a little boy about seven years old hung his head out the window and yelled in a singsong voice, "Nigger, nigger, nigger!" And I yelled back, "Your mama, your mama, your mama!" And my mama slapped her hand over my mouth to muzzle me. We didn't go back that way. We walked back home another way.

It made a difference to me. I knew there were white people because my mom worked for them. Before then, I had figured that the ones she worked for must have accepted the fact that she was Black and needed a job. So I guess I didn't ever get the point of racism. Not liking people that's not your color makes no sense. We're all human.

Did you ever feel limited growing up in the segregated South?

I didn't know I was being limited until I realized that some of the textbooks we were getting were textbooks that had been checked out before. You might get a textbook that four people already had checked out previously. And then, as I got older, I found out that those textbooks were coming from the white schools. So we were behind. But at the time, we didn't know we were behind. I don't remember ever getting a book where I was the first person to sign it out. It was always a used book from the white schools.

On integration:

Some of my friends got transferred to other schools. They got transferred to the white schools. By that time I had a baby so I wasn't really in school, though.

Integration was bittersweet. I think if we stick together as the Black community, we would be stronger than the white community, and they would feel very inferior. However, on the other hand, we're almost to the point where we almost have to be there at their protocol because they have control over so many things. If we don't follow their protocol and play by their rules, we might not make it successfully. However, I remember when we first started saying "Black Power," and making the little fist. We did that as teenagers just as a symbol of Black power. But if we think about it, what we were saying is, we got the Black power, *but* we've just got to put it together.

We can be doing well, but somehow, at some point in our navigating, the white man is always there to say, "Not so fast. You got one more hurdle to go." I realized that they just couldn't leave us alone. I wish they could meet us halfway and work with us. I think integration was a good thing in some ways, but then, I think that it was a way—in the long run—to control things more heavily from a white perspective. So now, they'll let us come and sit down and eat, but they would control how many could come, what time you can arrive, what time you can leave . . . all of this is by their laws. So, it's still a control thing. They offered it to us, but at what cost?

But I say don't let anybody second-guess you because you are Black. Because, at the end of the day, when a Klu Klux Klansman goes to bed and closes his eyes, he's the one that's got to lay down at night with what he did. To me, why are they covering their faces? If you are real about what you believe in, show me your face! If I put something on my face and cover up, you're going to call the police and say I'm trying to rob you. Now, they're still around, but without the sheets.

I believe Dr. King's dream is possible because I believe anything is possible. But it's possible with time. And you have to build it. And that's what we're doing. We're building it. So yes, I believe it is possible. Yes.

What would your message be to African Americans in the future?

I would say be strong. And never give up.

George after his dental school graduation.

INTERVIEW NO. 4

GEORGE CALEB McLAUGHLIN

I was born in Raeford, North Carolina. Hoke County. I grew up on a farm. The nearest house was probably an eighth of a mile away from where I grew up—the house I grew up in. The neighborhood was farmland. We were surrounded by white farmers and two Black farmers in addition to us.

My father was a farmer, a part-time butcher, and a part-time barber. I forgot who owned the land. It was a sharecropper arrangement. There was a total of eight of us kids, and I was the last. The baby. As a little kid, we worked as soon as we could get up and get out. We had our chores to do because we always raised pigs. One of my chores was to feed the pigs, feed the chickens. And then I'd go to school.

Initially I went to a little country-type school, the little two-room schoolhouse. And there were several of those in the county. And we would walk to the one that was closest to us, which was a mile away or so. We didn't start school until the middle of late September, and when we started, we did half-day. So you'd have to come home and have to gather the crops in the afternoon. And then, during the spring we did half-day so that we could help to plant the crops.

That was the way life was, so I didn't know any other way. The main thing was to get to school. Now, after I started school—in the beginning, when I started school— grammar school kids could not ride the school bus. There were very few buses we had, and only the high school kids could ride the school bus. We had a Black high school, a white high school, and a Native American high school in the county. That was the way it was you know, and you knew nothing else until later on in life, when you began to find out that things were separate and unequal.

All of my siblings finished high school. My parents . . . one, I think, went to second grade, and one went through fourth grade. They left because they had to work. My grandparents . . . my grandfather had a farm, and the kids had to work on it. Now, my father's father I never really knew. My mother's father, I knew. But my father's father had died before I grew up.

My grandfather had a farm, so his kids had to leave school in order to work the farm. Or not go to school at all. That was common. I'm not sure how many students started out in the eighth grade with me. But I think we started out with over 100 students in the eighth grade and we graduated 75.

How would your teachers have described you when you were back in school?

I was a pretty good student, and a pretty good kid. I didn't give people any trouble at all. And they didn't give me any trouble either, because I had four big brothers. And they had a lot of big friends, so nobody bothered me.

My parents made sure that I went to school every day. The fact that I was able to go to school every day was great. My mom said you go to school, you get an education. That's something nobody can take away from you. So they made sure that I went to school every day.

Math was good. It was my favorite class. We had recess. We played softball and base-ball and basketball. But recess was pretty short anyway. I don't recall exactly how long they were, but they were short. I know that. We had a band, and, of course, glee clubs.

For band, the school loaned the instrument. I believe that the PTA bought the instruments for the band. I'm not sure. The band wasn't that big anyway: probably 20 pieces at the most.

The whole thing is the sharecropper had to pay for any labor out of their half of the earnings. And the owner of the land didn't pay anything. If there was cotton to be picked or something like that . . . you know, because you were talking about cot-ton and tobacco, where you needed to get additional help to work it if the family couldn't work it. Let's say we were working with tobacco. There may be too much work for the family to do it. So the family would have to actually hire additional people, and they would have to pay them. Not the landowner.

That's the way it worked. And depending on the arrangement you had with the landowner, you may have to pay half or a third. In some instances, I've heard where people had to pay more than a half. If you didn't make payment, the money that you borrowed, you just had to flip it over to the next year. That's the reason my father was doing butchering and barbering to make ends meet and take care of the family. Help take care.

My mother didn't work outside the home, but my older siblings would do a little work outside. You know, there were peach orchards around. During that time, they would work there—gathering the peaches, apples, things like that.

The town of Raeford had little Black communities, and since there was no work for them, the only work that they had was farming. Some of the individuals worked at Fort Bragg, but most of them worked on the farm gathering the crops.

I have read a lot, and also heard stories from my own family, about how, at the end of the season, the sharecroppers would go in and speak to the landowner and tally the books, and those books were never fair. Did you have any experiences with that?

Oh, I was never involved, it was always my father. And I never knew what . . . what they did, because I wasn't around that. I was in school. So most of my time was spent at school. I would assume that my older brothers might have done some of that but I never really discussed it with them.

My grandfather was a good guy. I think my grandfather was born in the Pinehurst area, because there was a little area next to Pinehurst called Taylortown. That's where the Blacks lived. But what happened is supposedly there was this area that was set up as a resort, called Pinehurst. And it was a golf resort. And there was one guy and his last name was Taylor.

He was the one who got caddies and people like that for the golfers, and they named that area after him. Taylortown. And that's where my grandfather, or, I think that's where my grandfather, came from. I know that's where my mother came from.

My grandparents were not enslaved. They were born after the Civil War. My father's father, I believe he was born in South Carolina.

The unwritten rules were that everything was separate. You know, there were no restaurants or anything like that we could go to as Blacks. If you wanted to get a sandwich from a restaurant, as I recall, the only one in town . . . the only way Blacks could get food or anything in the restaurant was to go to a window that was on the outside. You could not go inside the restaurant. Same thing with the movies. They were all separated. And some of the smaller small towns, like Rich Springs, which was in the next county over, they had a movie with three different areas. One for Blacks, one for American Indians, and one for Whites. All in the same building, but different floors. The whites were on the first floor, Blacks on the second floor, American Indians on the third floor.

We just ignored it then. It was just a part of life. But we later became part of the NAACP. I don't believe Black people in my town voted. Oh wait, some did. Because I had some cousins that voted. There were just certain areas you didn't go, you know— you just avoided it. We knew what to do to keep ourselves safe. My parents always told us: don't go here, don't go there. You know, be back at a certain time. And we followed the playbook. And then, by the time I was 17 or 18, I was away at school. I was in Greensboro, and that's where I really learned about segregation and integration.

I had older siblings that went to college. I was the only one that graduated. I think some of it was financially motivated. And some of it was just being prepared. You know? But I think it was mostly financial. I got two scholarships when I went to school. I got one from a club at school and one from church. Which paid almost half my tuition. And each of those scholarships was $50. At A&T at that time, my tuition was $511 a year. That included all books—books at that time, we rented books, we didn't buy books. Books, laundry, food, lodging, everything.

My parents gave me the rest. That's the reason my father was working as a barber and as a butcher, part time. But basically full time almost. And then, I paid some of the tuition myself. I was a shoeshine boy in the barbershop when I was home. And then, when I was in Greensboro, I had two jobs. One, I worked at UNCG when it was University of North Carolina Women's College. I worked in the kitchen there. And then, I worked at . . . I guess you could call it a nightclub, in Greensboro.

I was a dishwasher at the college, and I mopped the floor at the end of the day. At the end of the day, after I got out of class at A&T, I would go over there and work, and I also worked there on the weekend. I don't recall ever interacting with a manager. I'd just go in and you know, we had the automatic . . . well, I guess you could call it . . . not an automatic dishwasher, but the dishes went down like a conveyor, and basically what you did was take them off after they would dry, and stack them and get them so that they can be placed on tables for the students.

I got the job through one of the students there at the college. You know, like a lot of things, their jobs would be passed down. One person would get ready to graduate and would replace themselves with somebody else.

My major at A&T was mechanical engineering. I liked math, and I liked machinery and things like that, and I knew that was a part of that: designing machines and things of that nature. So I decided to go into engineering.

What did your parents think about your major?

Well, like they didn't know that much about engineering. You know . . . like some of the people in town said, "Well, are you going to drive a train? What will you do with that?" My parents just wanted us to go to school. They didn't care what my major was because they didn't know that much about majors or anything, other than being a schoolteacher.

Coming from Raeford and growing up on the farm and stuff, Greensboro was kind of like a big city. It was a big city, and it was a *cold* big city. Going to Greensboro to go off to school wasn't bad because you had a lot of other students doing the same. Plus, there were about four or five of us from the high school that went there. And then because we had students from Fayetteville High School that went there too. But see, Fayetteville had I believe three Black high schools during that time. I know they had two, Chestnut and E. Smith, and I think there was a third one. Because that county, which is Cumberland County, had the main post of Fort Bragg. There were a lot of high schools over there.

How did you get to A&T when you were leaving to move in?

My parents drove me up there. It was a pretty straightforward paper application. I got letters of recommendation from a teacher and the school in general. One of the reasons I went to A&T was because of the band. And the band director that we had in high school was an A&T graduate. He had played in the band and the band would come there. The concert band from A&T came to our high school and played there during the spring a couple of times. And I always wanted to play in that band!

That was a part of the reason I went there. The other reason was my two older brothers had gone there. I played trumpet. I started off freshman year in the band. I only played in the concert band for maybe one year, and I played in the marching band two years.

It took up a lot of my time, that's the reason I only played two years. Because engineering took a lot of time. You know, we were in engineering drawing or something like that, all weekend. You know, we would be in the engineering building doing all kinds of drawings. Along with chemistry and physics and all those other courses like that, it just wasn't enough time to stay with the band.

But I had lasting relationships from the band. I even went back several years to do alumni band. I had a chance to travel in the marching band to Florida A&M. That I do recall, because that was my second year there. That was my second time out of North Carolina. The first time, I had gone to Maryland to see my aunt. And that was it.

They hired about, I guess three or four buses. You're talking about segregation during that time. So, I think we stopped in South Carolina. And we stopped in Georgia, on the way to Tallahassee. And we stayed in the dormitories at other HBCUs on the way down. There was no place else to stay. And I'd never gone south of North Carolina at that time. It was exciting because it was a new experience.

In regards to segregation, well, I actually realized that things were not the way that they should be. I realized that when I saw how the little white boys in the neighborhood had new things, and I didn't. And I realized how they looked down on Blacks rather than look at them as equal, and realized how segregation really played against you as a Black individual. I can recall my mother telling me when I was playing with them, because a lot of the kids were my age, she said, "Maybe you better watch playing with those little white boys." And I said, "Okay."

But then one day I realized what she meant when one of the little kids who was younger than I was—I was probably around 9 or 10 years old at the time, and then there was this little kid that was probably five or six, and then there were the older boys that were teenagers . . . and they had the little kid who was five or six come over and tell me, looking at some Black folks on the back of a truck, he said, "George those are niggers on the back of that truck." You know, and at that point, I didn't know how to take it. I just walked away. I was surprised and upset. And that was the last day I played with them. I realized then what my mother was talking about. And I never forgot it.

I would see the boys all the time after that. But I had no further interactions with them.

At A&T, I got involved in the sit-ins. I was not one of the leaders in it, though. I was more of one of the faces in the crowd. So the four guys that sat down initially came back to campus and said what had happened. The buzz was that they were going back down there the next day, or that afternoon, one or the other. I don't know how many it was down there. I know I was down there the second day. We had maybe a couple of hundred people, students who went down and sat down there at the lunch counter and refused to get up. What we would do is we would line up behind the stools of the students who were sitting, and when it was time for that student to go, they'd get up and then another student would sit down so nobody else could get to the stool. And that went on. I wasn't nervous at all. It was something new, and we didn't know anything about it.

We had white people yelling at us and things of that nature, but that was the way that things were. They yelled at you anyway, whether you were there or not. The big difference was that we had numbers. There were many more of us than there was them. We'd sit there and order, but nobody served us. So we'd just sit there. They ignored you anyway. You'd just sit there. They just looked at you anyway, the workers didn't say anything to you.

When you finished, some of us would leave, some would stay there. I went a number of times. But I wasn't there every day.

I heard of cigarette butts being put in people's pockets and that type of stuff, but I never had that happen to me. The other thing that I did was the stand-ins at the theaters. I can recall standing there in line, and a white guy on crutches tried to hit me with his crutches. And I had to jump back out of the way. He couldn't hardly stand up without his crutches, but he was trying to hit me with his crutch.

It was a segregated entrance there, I don't remember the name of the theater. But it was segregated like all the other theaters in the state. So we would try to say we don't want to go upstairs, we'd say we want to sit down in the orchestra level. So we would stand-in there in that line. And again, they wouldn't sell us the tickets for it. When you go to the movie theater and buy your ticket, you would buy your ticket for a certain level when you got there. The segregated level. It was a separate ticket window altogether.

Sometimes, it would be the same person selling the tickets. They'd sell the ticket out of one side to the whites and out the other window to the Blacks. And then the window was right by the stairwell. So you'd buy your ticket out that window, and then go upstairs and sit . . . which was a better seat anyway! But it was the principle of it. If I want to sit down here, I want to sit down here. Don't tell me I can't.

So we'd go to the orchestra line instead of the balcony line. The workers would ignore us, sometimes tell us to go back to the campus. They did the same thing as in the restaurants.

This only happened during my senior year. That was 1960. And the sit-ins really didn't last that long. I forgot how many weeks it was, but it really wasn't that long. Because what happened? They shut down the store. They closed the store. They closed it because we were trying to eat there. And no one else could do anything in there because there were so many students in there. So people could hardly walk in there and they couldn't run the business.

They called the police all the time. Matter of fact, my roommate just happened to be one of the ones that was arrested.

What did your parents think about you participating in it?

I never discussed it with them because during those times, there was no television. There was hardly any telephone. We didn't have a telephone. So, the only way that they could find out about it was through the newspaper. And it wasn't written about that much in the white newspapers. If you didn't get the *Afro-American, Journal and Guide,* or the *Pittsburgh Courier,* one of those Black newspapers, you didn't know that much about it. Now, later on, the *Greensboro Record* did carry some of that. But my parents didn't know what I was doing at the time. There was really no communication.

Now, when I graduated A&T, there were no jobs in the South for Black engineers. So, I came to New Jersey. Got a job at Raritan Arsenal, which is now Middlesex County College. And then, right after I got the job, they announced that they were going to close it. Then I got a job at Picatinny Arsenal. Because even in the North, there was hardly any jobs for Black engineers. Then I got a job at Picatinny Arsenal, and I was there for a while, and then I went to Fort Monmouth for a while, then back to Picatinny. From there, I decided to go to dental school. So I went to dental school.

When you were graduating and you were looking for jobs in the South, did you ever actually apply for any, or you just knew that there weren't going to be any opportunities?

I just knew that there weren't any. So I didn't even apply for it. Because we had one professor that worked for, I think it was Western Electric in Winston-Salem, and he was a part-time engineer there. And he was the only Black engineer they had. My professors knew there were no opportunities in the South. Closest to the South was probably Maryland, which was Edgewood Arsenal, I think. It was in Maryland, near DC.

There were no opportunities for me at home. But I didn't know that until I went all the way through it. And then I found out that there are no opportunities for Blacks. Just like there were hardly opportunities in any front-office jobs for Blacks. Hardly any. If I had stayed in North Carolina, I'd be taking a job that I was very overqualified for—if they would let me have that one. I probably wouldn't get any job at all.

My classmates and I discussed this. We did. But it was such a small number of us. For instance, in mechanical engineering in the School of Engineering, we started out with maybe 200 students, and we'd end up with less than 10. Students would leave or just change their major because they didn't want the rigors of doing it. You know, the math, and the physics, and the chemistry, and all that. So they would just change their major. And so when I graduated, I think it was maybe six or seven others in the group, mechanical engineers. And probably about the same number of electrical engineers. And most of us ended up in New Jersey.

There were more jobs because of the government jobs and the research that was being done in the government jobs. Because there was the munitions command at Picatinny Arsenal, and the electronics command at Fort Monmouth. But most of us went to Picatinny.

I had family in New Jersey. A sister and two brothers in New Jersey at the time. They left North Carolina for the same reason, to get work. You see, because in North Carolina, there were no jobs for Blacks hardly, not even in manufacturing work, because there were hardly any manufacturers. The biggest manufacturer in the Raeford area was Burlington Industries, which is a textile company. And there were no Blacks that worked there, other than in janitorial services or something like that. And that was it. Because my oldest brother worked there. He never ran a machine or anything like that. He was just there to help clean up.

If you could have gotten an engineering job here in North Carolina, would you have stayed?

Oh yeah. Absolutely. I wanted to stay. But knowing that there were none, there was no place to apply.

My father had died when I was in my second year at A&T. And my mother was getting ready to move to New Jersey. And she did move to New Jersey, as a matter of fact. So she got a job as a domestic worker to help me out. She was already living in New Jersey by the time I graduated. It wasn't hard to move. It was survival. And that happened with many Black families, not just mine.

You were part of the Great Migration. Did you experience culture shock in moving to New Jersey after living in the South up until then? And were there any differences that you noticed right away in terms of race relations?

When it comes to race relations, the differences were that you were accepted more readily as a person than you were in the South, in general. But there was still that covert segregation. You know, it was not as overt as it was in the South.

But when I started to work in New Jersey, there were a few Black engineers there already. So, I was able to talk with them, and they'd tell me a little bit about how things were. It was a good experience.

I knew some of the individuals that were still out there in the movement in the South—some were on the Freedom Rides. I knew one guy that was on the Freedom

Rides. You know, I knew one guy that knew the three civil rights workers that were killed in Mississippi. Chaney, Goodman, and Schwerner. He knew those individuals because he was on the Freedom Rides with them. He lived in New York. He worked for the Urban League, and my roommate was his homeboy. That's how I got to know him.

I read about it, but I really wasn't involved with the movement anymore once I left North Carolina. I got involved in the housing movement in Essex County, New Jersey. We would try to rent apartments in certain areas they wouldn't rent to us.

It was Essex County, New Jersey—West Orange. But it wasn't just West Orange. A lot of areas in New Jersey wouldn't rent to you, so the open-housing group got together. They would have a white couple go try to rent an apartment, and they would say, "Yes, we have an apartment available." Then they would send a Black couple in, and, all of a sudden, the apartment wasn't available. So I was part of the Black couple.

We'd go back and report it. There were just certain apartments that they wouldn't rent to you. Eventually, it desegregated. But I don't remember how long it took for that to happen.

I didn't feel that I was in a better situation being up North, per se. I just felt that the battle was still being fought. Because, many times in the South, it was overt. In the North, a lot of it is covert. So you were still fighting a battle. It just was of a different nature.

Back home in North Carolina, you'd hear about people being hurt. I never knew anybody who was lynched. But you'd always hear of people being beat up. There was one person in my town who was beat up and he was dropped off on his doorstep. I don't know if he died on the doorstep, or if he was dead when they put him there. But he had his arms broken and his legs broken. Not a whole lot of outright violence happened in my area of North Carolina—a lot was further south.

In New Jersey, I was still involved in with the NAACP, though. I'm a life member.

At one point, I decided that I just wanted to go in a different direction. I wanted it to be where I could do my own business. So, I figured the easiest way for me to do it would be to go into either medicine or dentistry. I had friends that were in dentistry, so I talked to them, and decided to apply to dental school. The lucky thing about that was when I applied, they had taken New Jersey Dental School and compressed four academic years into three years. I was able to do dental school in three years.

I wanted that level of independence and entrepreneurship, and I couldn't have had that as an engineer at the time. I graduated dental school, and did a general practice residency. That's the way I ended up in New Brunswick. I did a general practice residency at Middlesex General Hospital, which is now Robert Wood Johnson University Hospital. I did a dental residency there, and was going to stay for one year, but then I decided to open up a practice in New Brunswick. 40 years later, I'm still here!

At that time, I knew a lot of people in the community by doing a residency at the hospital. I got involved in the Dental Society, got involved in church. So, I knew a lot of people involved in the community itself. And so it wasn't that difficult to open my business. I got to know the people at the bank, and if I needed a loan or something like that, I was able to get it.

I considered moving back down South, but then I figured it would be too difficult to set up shop there and start all over again. I'm not sure if I could've gotten the loans and things like that in North Carolina. But I'm sure I could have started a practice in the South. I just didn't want to move. I didn't want to start all over again.

Do you think that Dr. King's dream is possible in this country?

I think it's possible. What we have to do is make it happen. And the only way you can make it happen is if you see something, say something. And the other way is through education. We have to educate more of us. That's what has to happen. Because the only way you're going to pull yourself up is if you're well educated.

Integration? I think it stopped the movement of Blacks becoming more independent. And what I mean by that is: before, we had our own communities; we had

George pictured with two of his dental school classmates.

our own businesses. We even had our own hotel chains. But then, once integration came—well, so-called integration, which is not truly integration anyway—we stopped going to our own Black businesses. And what happened was they of course went under. Because they couldn't survive without the clientele. And I think that's one of the things we have to get back to. We should get back to trying to build community, one community at a time.

We have to get ahold of our own colleges. We still have close to 200 HBCUs, and we have to support them and see if we can't move forward with them. Because integration was basically a hoax. Biggest hoax ever been pulled on anybody.

Mainly because it gave people a reason to stop helping each other, and that's what's needed. If you went to Greensboro, for instance, in the 1960s, '50s . . . you went out to Benbow Road, you would think that that was a big-time white community.

But it wasn't. Benbow Road was where most of the Black folks with money lived in Greensboro. There was even a Black hospital. At that time, I actually think there were two Black hospitals in Greensboro.

What I think happened was, I can remember when I was out there marching in the streets, we were marching *not* for integration, but for equal opportunity. That's what we were marching for.

And those are things that we talked about when I was at A&T, and after I got out, many times we would sit down and talk in groups about equal opportunity. That's all we wanted. Equal opportunity. If the white high schools had physics labs and chemistry labs, give us the same thing. That was it. Give us the opportunity to have the same thing. If we want to go to the white school, give us an opportunity to do it. But then, what happened? I think the media got ahold of it, and switched it around from equal opportunity to integration. Knowing that integration would be finite, while equal opportunity would be infinite.

My message again goes right back to education. You know, get yourself educated. Have a goal. As the saying goes, keep your eye on the prize. Make yourself better, and then make someone coming up behind you better. Always give a hand. You don't always have to have money. Sometimes you can just give advice. But the whole thing all goes back to education. Education, education, education. That's what I believe. Because, coming out of Raeford, North Carolina, if I hadn't gotten an education, I don't know what would've happened.

Johnnie represented Delta Sigma Theta Sorority, Inc. at homecoming in her junior year at Hampton University.

INTERVIEW NO. 5

JOHNNIE BOOKER

I was born in Forsyth, Georgia, and moved to Fort Valley, Georgia, at three years old. My grandfather was a chef at Fort Valley State University. My mother was a nurse. She was one of the only Black nurses in the area. My father was a welder. He was actually working on the World Trade Center when he died.

Since my grandfather was working on campus, they gave campus housing. So, I went to the campus nursery school and what they call the demonstration school, which was really the lab school on campus. In fact, I enrolled myself. I've always been rather precocious. And the school was next door to my grandparents. So, I would go over and play with the children. And my mother being a young person with a new baby . . . you know, my sister was a baby. So my mother was happy for me to find some way to go play, I'm sure. And, you know, times were free . . . Children could roam at that point. And I went over and I told the lady, that teacher, that my mother said I could come to school, and that she lived next door. And so they enrolled me in school, and my mother didn't know it until I came and told her that I was in a play and I had to have a pink dress and Shirley Temple curls. I told her at about three o'clock—she had to produce by six. It happened, though!

So you know, like I said, my grandmother had a cafe, my grandfather was a chef. Then, my grandfather retired from the school, and he worked in the cafe too. So, I continued, and then I finished. My last school went to the second grade, I think. So then, you had to transfer to public school, which was all Black. I went to segregated schools. All of my schools were segregated, you know. At four years old, I was in what was considered kindergarten today. And so, that put me one year ahead. And so when I went to public school, they tested me, and they put me in the fourth grade. I never went to the third grade. I was two years ahead, and I finished high school at 16.

During that period, my grandmother was very conscientious. And she would talk to me all the time. I never had a self-esteem problem relative to my color, being Black. She would tell me that if I got my education, and did well in the world, and even before that, that there was no one in the world better than me. That white people had an advantage because of their color, but that did not mean that they were better than me.

So I started from that point, in my mind, and in my heart, because that's what I was taught constantly. So, we lived in an all-Black community—my mother, my sister, and I. I walked past the white school to get to my school, which was like three miles away, every morning. I understood the rules. But I was protected from the rules. Even though there were rules, I didn't feel that they really applied to me. And my grandmother used to say to me that white people were stupid. They don't want us to eat at their restaurant, but green is the color, so they can eat at mine. Long as they got the money!

I never felt inferior. But I did have a resentment. I resented having to read out of books that had somebody else's name in it, because the books that the white kids had the year before, they passed them on to us. The desk had somebody else's name carved in it. And, you know, we went to school in some barracks. They were old army barracks that had big stoves in there, but white people had the brick buildings. We had one brick building, but we had these little satellite classrooms. But the teachers were very good. And they taught us Black history. And we did have the advantage of the college because the activities that they had at the college, we could also attend on occasion. And I remember Mary McLeod Bethune coming to the college. And they brought her to our campus, and we lined up. And she patted us on the heads and shook our hands. Yes, that was quite an experience.

The college made the difference. I had some good teachers, and then I had some teachers who were kind of prejudiced towards children whose parents were not professional.

And everybody that I've known that had gone to these segregated schools, they say that they experienced that as well. In fact, they told me: I was too Black to be queen. Homecoming Queen. A teacher told me that, and she broke the rules.

We had two sections of the 12th grade. Each section chose a person to run. I was chosen in my section. They told the girl in the other section that her parents didn't have enough money; now remember, these were teachers doing this. Said the girl didn't have enough money, her parents didn't have enough money. So she should decline in favor of a very fair-skinned girl with long hair in my section. And they broke the rules.

And the girl said, okay. You know, she was afraid of the teachers. And they told the freshman class members, and they kept telling people, that they'd never seen a queen as Black as me, and that I was too Black to be queen. So I lost. But I was the runner-up. And my mother said to me: "Don't be upset about that. And don't be angry with the girl. The *teachers* broke the rules. But you are going to be the sharpest thing on the floor!"

My mother spent every dime she had to make sure that I was dressed to the nines.

But that didn't bother me. I was always very outspoken, and I went to the teachers and said, "It is sad that you all, who are supposed to be training leaders of tomorrow, would break the rules, first of all." Then, I turned to the other one and said, "And what are you going to tell your daughter, who's blacker than me?" They just looked at me and said, "Oh, she's always been so fresh." So, you know, those were the kinds of things that happened in the Black community during that period.

We went to dances. We had dances, and got together in people's homes because we didn't really have any recreational activities. We had no city-based recreational activities. We had no recreation centers or anything that Black people could go to. So, we did it at home or at the school. I went to camp. I went to an Episcopal camp that was not too far from Fort Valley, and with kids from all over town. And I played in the band and we'd go to band clinics and we'd travel with the football team. That

Johnnie and some high school classmates.

was fun to us. And we didn't have any public swimming pool that we could go to, so we would go swimming in the creek that was not too far from Fort Valley.

We traveled within Georgia, but once we played at the Bud Billiken Parade in Chicago! We raised money and went to Chicago. And my mother was the chaperone. We stayed in a hotel. But we mainly traveled in Georgia, basically. They used to have what they call a band clinic with kids from all over Georgia. They would come to Fort Valley to the college for the statewide band clinic, and I met a lot of friends, people there that are still my friends today, from other cities.

Because my grandmother would say to me that white people were stupid, I'm 13, and I said to my friends, "Let me show you how stupid white people are." We went to the Dairy Queen. Now, everybody ordered from the middle window. But white people pay to the right. And Black people pay to the left. I didn't even have $1 in my pocket. There were three of us. And I said, "I want 12 hamburgers, 12 milkshakes, and 12 orders of French fries." And they fixed it. And then I decided to go to the white window to pay. And they said, "You know, you can't pay here. You got to get over there." So I said, "Well keep it, then!" And we ran.

Everybody was ordering from the same line, but then you have to go to a different line to pay. That's how ignorant it was. That's what I was showing them. Because my grandmother had told me that this whole idea of discrimination was ignorant. And then you know, we had bathrooms and they would say "White Ladies," and then "Colored Women." Note the difference. Ladies and women. And the water would say "White." And we'd go and turn the water on and say, "Oh, have you ever seen any white water? Let me look at white water. Let me look at colored water!"

So I was always pushing the envelope. We had to go upstairs to the movie theater. We paid 9 cents; white people paid 15 cents. And we would go upstairs and we would throw things down on them and spit down on them.

I was kind of fearful. I convinced my stepfather—my mother had gotten married by then—that I had turned 16 when I had really turned 14. All he knew was that I'd had a birthday. And my mother was at work, and I asked him, "Would you sign for me to get my license?" And he said, "Okay." So he signed and I got my driver's license when I was 14. My mother told me, "Well, because you're so fresh, you're going to be the errand girl for everybody." But she didn't know that that made me happy. I was happy to drive. So one of the college professors asked my grandmother if I could drive her to the train station—the train came to Fort Valley then—and take her car back home, and give my grandmother the key. So I'm in her car, I had dropped her off, and I'm driving back. I see this white man in this little rickety truck. I stopped because I didn't want to have any trouble. So then I get to her house, and a policeman is behind me. And he said, "Get in the car." I said, "I'm not getting in the car with you." I'm 14, now. Said, "I'm not getting in the car with you." Because I had seen Perry Mason, now, and I wasn't thinking about him. I told him, "I'll follow you."

I was scared to death. I didn't know what was up. So, I followed him to the police station. And when I got there, there was this white man—the man who I had stopped to let him pass, the one in the rickety truck. He said to the policeman, "I just want you to know how niggers act when they got a big car. She tried to run me off the road."

I said, "No, I didn't." I asked to make a telephone call. I wasn't going to call my mother because the glass was always full with her. I called my grandmother, who the glass was always half empty with. So, she came down. She was right downtown since her cafe was downtown anyway. And she said, "What's going on here?" They had given me a subpoena to come to court. And my grandmother came in to talk to the police officer, and she said, "Oh, no, he's lying." And she took the subpoena and tore it up. Now, that scared me to death. And then she turned to the police officer and said, "When did you get to be the policeman anyway? Anything can be the policeman, long as he's white. You used to be the iceman." She turned to me and said, "Come on. We don't have time for this mess. I got a business to run." And we left, and I never heard nothing else about it! But I was surely scared to death that day.

Because, see, the sheriff ate at my grandmother's cafe. She would always make him sit behind the potato chips stand. She wasn't going to give him the best seat in the house. She told him, "You tell all your people, they are not to mess with my children. If they do something, you bring them to me. Or you come see me. You don't have to bring them to me, you come see me." So there was no problem. And plus, he confided in her about all kinds of stuff. But she said, "You know, when he talks to me, he's just talking to Suzie in the kitchen." Although Suzie wasn't her name, but that was just, you know, like how they confide in their maids, like a piece of furniture.

But that incident scared me to no end! And for a little while, when I saw the police coming near the campus when I was in high school, I would be scared. But nothing ever happened from that, because, like I said, my grandmama kind of had him scared, you know . . . he had confided in her about stuff. I'm just going to tell you just the way she put it: "Always keep something on a cracker in your hip pocket." My grandmother was a mess!

My grandmother had saved her money and opened the cafe. She opened it in the mid-'40s, and kept it open until the mid-'60s, '65 or '66. It had a counter with stools, and it had one row of tables, about five tables, with about four chairs. And the kitchen was kind of over to the side. And then she had a room in the back where she had her telephone and a bed, because that was our babysitter. We had to come from school and go to the cafe. So, she had a bed back there where we could rest, or she could rest if she got tired before going home. The cafe, the building . . . it was a long place. It was kind of long.

She served soul food. The whole family had to help out there. My sister liked being in the kitchen. I didn't. So, I waited tables and cleaned up, swept up and kept the tables clean. I knew everybody's business in town, because I would listen to grown folks' conversation.

It was a neighborhood hotspot because everybody came. Field hands. People who worked in the factories. The college professors, you name it. Everybody came there. It was called Rogers' Cafe. My grandmother was Johnnie Mae Rogers. She served lunch and dinner. She didn't serve breakfast. She closed because she was getting old. And she'd kind of gotten sickly.

I knew everybody's business, but she would say to me, "Whatever you hear in here, you keep it. Because it stays here. This is the way I make my business; it's my money. We cannot talk about it. It's all our secret," she said. And so that's what we did. You know?

I saw my maternal grandmother every day. My paternal grandmother lived in Atlanta. That was about 100 miles away from us. I didn't really see her that often. In fact, I only saw her when my daddy came to Georgia, maybe once a year. But she worked for white people, you know, cleaning and cooking for them in her young years.

In fact, her father was the product of a white man. And they're kind of wealthy in Forsyth, Georgia. And she worked for her cousin. Her white cousin. And my mother said that every holiday. . . . My grandmother's father died very young, and her mother did too. And she was raised by her aunt. But my mother said that every holiday there would be a big box on their porch. Of gifts and clothes. So, the white man acknowledged him then, and he had their name. Had his name.

My grandmother accompanied the woman she worked for to the premiere of *Gone with the Wind*. And all of her memorabilia, when her house was hit with a tornado, all of her memorabilia was gone in the trunk that she had. But my grandmother was very fair, so she drove with her because she needed somebody to ride with her. And she told my grandmother, "They won't know what you are." Talking about her being Black.

Could she pass? I don't think she could have passed. She wasn't that fair to me, but white people don't know, you know what I mean? Black people can spot Black people easier than white people can. She couldn't pass to me. But she said that the woman told her, you know, they won't know. So she went with her.

My paternal grandmother was Mamie Brooks Merryweather. I don't really know a whole lot about her, my paternal grandmother, because I didn't grow up with her. In fact, my maternal grandmother did not like my paternal grandmother! She would say, "They didn't come from nothing, they ain't nobody, they haven't been nowhere, ain't going nowhere, and ain't doing nothing!" I mean, you know, that was my maternal grandmother. As I say, she was a mess! But, I saw her every day of my life during that period.

I didn't visit Atlanta a lot. But I, you know, would come up. I had a cousin up there that I would come up to see periodically, but didn't visit a lot. But I tell you what, that was also the time when Black people couldn't try on clothes in the store. My grandmother was a dresser. She was the first person I ever saw wear rhinestone earrings in the middle of the day. And she wore big furs, you know, big suits and coats and big fur collars. And there was a store called Goldman's in Macon, Georgia. It was a boutique. And they had gorgeous clothes. And although we—you know,

Black people—couldn't try the clothes on, they would call my grandmother. And she would go after the store closed, and we could try on clothes then. Isn't that stupid?

When I was eight years old, my grandmother got the *Atlanta Daily World*, the *Chicago Defender*, and the *Pittsburgh Courier*. Black newspapers. I went to the college library and I researched other Black newspapers and ordered them. It was a little store that had magazines, and I went up there and I ordered five other newspapers: the *Washington Afro*, the *Norfolk Journal and Guide*, the *LA Sentinel*, *Amsterdam News*, and it was one other one. I can't remember the other ones. I don't know, but it was five additional newspapers. And I read newspapers. I called it "Reading About People in Faraway Places," because I knew that there was life beyond Fort Valley. And I wanted to experience life beyond Fort Valley. People thought I was a little kooky.

My grandmother paid us for working in the cafe. And it wasn't much, but you know, she paid us. She wanted us to manage our money. She used to say, "You have to save in the spring because the winter *is* coming." But I took my money and I bought newspapers. And I ordered those newspapers from this little store called The Candy Kitchen. It was two Greek brothers who owned it. And then I got *Jet* and I got *Ebony*, as well. So I knew about life beyond Fort Valley by reading. And I would imagine myself being in these different places. So, you know, that was a way of entertaining myself and reaching beyond my environment.

We would go visit New York to visit my father in the summer. It was just a great big place. We went to Coney Island. We went to all the different sites. And his father lived in New York too. That's why he went to New York. His father lived in Harlem. They lived in Harlem. So we went to New York to see him. Oh yeah, we enjoyed it. We didn't go every summer, because he would come, and we would rotate it. Like he would come to Georgia. And then we would go to New York, because they would put a little tag on us and put us on a train. My sister and me.

We would go on the train, but we didn't go every summer. And we would go for maybe like a week to 10 days, and then we'd come back. My uncle worked on the railroad. He worked on the railroad from Atlanta to New York, and we would end up being on the train with him. He was a dining car waiter. And I know we used to be on the train with him.

He was really my mother's stepbrother. We would go from Fort Valley to Atlanta, and then we would change trains. We were in the Black car. And we would always go when he was going. Yeah, that was the way we went. And he saw to it that we got from that train to his train. I can't remember what it was called. . . . The Nancy Hanks . . . or the Silver Comet. It was something like that. I can't remember the name of the train.

Did you know anyone who was lynched or a victim of any other form of racial violence?

Lynching? I knew a man who they said was killed in jail with his hands handcuffed behind him, saying he was trying to break out of jail. That was a lynching. That was the only person that I knew. I remember hearing about it in the cafe. But sometimes I would filter some of that mean stuff out of my mind. I don't know. I remember that his name was Mr. Big Boy Scott. They said that he was trying to break out of jail. And people in the cafe said, "How could he break out of jail with his hands handcuffed behind him?" And they killed him. I didn't know of anybody that was hanging in a tree or anything like that, but there are all kinds of ways to go about lynching.

We didn't have a whole lot of violence in my area. I think maybe the college had something to do with it. I remember we had a Black doctor in Fort Valley. And he was trying to get a patient into the VA hospital. And that was during the time when you had to say "Operator" and you had to give the operator the number and all of that. There was no dialing. And he heard somebody say something about "It's nobody but that nigger doctor," or something like that. And he said, "What's wrong with you? I'm trying to get this patient settled." You know, he "talked back," as they say. He talked back to her. And he had a farm and when he came home, all of his paint and everything was poured out all over his farm, and his tractor and truck had been damaged. He left Fort Valley. And I don't blame him.

I left Fort Valley and went to college at 16. I turned 16 in July, and went to college in September. I went to Hampton. The principal of my high school, and the elementary school too . . . he was. . . . We had one Black principal here. He went to Hampton. He and his wife went to Hampton, and then their children were going to Hampton, and one of his youngest daughters was my friend that I met in nursery school. So I said, "I'm going to Hampton."

It was great fun. I did protests there at Hampton. Hampton was the second school to protest after A&T. But Hampton didn't make the kind of news that A&T did. But my sign said, "Khrushchev can eat here and I can't." Khrushchev was head of Russia at that time. I thought that was such a cool sign.

And my girlfriend and I, actually three of us, decided we were going to go integrate this tea room at this department store in Newport News. We dressed up. We dressed up and went to the tea room, and there was nobody sitting there. And the man came out with a big old hose and he said, "If y'all don't get out of here, I'm gonna turn this hose on you." And then, we ran outside. Kids were protesting, you know, Woolworths and all the other places to eat. And we went outside—all our friends were out there with handcuffs on them. And they were wet from being shot with a water hose. We flew back to campus!

But I did march in all the protests at Hampton. We protested at Woolworth's, places in the bus stations, you know, where they had places to eat, anywhere that wouldn't let us eat there will work. All the eating facilities. In Hampton and Newport News, we would march and we would have a lawyer. The lawyers would come to the campus and talk to us about what we should do and what we shouldn't do. They said that if they asked us to leave, then you get up and another group would come. Because if we stayed, we would be trespassing. NAACP lawyers.

They would have buses to take us into town. And we would line up two at a time at a certain site, and we would walk with our signs. And white folk would be screaming at us. "Niggers go back to Hampton," and all kinds of stuff. I always had a football player walking with me. I was too little.

We would be out there probably about three to four hours, you know, off and on. One group would come, and one would leave. Some students didn't participate because their parents would tell them, "Don't do that. Don't do this." So they would catch it when those of us who protested would get in from downtown. People were mean to them. They would put ketchup on their clothes or something else crazy to the students that didn't participate. It was expected that all the students would participate.

When I was sitting down at counters and everything, I was scared as the devil. I must admit that I was scared. But I didn't show it. And they'd say, "You know you can't eat here. We're not serving niggers," or whatever other things they would say. And then, the manager might come and say, "You got to get out of here, 'fore I call the police." So we would get up when they told us to leave. We'd leave, and then somebody else would come in. It would be at least 20 to 25 people, but you could only sit at the counter; see at Woolworth's, they only had about 8 to 10 stools. They weren't that big. We would go every weekend.

I never got the hose turned on me. Thank God. And nobody spat on me or threw eggs at me. I didn't get it, but others did. Maybe I was at a different place in the line, you follow me?

I was never arrested, and it's interesting, when I got my job at Department of Welfare in New York, that was one of the questions they asked.

I protested mainly my junior and senior year, because I finished in 1961. My mother was worried about me protesting. But my grandmother thought it was wonderful! My grandmother thought it was so wonderful that I did that. And she'd tell me, "Call me and tell me what happened!"

I was always against what the white people were doing. I was always against segregation. In my mind, I just knew it wasn't right. And that we should have some fairness. Because remember, I had read all these papers, now. For years, I'd read all these papers. I knew that stuff was going on all over the world outside of my little neck of the woods in Fort Valley, Georgia. Because a lot of times, people were afraid to do that protesting in Fort Valley, because they were state employees at the college. And the teachers were state employees—county and state employees. They would be fearful for their jobs. And the only other place they had, people worked in Warner Robins, which was an Air Force base. They worked there. And in my little town, they built . . . you know those school buses that have Blue Bird on the back? They were made in Fort Valley. So people worked there, too. Or they worked in the fields, or they worked in the packing houses, you know. So their jobs . . . they were fearful of losing their jobs. But there were no protests really going on while I was in Fort Valley when I lived there. Because Dr. King had not started the whole movement at that point.

After graduation, I worked for the Department of Welfare in New York, then I came to Washington, DC, after that. New York was just a bit much for me, particularly the Welfare Department. But with my recipients, my clients, I gave everything that was on the books that they could have. And I had a whole lot of families who were on drugs. Heroin was king then. And I had families of drug addicts, basically. And coming from Fort Valley, and then Hampton, I didn't know nothing about that! So it was a little bit rough for me.

Then, I had immigrants, mostly Polish, because I worked at East 68th Street. And they would say to me, "Are you one of them spics or one of them niggers?" And I would say, "I'm your social worker, and guess what? It will take me 20 minutes to get to my office and 10 minutes to close your damn case!"

The first time I encountered discrimination with regard to housing was in New York City. I was trying to get an apartment, and we'd go look at apartments that we would find in the paper. And we would get there and they'd say they weren't renting. This is before Fair Housing, now. So one of my colleagues and I said, "Okay, well, let's get our friend to go see it." So we get the white girl who worked with us to go and look at the apartment. And they told her it was open. They had told us it was rented already. And we said, "That's ridiculous, that's discrimination!" But we didn't know anything about any fair housing. So that was the first time I had ever encountered that. Because back home in the South, I knew where to live. I already knew that I was supposed to live in the Black community. But it was in New York City. And I was discriminated against for housing.

I had moved in with my dad when I first got to New York, but my dad was so strict. If a guy called and asked, "Is Johnnie there?" my dad would say, "This is a home, not a bar. You ask 'May I speak to Johnnie,' not 'Is Johnnie there." Which is right! But he was real strict, so that's why I was looking for an apartment. After leaving New York, I moved to Washington, DC. And I couldn't find a job. And I went to Adam Clayton Powell's office to get help finding a job. The woman said, "Well, the congressman gets requests like this all the time. Give us your resume." I did.

But then I went to the guard and asked, "Could you tell me who the congressman is from the Third District of Georgia?" Fort Valley was in the Third District at that time. And he told me, and added, "But he's a hard segregationist." He told me that his name was Tic Forrester. So I went to his office, and I said, "I'm here to see the congressman." They told me that he was on the floor of the House. I asked if I could wait, and they say yes. So when he came in, and he walked to his office, I followed him. By the time he got around to his desk, I was seated in front of him. And he said, "Well." He said, "How can I help you?" I gave him my resume and told him that I needed a job, I couldn't find a job, and that they told me that I should come see my congressman. So I told him I was from Fort Valley originally. He said, "Do you know the Pearsons and the Dukes?" Now, they were the people who were the big peach growers. They were the wealthy people. I said, "Yeah, my grandma used to work for them." Which was a lie.

He said, "And you can't find no job? You educated, you come from good stock, your folk worked for the Pearsons and the Dukes, and you presentable. I'm gonna find you a job."

So, he called his staff—a staff person—in, gave him my resume, and told him to find me a job. They had just passed the Manpower Development and Training Act. That was a Wednesday when I went to see him. Saturday morning, they called me and told me to report to this building at 9 o'clock on Monday. So, I had a job! And I started out as a GS-9 [author's note: a particular federal pay grade], teaching illiterate adults under the Manpower Program. How about that? A 9 at that time was unheard of for Black people.

It was very interesting. I didn't know a damn thing about teaching no adults, no illiterate adults. Some of them could read, some of them were functional illiterate. So I had to be very creative. I interviewed all my students; every one of them was older than me. I interviewed all my students one by one. And I made books up for each of them. I mean, it was hard work. But I wrote about their family: "My name is so and so, I live at this place, I have so many children, their names are," and so on. Each person had their own book. And we then would move up to different things. It was quite gratifying. I really enjoyed it.

I was working there when Kennedy was killed. Because one of my students had a transistor radio, and she was in the back listening. And I said, "Why, you're listening to a radio in this classroom?" And she turned it up, and it was talking about the president was dead. So that was very memorable to me, because that was where I was the day he was killed. Teaching. But I enjoyed my students. And I had people who could not write their names, so we'd practice that every day. They got paid to come. And I would tell them stuff like, "If you put an *X* on your check, I'm gonna stop your checks!" You see, that gave them incentive to learn how to write their names. I had to do all kinds of creative stuff, because I didn't know nothing about this! But by the time they left, they could write their names, they could write their children's names, they could read a few things. Some of them could read much better than others.

But we had a good time, and when they finished their program, I took them as a farewell to the Watergate Inn. Before the Watergate apartments and hotel was put up, there used to be a Watergate Inn. It was the place where the congressmen and everybody went. And I collected money and took all of them to lunch to the Watergate Inn. I told them to dress up, but don't put on hats. Dress up like you're going to church, but don't put on a hat. And I told the men to dress up in suits. So it was real gratifying. And from there, I went to work with the district government. And then, I got married during that period, got divorced, then came back to Georgia—to Atlanta—and went to graduate school.

In graduate school, as my field placement, I was assigned to the Southern Regional Council. And I sat in the hall. My desk was in the hall. This was my internship, now. My desk was in the hall, and the office across from my desk was John Lewis. The office above me was Julian Bond, and the one we worked for was Vernon Jordan. So you know, I've been involved in civil rights all my life.

My school was Atlanta University School of Social Work. And I was in community and administration. So that's why we were at a place like Southern Regional Council, which was a council set up for race relations in the South. And Vernon ran the voter education project for the South. And then, after I finished graduate school, I was in Atlanta when King was killed. In fact, I was working in the church helping to organize his funeral. I volunteered to go to West Hunter Church, and I was on the telephone. And I organized. Before he died, he was organizing the Poor People's Campaign. And a part of my project for social work was to organize the students—Black and white—to work with the Poor People's Campaign. The Southern wing of the Poor People's Campaign. So I did that as a project for school. From there, I moved to California, and worked for the National Urban League. Because Vernon, by that time, he had become head of the Urban League, and he asked me to join him. Well, I was first with the Community Redevelopment Agency, which was the urban renewal agency. I developed a social services program for them, and worked there for about three years. Then, I went to the National Urban League. I came back to Washington and worked for the National Urban League in Washington.

And the Urban League and NAACP had sued the financial regulatory agencies for their fair housing posture. And fair housing was part of my portfolio. Fair housing, minority business, and equal employment were all part of my portfolio. And so the financial regulatory agencies—FDIC, the Federal Home Loan Bank Board, and the Comptroller of the Currency—had to create these civil rights positions. And they called me in. Ron Brown, you know, who used to be head of the . . . the one who got killed in a plane crash, remember? Well, he was my boss. So, I've worked for some great people. And Ron called me in and said, "We've determined that you need to go get one of those jobs." Because they had to create these new jobs, you see? I didn't know a darn thing about no Federal Home Loan Bank Board. And he said, "You go over there and interview and get the job." And I did that, and I got the job.

I had to train examiners on how to detect discrimination in lending. I had to go to examiner school and learn how to be a bank examiner in order to develop a program, and that's where I had my big discrimination complaint. That I lost. I did all of the development of the program, and when they wanted to make it bigger and broader, they hired a white woman over me. And I filed a discrimination complaint. 'Course, I lost. But then she left and went to HUD, after being so mean and nasty to me. And then I went to HUD later. And talk about just desserts? I became deputy assistant secretary, and she was three levels under me. And she begged me to take her because her boss was mean to her like she had been to me. And I took her. And worked her like a junkyard dog. I wasn't nasty to her. But I worked her. And we did a lot of stuff, good stuff.

Then, I became vice president of Resolution Trust where we cleaned up the savings and loan scandal. My job was to develop a program to assure that minority- and women-owned businesses got contracts. And we did 48 percent under my program. Nobody had ever reached 48 percent. So you see, I've done civil rights kind of stuff all of my life.

We were in an encounter group session, believe it or not, with the white students [when the news of Dr. King's murder broke]. And somebody knocked on the door and said, "You've got to break this up, you got to get out." I said, "We can't get out, leave us alone." Because we were really dealing with some Black and white issues, because we had white students. But we were all students dealing with things in our little encounter group. But they said, "You've got to get these white people out of here"—whoever that was knocking on the door said—"because the folk are getting ready to riot." So, we took our coats and put them over their heads and walked them through the campus to the dormitories and to their cars so they could get out of there. And it was just chaotic.

It's hard to even relive that. So then, they wanted to organize. They were saying that West Hunter Street Baptist Church, which was right down the street at that time, was going to be the headquarters. So I volunteered for that. But my friends were getting ready to get on a plane—they wanted people to get on a plane that was going to go to Memphis to march. By then, I had a child, and they were telling me to come on and that I had to go. So I went to get on the plane, and as they would call one group, I would move backwards and let people go ahead. I wasn't going to no Memphis!

And my friends went to the Poor People's Campaign in Washington, two of them, and stayed out there in those tents. But I did stuff here, because my son was four years old, so I couldn't do that. And you know, we did research for them with the voter education project as students, and then, my second year, I went to Winston-Salem, North Carolina, to work with the Urban League, who only had two employees. So we really became the employees of the Urban League.

Later, I had to go and learn how to be a bank examiner. I went to what they call new examiner's school. I had to learn what they do in the back of the house. There was a real smart white boy who liked to travel, so I asked him if he wanted to work with me. He knew bank examining back and forth. So we developed a real training program. And there were only two Black examiners in the country at that time. Two Black examiners.

Okay, by that time, you had the Community Reinvestment Act that was being developed. I served on the interagency task force to write the guidelines for the CRA. We

Johnnie during her professional years.

had what they call the Home Mortgage Disclosure Act, which that was already in place through HUD, which showed the location of loans that each financial institution made; and we developed nondiscrimination guidelines. So, we had those three instruments. So when the examiners went into an institution, and they looked at the loans and the patterns of the loans using those instruments, you could tell if they had redlined certain areas if there were no loans in certain areas of the census tracts. So, they would call me. And we would set the scope of the exam: how far to look, where to look. And they would write their reports. And then, I would take it to what they call supervision. If my recommendation was that the bank be . . . not censored, but dealt with. I can't remember what they call it now. This is my 80-year-old mind! I turned 80 in July.

So that's what I did for a number of years. And after I got the program all set up, then they gave it to the white woman. But then I got it after she left. So I did consumer affairs too. So when they would close an institution, I would have to go with the examiners to make sure that the customers were really treated properly.

And so that, you know, from social work to that, was quite interesting. And then the Resolution Trust was when they closed 700 savings institutions. And we were liquidating the assets. And as I said, my job was to ensure that minorities and women got contracts. Because we had $650 billion dollars in assets. And I did 48 percent. And after. . . . Oh, and I sued them too.

Did you experience any discrimination in your professional roles?

Well. $5,000 was quite a bit of money to give as a bonus in government at that time. And they gave all of the vice presidents except me $5,000 and gave me three. And they were so stupid because EEO was under my portfolio too. I just called the lawyer in Washington that wins all the cases. And, in less than two weeks, I had six figures in my checking account!

Because I had to testify before Congress a lot too, see. Because, you know, this was a congressionally created agency. And so, they didn't want me to go to Congress and say that they had discriminated against me, right. I had a good staff that got me prepared to testify. I thought at first that it would be intimidating, but they made me feel comfortable. And welcome.

Okay, so then I retired. One of the stipulations of my settlement was that I had to retire, but it was over anyway, we were transferred to FDIC, and they hated me over there anyway. But did I care? No. I've never really cared about what people thought about me when I was doing my work. Because let me tell you, when I was at the Resolution Trust, Congress made them put me on the policymaking committee. I was the only woman and the only minority. It was all white men. And they would try to do stuff when I would leave town, underhanded stuff, you know, behind my back, and do stuff for white people that they weren't going to do for Black people. And I was very outspoken. One time, I told them that they thought their sheets were invisible, but that I could see them.

Also, this was before cameras. The security guard and the janitor, I'd tell them where to find the document, and they'd go get the documents and bring them to me hidden in between the pages of the *Wall Street Journal*, and I'd copy them. And then, they'd take them back. So I would know exactly what they were doing for white people that they weren't doing for Black people. And they would wonder how I got that information! And there was the secretary who worked for one of the big boys who would bring me stuff she typed. She'd say, "I'm bringing you this in the name of Mother Africa!" We called her Mother Africa. I don't know her name to this day! So, that's how we get 48 percent. You follow me? Plus, I developed a program where if a major company was going to bid for a contract, they had to have a minimum of 10 percent minority or women participation. If they didn't, they were noncompliant. And their bid was thrown out. They said that was unconstitutional. And if they did 25 percent, I gave them bonus points on their technical and cost proposals. And if they gave them 40 percent, they got a bigger bonus point, and if they did a joint venture, oh, it was home free. But . . . it might have been a little unconstitutional. But, in the federal government, you publish in the federal registry. So people can comment. So, I never made my rules final. They were interim until we went out of business. So, if they were interim, people can continue to comment on them. So, how can that be unconstitutional?

It was really interesting that my first chairman had been the chairman of American Airlines. He was a staunch Republican. And he would let me do whatever. Because he didn't want the Congress on his butt. Because Maxine Waters would call up there and chew him out. And then, when the Democrats came in, that's when all the "unconstitutional" stuff started coming up. In fact, they sent for me at the White House and told me that my program was unconstitutional. I said, "Well, this is interim. These are interim rules." They sent this lawyer—Black lawyer who was very known in

Washington—to tell me to cease and desist. And she was going to show me how I could change my program, which was working. And I said to her, "Go get your 12 pieces of silver and get the F out of my office." So, they said I was crazy.

After I retired, I did consultant work with the guy who was head of procurement in the White House, and we wrote the empowerment zones, contracting rules with the Commerce Department, which eventually became what they call the HUBZone rules. And Coke recruited me to develop their supplier diversity program after they had had a discrimination complaint against them. So I developed that supplier diversity program and I stayed there for 10 years and I retired 10 years ago.

While I was in grad school, they were doing voter education for the voter education project. King was organizing the Poor People's Campaign. Okay, and I also marched in the March on Washington. The original one, and the next one. I marched in the March on Washington. I told my students—see I was working at that school then—I told my students don't come to school tomorrow. And they were happy not to come to school! I said don't come to school, don't worry, it's not going to affect your check. My friend and I went down early. And we said at first, "Oh, it's gonna be a flop, we don't see anybody!" It wasn't that many people at first. And we were standing there, and Peter, Paul and Mary were performing under a tree. And we were watching them. And then we looked back and the droves of people started coming. We saw people in wheelchairs, and on crutches. I mean, just people were coming from everywhere. And yeah, we're at the March on Washington. The original one. And then, we marched so far, we got so tired, we said, "We're going home to finish watching on television!" But I mean, we were so excited. I mean, it was just so exciting.

And the day that Kennedy's cortege came through Washington, my same friend . . . we always did everything together. We went down and it was just so crowded, we said we got to go down to see the president and see Little John John [author's note: the president's son] walking behind him. We got down there, and we were just way in the back. And these two officers were saying, "Let me through, let me through!"

and I said, "Let's get behind the police." We got behind the police and walked up to the front and stopped. We were in the front row. And I told my friend, "Don't look back, because people are going to be mad!" And we saw the cortege go past. I mean we did a lot of stuff.

What was it like when integration happened? What were your thoughts on how it unfolded?

It was exciting to see public spaces integrate. You know, we could do new things and go explore places where we couldn't tread before. It was exciting. But my grandmother said, "You know, integration ruined Black people. The mess they're doing today? They never would have done that mess had they not been hanging around with white people!"

I could go to Atlanta and we could go to the movies and not go upstairs. You know, that kind of thing. We could go to the same place and pay at the same window. Everybody could use the same bathroom. I remember that I told my mom I was going to become a Freedom Rider. And she said to me, "If the crackers don't kill you, I am. You better stay in school."

John Lewis and I were friendly, you know, forever. And my granddaughter when she was nine, when we saw him on the Vineyard, she went to him and asked him to speak to her school. She's a little forward, too. She went up to him at Union Chapel, and said, "Mr. Lewis, I'd like for you to come to my school to speak to us. Because I've read about you, and I know all the good things you've done." And I said, "John, that's my granddaughter." And he said, "Oh, my goodness, you are just like your grandma!" And he gave her his card and told her to have her teacher write him. And what the school did—it's an Episcopal school in New York—they made him the Absalom Jones honoree, and then they sent the children to his office. And so, of course, from then on, my grandson and granddaughter said that he was their friend. "Our friend John Lewis" is what they called him.

I didn't attend Dr. King's funeral. That was by invitation only, and I was a lowly student. The riots? Well, you know, the news showed every other city, but it didn't show

Atlanta. It didn't show Atlanta rioting. It kind of kept that quiet. But I remember telling people, "Don't burn no buildings! If you're going to burn something, go burn the credit bureau and everybody will be free!" You know, that was before computers! Why are you going to burn your neighborhood? Burn the credit bureau. And your mama and everybody will be free.

I stayed on campus during that time, and the campus was pretty quiet. Except people were trying to volunteer as much as they could to do whatever they needed to do. You know, everybody was sad when he was killed. It was just a sad time. It was like a dark gloom was over the world, it appeared to me. It was just such a sad time.

Do you believe that Dr. King's dream is possible in America?

At one time I did believe that Dr. King's dream was possible here, but now I don't know. There's so much division. And Trump kind of was the catalyst for bringing back all of the old vestiges of hatred and racism. It saddens me to see this. I think that all of it, too, is related to us having a Black president—two terms of a Black president. Backlash. I mean, that's a part of it. That helped to generate the hatred. Because, see, it was latent. And Trump said, you don't have to be latent with it. Let's bring it on out. And that's what they did. That's what they are doing, rather. It's current . . . it's as we speak. And all the other -isms that go along with it. I thought it could be, and I still think that it may be, and I think that we just still have to keep the faith. And go to the ballot box. That's the only place we can get them. And they know that. That's why they're making all these crazy laws.

It is very scary, very scary. It's sad, but it's something we have to live through. But I'm very happy that my grandchildren are very clear on who they are.

People are afraid to challenge the status quo. I challenge the status quo. I have never been afraid, even when I needed my job. You have to be willing and able to stand up for what you believe. And you got to push it.

At Coke, when I first came here, white women and white men told me that if they use a minority or a woman, that they would get an inferior product. Okay? And I said to one white woman, "You know, a lot of men think that women ought to be barefoot and pregnant on the edge of town, and I think you're one of those women that should be, if that's the way you think." I'm very outspoken.

And they couldn't stand me at Coke. And I'd say to them, "Let me get the correct spelling of your name. Because if you don't believe in this program, I think I have to report you." I did stuff like that. And they'd say, "Oh, she's such a bitch." And when I was at the Federal Home Loan Bank Board, there were only four Black people in managerial positions. And I was in an elevator—this was pre–Clarence Thomas and Anita Hill. I was in the elevator and I felt somebody touch my butt. And I thought maybe I bumped into somebody because the elevator was crowded. And I felt it again, and turned around, and it was this white man looking cheap. And I broke his glasses on his eyes with my fist. Cut his face. Then cussed him out . . . I said, "You bastard. You touch me again, and I'm gonna pick up your check every two weeks." So they labeled me as crazy. I didn't care. I get the job done. And they knew not to mess with me.

I've really been that way all my life. Just like when I challenged the teachers who said I was too Black.

I grew up in the AME church. Sunday school. Vacation Bible School. I was very active in the church. And I was at the Metropolitan AME church. I was a steward, which is, you know, an officer. Ernie Green from the Little Rock Nine was there, Vernon Jordan went to that church, and Gwen Ifill. A lot of people went to that church. But anyway, I was a steward. And we planned the 160th anniversary for the church. Ernie Green and I were the chairs, Gwen Ifill was the emcee, and Bill Clinton spoke for the anniversary. Bill Clinton used to do his two prayer services at our church during his inauguration.

What message would you give to African Americans now, and in the future?

My message to them would be always believe in yourself. Always strive to do better each day. Love yourself and be true to your people and your heritage.

Johnnie as a freshman at Hampton University.

INTERVIEW NO.

6

OLETHA
BARNETT

W*hat's your full name and where you were born?*

My full name is Oletha J. Barnett, and I was born in Morris, Oklahoma. I grew up in Okmulgee. Oklahoma. Part of the time in Okmulgee, Oklahoma, and part of that time on our farm in Morris, Oklahoma. Morris is 12 miles south of Okmulgee.

Can you describe your childhood home and neighborhood?

We had a 160-acre farm, and there were no neighbors per se, other than farms that were distanced from us. On the farm, we had cows, horses. . . . Mama had chickens and various things. And in the little town where I went to school, the neighborhood was segregated. It was a quiet neighborhood, and there was the Black part of town and the white part of town. It was completely segregated. I grew up in a segregated elementary school and high school, and they did not integrate until the year after I graduated from high school. And it was a neighborhood where everybody knew everyone. It was a small town. I think the population at that time was around 13,000.

On the farm, it was just our little world and we were happy. We could roam the land. And we had ponds where you could go fishing. My mom and some of the siblings would go fishing; I didn't particularly care for fishing. My older sisters and brothers worked the land, but the younger ones didn't, because by then my dad was hiring people to work the land. I do remember one summer, once the older ones were gone and married—see, we were much younger—he decided that we should work it like the older kids did. But we didn't do so well!

I grew up with six sisters and three brothers, but I have 22 siblings. My dad was 20 years older than my mom, and there are two sets of us. And so that's why I say "the older group" did the farming. By the time we came along, some of the older ones were in the same age group as my mom. So, 22 total, I grew up with nine of them. Out of the first set, there were 12 of them, and there are only three of them left. And, by God's grace, my oldest sister is still living. She's 103 years old. Longevity is in our family, and I hope I'm one of those.

Where do you fall in the order of the siblings?

I am the fourth from the end. Both my parents had been married before, and I'm the first of the last set. There are three younger than me.

Did you have chores on the farm?

Not really . . . I'm trying to think of what chores we did. Because like I said, he hired people. We just went to school. By the time the younger set came along, Mom and Dad were older. And so, they weren't doing the same kind of farming that we had done at one time. Now, my mom did do canning, and most of the older siblings would help with that. I'm sure I did some chores. I cleaned up the house.

What all were y'all growing on the farm?

We grew peanuts and we grew cotton. It was 160 acres of land: 80 in one spot, and 80 in another spot. They weren't together.

How were your parents able to purchase this land?

My dad was quite phenomenal. But he was much older. And he purchased that land before they were married. That was during his first marriage. And he farmed, sold cattle, and various other things, and was able to pay for the land in a time when you didn't have a lot of Black landowners.

He came from Montgomery, Alabama, when Oklahoma was not even a state. He was born in 1896. There was a race incident. I can remember my dad telling me about it. There was a racial incident in Montgomery, Alabama. One of his uncles was a mail carrier. And something happened. . . . He had gone into a store to warm himself in the wintertime. And there was a white man who slapped him. And so, as my dad put it, he defended himself. And they left early the next morning on a train, and ended up in Oklahoma Territory. It was not a state.

There's a quite interesting story that goes with that, because you got to realize that at that time, it was early 1900s, around 1907. At that time, obviously, you're going to lose track of your family in Alabama if you're in Oklahoma. I can remember there was a traveler who had come to our little town of Okmulgee, and I believe my dad may have been in his late sixties or early seventies. And there was a lady in Montgomery, Alabama, who was wondering what happened to her family all those many years ago. And if there were any Barnetts in that little town. And someone had directed her to our home in Okmulgee. So, my dad wrote the lady and named all of his people. One of those people that he named was Aunt Honey. And amazingly, she actually turned out to be his Aunt Honey, which of course was not her first name, but that was the name he remembered. After that, one of my sisters flew down there with Dad, and that's how we got reconnected with the people in Alabama. That was my dad's very first time being back in Alabama since then, and he told me, his church was not there, but the tree outside the church that he used to play under was still there.

When we reconnected with the Alabama family, people would say, "Well, actually, you all are Smiths, not Barnetts." My great-great-grandfather's name was Dick Lewis Barnett, but he was a slave owned by Sol Smith. He was what they called a house n-i-g-g-e-r.

Well, he ended up joining the Union Army. He had gone to war along with his master, who fought for the Confederacy. Like a lot of others, when he had the chance, my great-great-grandfather escaped and went to join the Union Army. Years later, he was attempting to apply for the government pension as a Union Army veteran. As a part of the process, they wanted to take a deposition from him to find out how a slave ended up in the Union Army.

Oletha's great-great-grandfather, Dick Barnett, and his wife; photo courtesy of the U.S. Department of Veterans Affairs.

That happened a lot—a lot of enslaved people went to join the Union. But not a lot from the Deep South. Is that what raised their antenna?

They took the deposition because of an issue with his name. He had always gone by Lewis Smith. Then one day, he learned that white people took the last name of their fathers. See, he'd never known that. As a slave, the people he knew had the last name of the slaveholder. Well, his mother told him that his father's last name was Barnett, so he took the last name of Barnett after the war. When he applied for the pension, he applied as a Barnett, but when he served, he was under the Smith name. So that's why they took that deposition, they wanted to see if it was really him. His deposition can be found in the National Archives.

Another thing about this is the way we found out about the deposition. My nephew was in therapy, and his therapist was a young white man. After learning more about our family, the therapist told my nephew, "We might be related." Turns out that we were, and it was actually the young white man who told us that there was a deposition from my great-great-grandfather. This was some years ago before we had ancestry services and all these tools. So the Blacks and the whites are connected in a lot of ways, right? Slavery forced us to be connected.

I also remember that my dad hated the military. He always hated the military, and it's because of how my great-great-grandfather was treated, and how he had to fight for his pension.

So when your family fled Montgomery, who all left?

It was my grandfather, my dad's dad. And then there was my dad's first cousin, Thomas. I don't know who all left, but those were the two people that I knew. They ended up in Oklahoma. There may have been some who left, and later ended up in California. Because my dad's brother, Uncle Alexander, lived in California.

Why did they have to leave so suddenly?

Well, you gotta remember it's late 1800s. And we're talking about Montgomery, Alabama. And so, we know why they had to leave. For fear of their lives. I know they had to get out of town. Yeah.

What was school like for you growing up?

I grew up in a segregated school. And I just thought school was wonderful. All of my teachers were Black. All of the students were Black. The teachers knew our families. And so we just went and learned. I later learned from children who had gone to the integrated schools that it was totally different for them. Because our teachers always pushed us, and encouraged us to go to college, and told us we could be anything that we set our minds to. However, as I understand it, at the other schools, they didn't have much expectation for the Black kids. They didn't talk to them in the same light. In fact, one person I know was told as a student that, because of the curse of Ham—which we know is a lie—that Blacks are inferior, and so he just needed to accept the state that God has made him in, to be subservient to the whites.

I loved math, because my dad loved math. He also built houses. Because I liked math, I majored in math in college. Math was my favorite subject, and my dad and I did math problems; I think he did that just because of his building and all.

I had two favorite teachers. My fifth grade teacher was Mrs. Jones, and she was my favorite. And my absolute favorite was Mrs. Rodemore, my sixth grade teacher. And I just loved her. When I graduated from high school, it had been many years since I had seen her. And lo and behold, to my amazement, there she was. And she brought me a gift after all those years!

They kept up with us. The teachers. They took a genuine interest in us.

What did you do for fun when you were a kid?

I read. I loved to read. I'd just curl up with a book and read. Of course, fun was built in. Because we had a house full of other kids. And so we played jokes on each other and looked at TV, and read, you know, things like that.

We did not have a lot of social events at school. The only thing I'm kind of remembering was a Halloween party. Mom had let us go to it, and Daddy found out when he got home. He came and got us and he said Halloween was foolishness. So they probably did that every year, but we didn't get to go.

Osage Avenue Christian Church in Okmulgee, Oklahoma, is where I grew up. And my grandmother was one of the founders of that church in that little town. And I can remember the older people there would always say I reminded them so much of my grandmother, my father's mother.

The grandmother to which I'm referring was dead when I was born. I did know my dad's dad, and my mother's mother, my granny. I was very close with those grandparents.

My grandmother was at our house every day. She lived on one street and we lived on the other. She'd come down that alley to our house. Then, there was a time when she lived across the street, so you know, it was seamless.

Even my great-grandmother, when I say down the alley, it was my great-grandmother's house. My granny was down there a lot with her mom. And my great-grandmother went to bed at 8 p.m. every night. And she had a telephone, but the neighbors didn't. So, lights out at 8 p.m. I knew the lights were supposed to be out, but I tipped in there when Granny was asleep. And so, I turned the light on so I could read. Then, there was a knock at the door and a neighbor wanted to use the phone. She figured Granny was up because the light was on. Right then, I knew I was in trouble!

In reference to my great-grandmother, I didn't realize this until I was an adult for many years . . . she would love for me to read to her. And I would read, and I would look up every now and then, and she had this smile of joy on her face like no other. I would read, and I would love to look up and see that look on her face. And you know, I was probably 40 years old or more before I realized what that look was. She couldn't read.

She could not read. Based on her time of life, when Blacks didn't go to school—and in fact, at that time, it was illegal for us to read and write. So she just loved the fact that her great-granddaughter could read. Yes, she loved it.

And my grandmother also could not read. She would write an X for her name. My granny was born in the 1800s, and she would make an X for her name since she couldn't read. And I find it interesting that there was a mindset that Blacks were illiterate. But that was set in motion by society making it illegal. Right.

Did your great-grandmother or others talk about slavery?

You know, I was reflecting on that question pondering that, but I don't remember them talking about it. And I don't know why. Maybe they wanted a better time for us, and not to remember what had happened. My great-grandmother had been a slave. And she was referred to as a Choctaw Freedman. Grandma Harris.

And she never spoke of it. She would cook for us and do things with us, but she never spoke of it. Nor did my grandmother. I don't know if there was shame associated; I don't know why. It's even like the Tulsa riot that happened about 20 years before I was born. We are 35 miles south of Tulsa. My sister Ruth said that she heard Mom and Dad whispering about it once. And, even after all that time, they would whisper. It was almost like the Black people that I knew who were living in Tulsa around that riot time had decided not to discuss it. But you can just imagine that, here you are in this thriving community where money was turning around 18 times, and the majority culture is looking with hatefulness and jealousy. Greenwood—they called it Black Wall Street. It was a *thriving* metropolis. Businesses everywhere. And they bombed them.

And not only did they drop bombs on the community to make sure it didn't go any where, but they also came in and built a freeway over it and cut it off. You couldn't even drive all the way through it like you used to. They closed off whole streets and everything. And so there was a lot of hopelessness, helplessness. But I do not recall any story that my grandmother or my great-grandmother told like that. And they probably would not have told us as kids.

You could be lynched or anything else for even raising the issues. And so, there was a chilling effect put on it. And that's why there was a quietness. There was an acceptance of the plight and the condition, I believe. You know the letter, Willie Lynch? The making of a slave, how you break down a person. Their emotions and their psyche, and everything else. And so . . . and that's why you saw a lot of Black elders with their heads bowed down, and you had this rule in the South where you couldn't

On the left, Oletha's father's side of the family, including her brother Carl, her father, and her grandfather Frank (son of Dick Lewis Barnett). On the right, Oletha's mother's side of the family; from left: Oletha's grandmother, great-grandmother, her mother, her sister, and her nephew.

look a white person in the eyes, and so their heads would be down. And that was passed down in order to protect us. I don't even think it was that they were trying to forget it. They were trying to protect us.

Here's the thing to remember about Jim Crow. There was a period of time when Jim Crow was legal. But never forget that the baggage of slavery was passed down. Jim Crow is still with us, just in different ways. When you change the law, you don't change the hearts. Jim Crow is still with us in a different form. I'll give you one example. After the Civil War, and after Reconstruction, they brought in the Jim Crow laws and the Black Codes, and voting was a huge issue. They did everything under the sun to keep us from voting. The 14th Amendment gave us the right to vote, but no, we still got to have special legislation. That's still the baggage of Jim Crow. And then, even before 1965, you had [to have] all those other interim laws trying to give us the right to vote. Getting rid of poll taxes and literacy tests, and all of that. Even today, you still see the suppression of the vote.

So, it's still with us. We still have that as an issue. That's part of the baggage of Jim Crow; it's still with us, make no mistake. Passed down in the psyche of the whites, passed down in the psyche of the Blacks.

When you were growing up, were you aware of any unwritten rules that govern race relations?

There are so many, you can't even envision it. There was an incident that happened with me. That was an unwritten rule, but it came about as a result of Jim Crow and segregation and the hatred of Blacks. Here's a little story: a number of years ago, I was in Maryland driving to a friend's house. This was before GPS. I realized I was on the right street, but going in the wrong direction. So I make my little U-turn in the street to go in the other direction. And my friend who was riding with me said, "What is wrong with you? Why did you make that U-turn in the street, instead of just coming up in somebody's driveway and backing out?"

See, it had floated up from my subconscious. You don't know what's in your psyche until something triggers it. I was always told as a child that you don't turn around in the driveway of a white person's home, or they will shoot you. And so that floated up from my subconscious. I believe that it's untold, and we can't even scratch the surface of the impact of it. That unwritten rule, see, my mom had told me that to protect me. But I wasn't even aware that I was operating from my subconscious until somebody raised the issue. Had that issue not been raised, I would have gone along without ever thinking about it. Thinking about getting shot at the time, I was just acting on what I knew.

Once, we were driving near Henrietta, Oklahoma. And my mom said, Henrietta used to have a huge sign on Main Street that said "N-I-G-G-E-R, don't let the sun go down on you in Henrietta." It was a sundown town. A sundown town is a town where Blacks have to be out by before sundown, or you would be hanged; in fact, a white woman told me that her mother would drive through a town called Poletown to take her to school every day. And she once asked her mother why it was called Poletown. Well, her mother told her in a matter-of-fact tone that it was called Poletown because if Blacks weren't out of town before sundown, they would be lynched from a pole.

So, people talk about the South, but when Blacks escaped to the North, there were a lot of those Northern places that had sundown towns, also. The North may have been different from the South, but the North had its own racial issues with sundown towns, and so much more. It's just steeped throughout the country, and it's an ugly legacy of the United States of America.

My college, Langston University in Oklahoma, was predominantly Black. One of my professors said, "If you got to drive through the South, you'd better get through the South before it's dark." And the college president's wife told us that they were driving through the South. The president had a new car, and they got pulled over. Today, we would call it "pulled over for driving while Black." They pulled him over, and were questioning him because he was in that new car. She said he kept saying, "Yes, sir. No, sir. Yes, sir." You know, answering meekly because you don't know what's going to happen in those situations. And so, that was a rule. Get through the South before dark. That's what our professors were telling us.

Now, here's something that happened just last year. My sister had a man drive into the back of her car. He hit her. He was an older white gentleman. He hit her and drove off. So she's following him and honking her horn, and he's just going, ignoring her. She called me while it was happening. So, they finally got to a place where he had turned and pulled over. He was an older man, and he said he didn't know what had happened. He said he couldn't see well and had lost his wife, and I don't think the man even had a license. And so, she called the police to have a report made. Well, about three or four police cars pulled up.

I'm still on the phone. The police pulled up and began yelling at her, and it was as hateful as could be. They were telling her that they didn't believe he had backed into her car, that she already had that dent, and everything else. This man had admitted that he had backed into her. But they see the white man, they see this Black woman, and they hadn't even gone to talk to the man. The man didn't have insurance with him or anything else. So, is Jim Crow still with us? Laws change. Hearts don't.

Were there colored and white signs in your town growing up?

There were. Everything was fully segregated. At the Black school, we would sing "Lift Every Voice and Sing," the Negro National Anthem. We did it at one of the graduations, and the school board forbade us from singing it. So, we had to stop singing it in school. We fully had Jim Crow, and even after Jim Crow, we had Jim Crow. Still had poll taxes and a lot of other madness that went on.

Did your parents vote?

Oh, yeah. My sister and I were laughing about it not long ago. Because Daddy was a Republican and my mother was a Democrat.

Well, the Republicans used to be the Lincoln party!

Yeah, that's exactly right. And you know, when Lincoln was assassinated, he was Union and his vice president was from the Confederacy. That's why the South didn't progress well, because they were slaves in every way except by name.

Yeah, I often wonder how things would be different if Lincoln hadn't been assassinated before he was able to fully roll out his presidential plan.

I wonder the same thing. And, *The Birth of a Nation*? Was it Woodrow Wilson, you had the president of the United States praising the Ku Klux Klan. Woodrow Wilson was a Democrat, friend of the KKK, and racist. They had a private screening of *The Birth of a Nation* at the White House. He praised the Klu Klux Klan. And that was the president.

The same white woman who told me about Poletown told me there were people in the Klan that she loved. Obviously, she wouldn't identify them. But you didn't know who was in the Klan. There were policemen, public officials, elected officials, politicians . . . many of them were in the Klan.

Did you ever know of anybody who was lynched?

Not personally. And when I was a kid, if I heard something unpleasant like that, I would just kind of bury it as though it didn't exist. So, I don't know what's down there subconsciously. But in my hometown, there were a group of sanitation workers. Most of them were white, and there was this one Black man who was a sanitation worker. He was killed. They claimed it was an accident, and that they didn't realize he was back there, and he got chewed up with the trash and killed back there. And my sister said she was talking to this white woman, and the white woman said, "It's shameful what they did to that man." And then the white woman quickly shut up. And so my sister said that they killed him. On purpose. The story I heard on it was that they killed him. The white people in the town would have known what happened.

Were you ever afraid for your safety as a young person?

In my segregated world, I was not afraid. There were generally no whites in our neighborhood unless it was like the milkman or someone. But the only time I felt fear in my neighborhood was one time I was walking from the store, and this white stranger was driving on that street. He said something really, really nasty to me. And it scared the life out of me, and I ran like crazy. Ran home. And my sister said, "You should have got his car tag." And Mom said, "No, baby, you should have done just what you did." Because he could have tried anything.

When I was in college, a group of us went to Houston, Texas, and we ended up in a restaurant. There were some white people who kept shaking our table and doing things like that. This was the early '70s. Now, that was one time I was terrified. But some of the guys, the students I was with, they weren't taking it. Some of them were from the Northeast, and they weren't going to take it. They would have shot.

If anything had happened, they would have done something. And I was terrified. I was thinking, my mama and daddy didn't send me to college to go off to Houston and get shot.

But they insisted on staying. And so we ate, but I didn't enjoy my meal because I was afraid. But the others I was with, they weren't afraid. They were used to confronting directly like that. And the white people were saying derogatory things, but when the guys in our group showed that they weren't taking it, they eventually shut up.

I remember my ex-husband and I going to a little fast food place to get some food, and I was sitting in the car while he got the food. And there were some white men in a car next to me, and they looked at me and started saying all kinds of racial, ugly things. And when my husband came out, I didn't say a word because I didn't want to have any stuff up in there. I recognized that I wasn't the issue, they were the issue, they had bitterness and hate in them. And I wasn't going to put myself at risk because of somebody's bitterness within.

I still think it's amazing that your family owned so much land as Black people at that time.

Yeah, it was by God's grace, and was by my dad's hard work. But you know, what I do remember is that my dad was *always* concerned about someone misplacing the deed. He was older then, and he was just really disturbed in his spirit about misplacing the deed, and that the white folk might try to take his land. Yeah.

There were other Black landowners in my dad's age group. I was just thinking about the Hills. They had land not very far from us. Anita Hill's family. My younger sisters and brothers were in school with her. And at that time, Oklahoma was only about 6 percent Black. Was it racist like other places? Yes.

How did you end up going into the law?

Oh, a friend wanted to attend law school, and I thought it was a neat little idea. So, I went. That's pretty much the long and short of it!

My initial plan was to be a math teacher, and after I graduated from college, I ended up working at a bank. I supervised tellers and new account representatives in a small town in Oklahoma.

Then, right out of law school, I worked for the federal government in Washington, DC. After that, I worked for the federal government in Fort Worth, Texas, because my parents were getting older and I wanted to get back near the Texas-Oklahoma area. I worked in the state government in Texas after I left the federal government, and then I've done some private practice. I've kind of run the gamut of all of it. Yeah. Then, I retired for the ministry. I went to seminary in Dallas. And now, I teach conflict resolution and racial reconciliation at two Bible colleges here in Texas, and I also run a business.

When I worked for the state of Texas, we had one Black supervisor. My nephew would cut his yard; he had a beautiful home. His wife was a doctor, and his home almost looked like a mansion. And I asked him, "Why do you drive this old truck to work? You got all those fine cars and your big home." He said, "Oletha, if I drove this car to work, white people would try to take me down. They're not gonna let you get ahead or try to do better than them. And that's why I drive this truck."

Now, there was another lady who worked a menial job. And they had no reason to fire her. But she was able to go out and buy a new car, after working. Well, they fired her. She bought the car and they fired her, and they said to her, "We don't know how you going to pay for that new car you got." Yep. "We don't know how you going to pay for that new car you got."

You know, there's hate in the world. But if you get hatred in your heart, then evil wins. You've got to put it in perspective and recognize that they don't know who they are. And they don't know who you are. My father would always ask me, "What makes one man think he's better than another man?" And I'd say, "Well, he's not, Daddy. He's not." And that answer always satisfied him. And so, instead of telling me stories about what happened to them, they were instilling in me that nobody is better than me. They wanted a better life for us than what they had, and they made sure we knew that there was nobody better than us.

Were you involved in the Civil Rights Movement?

No. Of course, we did have . . . you know in 1968 we had the marches and all the things. And I saw on TV, the water hoses being turned on people, the dogs being turned on people, John Lewis, Bloody Sunday, the Freedom Riders, all of that. But I was a little country girl from Okmulgee, Oklahoma. However, God didn't call everybody for civil activism in the same way. One of the things I do now is teach peace and reconciliation. So am I doing it? Yeah. Not just for Blacks but also for whites, because they don't know what they don't know.

I can remember I was in school one day, and a guy who was kind of a class clown came in and told my teacher, "Ms. Hayes, Dr. King was assassinated." And she said, "Don't say things like that!" She thought he was playing around. But it turned out to be true. And I remember everybody was glued to the TV. I was a senior in high school. Obviously, there was much talk about it, much solemnity about it. At church, everybody was grieved about it.

Did y'all get any of the Black newspapers?

Yeah, *The Oklahoma Eagle*. It was out of Tulsa. *The Oklahoma Eagle,* and every Black household got it. We had the Black church that kept the community connected. We had our Black newspapers that kept us connected. And even during slave time, it was the Black churches that kept even the slaves connected. And then they would talk about some of the old songs like "Steal Away to Jesus." The slaves would be singing, and that was a sign for them to say, "We're going to have our church meeting in the swamps tonight." And there was "Couldn't Hear Nobody Praying" to let them know that it was successful and the master didn't even know they were out. It's creative genius.

But God did not make any lesser people, period. I'm a strong Christian, and my intent in sharing this is to say that there is great evil that has been perpetrated against Black people. But you also had white abolitionists, and Quakers. So it's not all evil. My point is not to attack anyone, but just point to the truth. And a lot of the stuff that they're saying, and have said throughout history, *is not true.* I mean, you have Michelle Obama being drawn as—compared to—a monkey by some white people. That's been passed down. All that is still with us, it's been passed down.

This is my belief on it. The Bible says that Abel's blood cried to God from the ground. You think that the blood of all of those slaves who were thrown over the ship, or were hung, or the Martin Luther Kings and the Medgar Evers, you name it. Their blood cries to God. George Floyd's blood cries to God from the ground. But there is a change. Because never before would you have ever seen everybody marching with Blacks during that shutdown based on George Floyd's killing. So God is doing a shifting.

There's a huge evil connected with race in this country. And so, we're imploding from within. That's my position. We're imploding from within because of sin.

What was it like when things became integrated?

Well, I'm Black, and I had a great childhood, and I love being Black. And so, I'm going to show you where integration was not necessarily a great part of my life. My elementary school was Black, my high school was Black. My college, Langston University, was predominantly Black. The first time I went to a predominantly white school, I was in my fifties, when I went to seminary school here in Dallas, Texas. Dallas Theological Seminary.

So here I am, coming out of a Black college, ended up working at a bank in Oklahoma and there were racists there. But I had to move on and bury it because I wasn't much in a position to say or do anything, and we didn't really have the civil rights laws to the extent that they were actionable at that time. I didn't even really know what my rights were for the most part. So trying to work in that environment was tough.

When I was in high school, we had to go compete with some other schools on some things. And so, they put our little school up against some really big schools. And our teachers said that they did that to keep us from winning, because we would have taken it away. Our teachers had really prepared us! But we were being put up against schools with hundreds of kids, and we were small. And our teachers wrote and told them that they put their students with the wrong group. And they wrote back and said, "We reserve the right to put you where we want to put you." That's the school system saying that. The educational system in Oklahoma. They told us they would put us where they wanted to put us.

Near my hometown, there was a white Christian church, and one summer, they decided that they were going to let some of the little Black kids go to their camp. That was my first real experience with race. I was about 12 years old. And they were not kind. The white kids were not kind to us at all. And if I had left there, and hadn't met one little white girl who was nice, I would have thought all white people were like that. She lived in the same town as we did, and she was nice. And she wanted my address. In our little town, we probably lived 10 minutes walking distance from each other, but we wrote letters. You know, Black part of town, white part of town, never the two should meet. So even though we lived close to each other, we wrote letters.

Sixty years later, I get this ping on Facebook Messenger, and it's her. She'd been looking for me for years, and we reconnected. Then later on, I was kind of disappointed after I saw something that she had said about the protests connected with George Floyd. It was just kind of sad to me that she didn't grow up to be who she appeared to be when she was a child.

When I was in seminary school, and Obama was elected, one of my professors said, "Well, at least maybe Obama can get the boys to pull up their pants." I heard it mentioned that there was another professor who said to some young Black students, "Settle down and quit acting like some little monkeys that just got off the boat from Africa." And then there was another professor in seminary who, after the police had stopped his child, said, "My son has blond hair and blue eyes. Why would the police stop somebody like that!" It did give me pause, but I just moved on, because I'm used to it.

I don't want to give the impression that I don't stand up for my rights, because I pretty much always have. Because I do . . . I've had to confront racism. And I have done that. But I admire the younger generation. You all are tough. If something is racially insensitive or culturally insensitive, you will call it out. And that's a good thing.

It's because we are privileged to live in a time where we can be more bold, because of previous generations working to make things better for us. Do you think Dr. King's dream is possible in this country?

(Very long pause.)

I think that it is possible to a degree. And I think the younger generation will do much better with it than we will. There are some in our generation, Black and white, who I think have the right heart and mindset. But I think the younger generation will do better.

I see things getting better down the line, but in order for them to get better, we had to be where we are now. For this thing to have surfaced to the degree it has surfaced, it was there. It's kind of like the iceberg: you're seeing the tip, but that thing was deeper. The iceberg of racism is underneath, and if you don't know it's there, you won't be able to fix it.

Regarding integration, it had to be done to some degree. You couldn't sit there and not do it. You couldn't sit there and not do your Selma march and not fight for your rights. Dr. King did it for his season in his time and for his generation. The Freedom Riders, the counter sit-ins, the Bloody Sundays, it had to be done. We've paid a cost for freedom. And we continue to.

Those who have a heart of racial division and strife and separation and racism, that's evil. We have two countries. It still goes back to the love of the Confederacy, and then those of the Union. That's why they say, "Away in Dixie," and why we ended up with all those huge monuments to the Confederate soldiers. In the United States, the heart for what we believe didn't change. Those who believe in racism still do. Those who believe in equality still do.

This is not just history, because the baggage of it is still with us. A white woman once asked me, "Do you always feel Black?" Well, that's all I know! I'm Black. That's all I know. But when I had that situation with the U-turn in Maryland, and I realized what I had done, I thought that if you can "feel Black" in a particular context, that moment would have been it.

Learn about history, but don't become bitter about it. Take the creative genius that God gave you, and make the world a better place. Don't become bitter. Become better.

INTERVIEW NO.

NO. 7

PHYLLIS
TAYLOR

My dad's mother's name was Julia Allen and his dad's name was Charlie Allen. My grandmother's name on my mother's side was Phyllis Coles Lecars. And my grandfather was John Henry Lecars. My mother was Corinne Lecars Allen. And my dad's name was Booker T. Allen. I grew up in a section in Richmond called New Town. We were approximately in the area where the Maggie L. Walker High School is now. There was two parts to New Town. One part was called New Town, and that was the section on Moore Street and Lee Street, and it ended at Hermitage Road. And the other part, which we did not call New Town, was called The Hill. And that's where the Black neighborhood on the other side of the railroad was. And it was on a hill. And that's where our church was. And it was started by my grandfather and grandmother, along with 14 other people. And it's called St. Paul's Baptist Church.

But in the area that really was New Town, there was a church called First Union Baptist Church. And my grandmother and grandfather were formally members there, and they, along with the group I told you about, asked to start a church of our own, and that's what became St. Paul's Baptist Church. And it was started on Thanksgiving night. In 1909. And most of our family still have family members that are part of St. Paul's, including me. I was baptized when I was five years old, became a legitimate member of the church. And I'm still an active member at my tender age!

I've held a number of positions in the church. As a member of St. Paul's for years, our pastor at the time, Reverend J. A. Mosbit, had a lot of confidence in the members and in the young people who were growing up in the church. Before he became pastor, whenever we would have an activity or something, they would go out into the community and get people to be in charge of it and sponsor or train the people who were going to be a part of it. But once he became pastor, he said, we will no longer be going into the community of neighbors to secure people to do our work. We will be doing it ourselves. So, the members started using their talents, which were many, and were very effective to start having programs in the church.

One of the main things that we did have growing up was what was called the Baptist Training Union—the BYPU—which met every Sunday evening at six o'clock. He was a very forward-looking minister who would make the young people feel comfortable. So, he allowed us to have activities in the church that other churches would not allow, for instance, debates, quiz contests, oratorical speeches. . . . So, we got a lot of training. We also had youth choir. But he was saying to the congregation that, once a person is baptized and they fellowship into the church, they are full-fledged members, regardless of their age. So, at 10 years of age, I became the church secretary. And I served for 25 years in that position. We had a youth choir. And I have pictures of that choir when we were growing up. Some of us were in early teens and some are younger. And we were all in our robes and caps, and we were looking mighty good, if I do say so myself!

What skills and opportunities did you receive from growing up in church in the segregated South?

Oh, it was like talent being developed. But we didn't realize it at the time. We joined when we were five, my first cousin and I. And during that time, it was a tradition for churches to visit each other. And when you went to the other church, they would have someone to give the welcome and somebody to introduce the pastor. So, once we became official members at five, whenever our pastor would go out, he would be so proud of us he would have one of us to introduce the speaker, and the other one to give the welcome. And we knew that you better be prepared because you are going to be called on.

We also had some citywide organizations, and we were chosen to go to them and represent the church in the youth department—not only in Richmond, but throughout the state of Virginia. That gave us a talent. And then we had a General Baptist Missionary Society, who had a radio program on Sunday morning. And I was chosen to be the youth participant on that program on Sunday. We had talent shows, also. At the time, you didn't charge money in the church to see those things, but we always took up an offering to help finance the church and help finance the activities that were sponsored for the young people. We also got quite a bit of encouragement from the senior members of the church, because even if you got up and tried to do something, and you may not have been real good at it, they would say, "Yeah, chile, go on chile, do it!" They would encourage you.

My mother was a seamstress. So she made all of my costumes. And she made a lot of them for our kids in the neighborhood. When we would have events, she had to turn people away because she could make all those costumes they wanted!

And another event that our church sponsored, which was city wide, and the tickets always sold out, was. . . . You know, we could go to the beach every summer, but this was during the years of segregation. And so the Black beach was called Bay Shore. And the white beach was called Buckroe Beach, but you could not go on Buckroe Beach. But my uncle worked for the railroad, and he persuaded them to let him have a train for that whole day, so that we could take people to the beach. And so what happened, we would take the train, we would have seven or eight coaches, and sell tickets to go to the beach for the day. You'd go in the morning, and you come back in the evening. Ours was so popular, and so well received, that one of the social clubs, called the Devils, decided they were going to do it. So, the railroad would only let two groups do it. Our group would go in the morning, and when the train came back to Richmond to put us off, then the Devils would get the train. And they would stay until midnight. And we went the first Saturday in August of every year. If you didn't get your ticket by maybe . . . I'll say July 15, you weren't going to get no tickets to go with us. And lot of people didn't want to go to with the Devils because they were having drinking and you know, alcohol, and they were just carousing. So they didn't want to be bothered with them.

But our tickets, you know, they knew they were going to do very well. Everybody would be well behaved. And so they were very anxious to get our tickets and those are the ones who took the children as well. So the adult tickets were one price and the children for half price.

The Sunday School really were the sponsors of "the excursion," we used to call it. And those kids, if you came to Sunday School every Sunday regularly, you could go free. And your parents would have to pay a small fee, but their fee would be smaller than the regular people's fee. It was maybe a dollar or two. Five dollars at the most.

What was the beach day like?

It was interesting because they had a refreshment car. And so they were stocked with all kinds of sodas and potato chips, all kinds of snack stuff, sandwiches and everything. They made sure that it was well stocked. Nobody could have alcohol on the train with our knowledge, but you know, some people did sneak the alcohol! But they would hide it if we came along. So it was a fun time. And when you'd get down to the beach, the Black side of the beach, we had a member's daughter who had a restaurant. We called her Ms. Sitter. Everybody was gonna go to Ms. Sitter's restaurant sometime during the day and get some fish, because that was her specialty. You got to get some of Ms. Sitter's fish before you leave the beach, although it was traditional for everybody to pack a basket. Very rarely did they pack sodas because there were plenty of them in the refreshment car. And we talk about it now, and we don't understand why none of that stuff spoiled! Because now they say you can't leave stuff out. But that stuff stayed out all day! We had deviled eggs. We had potato salad. We had slaw. We had everything that you have now, but nobody ever got sick of food poisoning. So we don't know what's the difference? We didn't worry about any of those things back then.

Some of the activities that we had in the church was, we had the Camp Cary for the young people. And it was for girls only. And every year, for a month, the General Baptist Association would rent what was called Pocahontas Park. And they would have a camp where your church could send as many girls from 10 to 16 to the camp to stay a week. Okay? That was an activity, which was very beneficial, because you got to meet kids from all over the state. And also, you got to use your talent. And you got to study the Bible. I got to go when I was a young child, and my kids got to go when they were young as well. And they remember some of our leaders from that time, that had such a great influence on their lives.

And we also had a citywide group of junior missionaries, we called them, and they met once a month. So that gave you a chance to meet kids from all over the city. And even till they passed away, you know, we would get together for different activities just like a reunion, because we remembered growing up together. And those were some things that we did, because all of our activities were sort of limited during that time because of segregation.

Did you ever interact with white churches?

I had a mentor named Emma Hicks. And I don't know how she made the connection. But she became connected with the National Conference of Christians and Jews. And they had a youth department, which was all white. But she insisted that they could not be a National Conference of Christians and Jews if they didn't have any Black representation in it. So she got me to be the representative for the Black churches in Richmond. And once a year, they would have a conference in what is called Rosslyn, which is an Episcopal community center. And it was all segregated, as far as I know; I never knew any Blacks to go there. But the National Conference of Christians and Jews would use it for their youth meeting once a year, and I got to go. And the interesting thing was that I was a participant there, and I knew no discrimination. I felt no different from any other kid. But the minute we left there, and came back to the city, I knew I was Black.

How old were you?

I was between eight and 12.

Did you go that one time, or you went several times?

Several times. But we only had one meeting per year. It was something that you did on a yearly basis. I was the only Black person there, and they even elected me the vice president of that youth group eventually.

So how did your parents feel about you being in this role?

My mother was a person who believed that you had to be exposed to experiences in order to be a well rounded person. And so she made sure that when Ms. Hicks had anything that would be beneficial to youth, she let me go, and she made sure I was dressed appropriately, because, as I told you, she was a seamstress. So they were very happy to have me to go. And when I was in elementary school, I went to school, and because of my gift of speaking so well, they would let me go represent our school at different activities like the Red Cross meeting for the city's schoolchildren. All of those activities were segregated—we did not have an integrated Red Cross for youth—but Black youth from all-Black schools would come to this particular meeting once a month. And your teacher would be your person who escorted you to the meeting. And they would plan the activities for us to do, but they were all segregated.

When you were representing the church, did you have any Black adults come in with you or it was just you?

This lady, Emma Hicks, she would escort me to everything that I went to as a youth. My mama wouldn't let me go by myself. First time I ever went by myself to a conference—and that was in connection with the National Conference of Christians and Jews—I was chosen as one of the delegates to a national meeting, which was held in New York City. My mother let me go by myself because I had an aunt that lived in New York, who was like my godmother. So she was going to meet me at the train and make sure I got to where I needed to go. And that was an excellent experience, because you had people there from all over the world, all nationalities and everything.

You said that when you would go to the yearly meeting, it was a great experience. But as soon as you got back to Richmond, you knew you were Black. Can you talk more about that?

Well, you know, like I said, she would take me to the meetings, and I would feel so good. You know how you feel so special and everything. But once you got back into the real world, and crossed the city line, I knew right then that segregation would rear its ugly head because you had different signs, and, you know, different community borders that you weren't supposed to go across.

Back some years ago, First Baptist Church on Monument Avenue in Richmond... white church. Well, they used to send missionaries to Africa. And when some of the African people came over here, to live, and they tried to join the church, they refused them because they were Black. And the pastor at that time, Dr. Adams, said what a testimony that would be if we go out to convert people and bring them into the Christian fold. And we are all supposed to be sisters and brothers. And yet, still you don't want them to be a part of this church—I refuse to be a part of this church. And so they allowed them to become members. But before then, they did not have any Black members. And if you went to that church, you could not sit with the white members. You had to be in the balcony or something.

So for you growing up as a young girl in the church, what was your favorite thing to do?

Well, I guess we used it as a dating source because all the boys and girls could get together on Sunday without anybody restricting you from having a conversation with your favorite person. So it was like a social event: everybody who lived in the neighborhood would go to our Vacation Bible School, even if they did not belong to First Union. Because I told you our pastor was so lenient. So he let us do things that were interesting to kids at that time. And then of course, if your boyfriend knew that you would be at BYPU, they gon' get there too, because see, that gives them a chance to talk to you on the sly. You couldn't go nowhere or do anything, but you could at least talk to each other and wave at each other across the aisle. And that was 'bout the limit of what you could do at the time. Because you were never allowed to date until you were at least 16 years old. And you know, between 12 and 16, there's a lot of interesting things going on.

So you said your mother was a seamstress; what did your father do?

He was a porter for the railroad. The RF&P. And so that was another enjoyable experience during my years growing up. Because if you worked for the railroad, the railroad would give you a pass according to what routes they used. And the direct route from Richmond was from Richmond to Washington, DC. So my dad had a family pass, which all of us had copies of. And we could ride the train, no matter how many times we wanted to, any day of the week, as long as it was between Richmond and Washington. So one experience that we learned doing that . . . they had the Black coaches, and the white coaches. What I'm saying is one was for Black people, and one for white people. And from Richmond, to Washington, DC, if you rode the train, you had to ride in a coach for Blacks. Once it got to DC, they would have an exchange of coaches. And all the coaches would become desegregated then—you ride anywhere you wanted on the train.

One of my most memorable experiences was the time when I went past Washington, DC. And then they go through this tunnel and then they say they got to switch engines. That's what they used to say. But actually, they were fixing the coaches so they would be for anybody who wants to ride there. And so you get off the train, and then when you got back on, you can sit anywhere you wanted to. Now, if you were going South, they did the same thing: they stopped in DC. But when you got back on, you were going to be in a segregated car.

And one good experience that came to mind, because you asked me to think back over segregation, so one time—this only happened one time—my mother decided she was going to take me on a long train trip so I could experience that, because she always wanted me to be experiencing new things. So she got . . . you could get a pass

Phyllis's parents, Booker T. and Corinne Leecost Allen.

to anywhere in this country, on the railroad, but you had to get special permission. So my dad applied for us to go from Richmond to Miami. And it took two days and nights to do it. But we got on the train. We didn't have to worry about it because we were already segregated since we were going South. Now if we'd been going North, it would been different. And it was one of the most interesting experiences.

But you weren't allowed to eat in the dining car after . . . I don't remember whether it was North Carolina or South Carolina . . . must have been after you got out of North Carolina, you couldn't eat in the dining car. Because that's what the segregation rules were. You couldn't eat in it. You could buy food in it, but you couldn't eat in it, there in the dining car. But because Dad worked for the railroad, and his friends knew the porters and everything, they would bring us good food from the dining room. And I remember that because we would not have had it if they hadn't brought it to us. So that was a wonderful experience.

So your dad was a porter? What kind?

Yes. He was a baggage porter. He was in charge of baggage.

Do you know if it was difficult for him to get that job?

I really don't know. Because you know, I was a child. And things like that weren't important to me back then. Although I know, porters were the biggest jobs you could have. Those that worked on the railroad fixing tires, and, you know, changing the rails and all that stuff, wasn't quite as sophisticated as the baggage porters.

Do you have siblings?

One, I have a sister, and she's still living. And she is 94 years old now.

Did you know your grandparents growing up?

I knew my grandmother and grandfather very well. That's on my mother's side. On my dad's side, I only knew my grandmother. And I knew her very well. We visited them every summer. And that was the interesting thing. They were sharecroppers. And I remember when we went down to visit, a lot of kids in my neighborhood would go spend the summer in North Carolina or wherever their parents came from, because they didn't have any babysitters. But I grew up in a different environment. But anyway, we went to North Carolina to visit, and all of my cousins were out in the field picking cotton and tobacco. But they knew better than to send me out there because I was a sickly child. They'd say, "Phyllis will never make it if we send her out there!" So one week a year was enough for me. You know how people love to go visit? Not me, not down in North Carolina, no. But when my grandmother used to come visit us, we'd be happy because we didn't have to go down in those parts. But we had to go at least once a year.

One time, we went during the wintertime. I can't remember whether somebody had died or what, but we did go during the wintertime. And that was another experience I'll never forget, because they heated the house with fireplaces. Well, of course we had stoves in our house. And so a fireplace was just a showplace as far as we were concerned. And so when I went there, and everybody's sitting around the fireplace, and I thought it was so interesting, you know, to see the fire and everybody sitting around it, trying to keep warm. But I discovered that sitting around the fireplace might be fun. But the front of you was burning up, while the back of you was freezing!

Did you have any special memories with any of your grandparents?

The only thing I can think of is that with my grandfather—my grandfather on my mother's side—I was his favorite. I didn't realize it at the time. He favored me over all the other grandkids. And so it was tradition in the family for my grandfather to take my grandmother shopping every Saturday night down to the 17th Street Market. And so we would get in the truck and go down to the market. And he would say, "Phyllis, you go ahead and do what you need to do." I was named after her. I would sit there in the truck. And as soon as she would leave, he would say, "Come on, Phyllis," and he would take me out to one of the seafood places that sold seafood, and buy me a bag of shrimp. And we would come back to the truck and sit and eat all that bag of shrimp. By the time my grandmother got through shopping, we were lucky if we had any left. It was so much fun! And I never forgot that.

There were a lot of first cousins, and my grandma kept a lot of us, and if we had spats—if somebody did something to me—he would punish them. But then if I did something to one of them, I never got punished. And I say, I'm surprised my cousins still love me because of that! This is in my memory all this time. I forgot to hold on to other stuff. But I didn't forget that.

What about your schooling?

The schools that I went to, I lived up near where Maggie Walker is now, and at that time when my mother was in high school, there was only one Black high school in

Richmond. And all of her family went to Armstrong High School because that was the only high school. And all of the kids from all over the city came to that high school. And how they handled it was they had two periods of study: the morning study and afternoon study. The kids who were freshmen and sophomores, they went to school in the afternoon. And the children who were juniors and seniors, they went in the morning so that they could go to jobs in the afternoon. And then, in the 1930s, they decided to build another high school. But they built it for the purpose of teaching trades to Blacks. And that's what school was all about.

I lived right on the block next to the school. But my mother and her sisters insisted that their children go to Armstrong because they wanted us to get what they called a better education. But we'd walk past the other school, walking past this good school, down to Armstrong. But it was a social event for us too. Because walking down, you picked up people along the way. And so all of us were friends. And then we would pass kids going to Walker, because we were all friendly. But we were on different sides of the street. I don't know why we never were on the same side of the street! And so we would wave at the kids going to Walker, and they would wave at the ones of us going to Armstrong. And it was a friendly thing.

Well, the highlight of those years was the Armstrong–Walker game. It was a football game between the two high schools, and that was the social event of the Black community. I don't care where you were in the world. On Thanksgiving, you came home to Richmond, because you had to go to the Armstrong–Walker game! It was such an event that if the white people told the Blacks they hired that they couldn't be off on Thanksgiving Day, they would say, "Well, we quit!" They would quit their jobs because they were determined they were going to be at that game.

And that was the fashion show of the year. Everybody was trying to outdress the other one. Everybody wore either green and white, or orange and blue. And you couldn't be on no sidelines, you had to be one or the other during that weekend. Those were the schools' colors. Walker was green and white, and Armstrong was orange and blue. And remember I told you my mother was a seamstress. She made me this skirt that was blue with pleats all around. And in each pleat was an orange panel. And I wish to this day that I knew what happened to that skirt, because that would be really something worth saving! But I don't know what happened to it. And when I'd walk—you know how the pleats will do, they just move and peek out. Oh, I still think of that skirt even now! Now that was so much fun.

But that was the social event, we call it, of the century, because everybody was going to get off to go to that game. We had more people at that game than any other activity that was held at the stadium. And that's where the game was held. And then when one of the superintendents came in, because they started integration, they decided that there weren't enough people to sustain each high school individually. So they grouped them. And they did away with the Armstrong–Walker game. And it has not been the same. People still mad about that, people who are still living and remember it, even if they weren't even students at the school—they still mad because they cut out Armstrong–Walker.

This reminds me of the whole debate between Booker T. Washington and W. E. B. Du Bois, the talented tenth and all of that. Do you know why your parents would have wanted you to go to Armstrong . . . can you talk a little more about that?

All of us within that social circle went to Armstrong, and it was because they knew we would get more education after high school. They had schools back then called "normal school" that you could go to, but they were planning for us to go to college. And Armstrong was the college preparatory school. And we did get a good education at Armstrong to prepare us for college. But then, when the neighborhoods changed, because they brought the expressway through Richmond—we call it the Downtown Expressway—and 95 cut through the heart of Richmond, and it affected mostly Black residents. And as a result of that, people had to move to different parts of the city. The majority of the people moved to Northside. That was when professional people wanted our kids to go to college too, so they changed the curriculum so that both schools could have college preparatory. Armstrong never became the trade school, but Walker still had the trade plus the college preparatory. You could do either one at Walker, but you couldn't do that at Armstrong.

What did you and your sister end up doing after high school?

My sister didn't go any further. I went to Virginia Union for a couple of years. And then I got married and my education stopped for a while. And then I decided to take up schooling to be a secretary. And then after that, I got to be a professionally certified office person, by going and getting an associate degree.

Let's see. One thing that really helped us as Black people, I think, was World War II. Because when World War II came, everybody that was able had to do something to help with the war. And before then, most Black people had menial jobs. But those like my mother, who had talent for sewing, she used her talent to help make parachutes. So she got a good paying job, and was able to save that money so that we could buy a home and all that good stuff. And a lot of women, too, went into the manufacturers and factories, to do whatever they needed to make the war materials that were needed at that time. So after they came out of the war, they had accumulated funds, because you didn't have many places to spend the money and everything. And then when the soldiers came back, they were given an opportunity on the GI Bill to get some education beyond what they would have normally gotten if they had not gone to war.

And so Walker had all the different trades, like automobile repairs, and even got to the point where some of these things were put into the colleges like Virginia State, so that they could get degrees in those particular things. And that helped a lot. They were able to come back to go back to school; some of them became teachers or lawyers, even doctors, because their education was free. And they could pursue it. And it helped them to be trained to do something that they really had wanted to do but just couldn't afford to do.

Phyllis on her wedding day, 1948.

And that was another thing that changed the social events. Because when the soldiers came back from the service, the young ladies who were in school with them before they went, they had moved on to something else. So the younger ladies were in Walker or Armstrong. And so they met each other. By that time, I was in college, and they were all coming back. So they married a lot of those guys. Although they were older. Before that time, you rarely ever married anybody more than a year or two older than you. After that time, they were three and four years older.

We had a lot of different activities that were a result of them coming back and facing life and thinking differently because they had a broader view of what the world was like. Some of them went overseas and they saw how the people lived and everything. So they wanted to make vast improvements in how they lived.

Even after we integrated, we still had segregation very open in Richmond. For instance, I worked for Richmond Public Schools, and a job came open for me at what they call the plan services. When I went to work there, which was the headquarters for all of the maintenance of the schools—like the grounds, the flowers, the buildings, plumbing—everything pertaining to schools were in this particular building. And the person who was in charge was a white person. All of the purchasing for Richmond Public Schools was done by whites, no Blacks. You know, when you were ordering something, you didn't worry about who was doing it, or how they were doing it—you just ordered it. And the same thing when you needed a repair in the school—you just called, never thinking about the fact that these people are white.

So when I was offered the job to go there to work, it was my first experience with total racism. And that's all it was. All of the employees were white, except about 3 percent in that particular unit of the school systems. Only about 3 percent were Black. One of the things that was under that was the custodians, and that was the one thing that was headed by Blacks. Well, I went to work for the man who was the head of the whole department. I went to work for him as the secretary. And when I got there, one of my responsibilities was to keep the payroll. But I could only keep the payroll for Blacks. Not whites.

And before I got the job, they had three people doing it. When I got there, those people had left, and they were never replaced. So I had to do the job that three people were doing. And we had ladies in what we called the radio room. And their job was to answer the phone and take the calls. . . . Like when I was in the schools, I would call and tell them what I needed done, or call in to order supplies. So they would answer these calls. Across from my office was the radio room. And every time a call would come in for the Black supervisor, one of the white ladies would be complaining about it, you know? And then she kept saying, "Why can't Phyllis take his call?" But she never asked me to take any white person's call. My boss was trying to keep peace with everybody and keep everybody pleased. So he would just say, "Just ignore it, ignore it." But one day, she caught me wrong. And the Black came out in me! I got up from my desk, went over to her in the radio room—and there were two other white ladies working with her, but the two of them were just as nice to me as they could be. But for some reason she decided that I needed more work to do when

I already had the work of three people. And I said, "Look, Audrey"—I pointed my finger, and I said—"If my name come out of your mouth one more time, I'm gonna give you a knuckle sandwich." And that was during the time when they had the program on TV where the man said, "I'm having a heart attack," and he used to tell his son all the time that he would give them a knuckle sandwich [author's note: This was *Sanford and Son!*].

And so I told her that's what I was going to do to her if my name came out her mouth one more time. And of course, I was through with it after that, and went and sat back at my desk. And I thought about it and said to myself, well, if you don't speak up for yourself, you'll never get anywhere. So that was that.

There was a white guy who was in charge of growing the flowers for the schools, and, you know, that type of thing. And every day when he would come back from inspecting whatever school he went to, he would bring flowers to the ladies in the department. And he would give everybody some flowers, except me. He never gave me any. And so the different secretaries, who were white, would say, "Well, you didn't bring Mrs. Taylor any." He'd say "Oh, I forgot!" and every day it was a different excuse. So you know, I'm not dumb . . . he thought I was dumb, but I knew what was happening. So anyway, he caught me wrong one day.

So here he come, and Ms. Emily asked him, "Where are Mrs. Taylor's flowers?" "Oh, I forgot. I will go out there now and get some for her." So, he did. He went out and came back and brought the flowers to me and offered them to me. "Here, Mrs. Taylor, here are your flowers." I told him, "I do not want any flowers that you put your hands on, and don't leave them in my office, either." I didn't want flowers from him when he clearly didn't want to give them to me. And I was through with that. So, there were things like that. Those were the kind of things that would happen regularly.

Then, I got a Black boss who was head of the whole department, because the white person resigned. But the white counterpart upstairs in the building had a secretary.

She wasn't required to do any of the things they would ask me to do. He wanted me to keep doing all the other things, like being in the cafeteria, being the cashier, being helpful, doing all kinds of extra things. They wanted me to do them to keep the peace, but I don't care nothing about peace when I'm being mistreated. So the white boss kept telling my boss, "Tell Phyllis to do so and so, tell Phyllis to do so and so." Of course, I ain't paying attention to him, because I wasn't planning to do it! But why am I expected to do these things when the one person who has the same position I have is not required to do it? So I told him, "I will tell you right now. Don't ask me to do that anymore. I don't plan to do it. And I don't care. Until Alice (which was the white lady) is doing it, I will not be doing it either. I don't care what you do. You can take me downtown, you can do anything you want." The superintendent at that time was white, and he would come up to visit the department. He came in about two days later after I had told the white boss that I wasn't going to do any of that. He walked in the door and said "Ms. Taylor! Are they treating you right up here?" I said, "I'd rather not answer." And he had a very loud, boisterous voice. And he said loudly, "I'm letting y'all know that Ms. Taylor is my friend. And if any one of y'all mistreat her, you will have to answer to me!"

One thing that was a startling thing to me when I went to this particular building was that every office in the building had a Confederate flag in it. Can you imagine? Then, we got a Black superintendent, and he had no knowledge of it at first. When he came to visit for the first time, they were taking him on a tour of our building. And every one of the offices had a Confederate flag in it. He said to my boss, who was Black, "Archie, what is going 'round here? Why are there all these Confederate flags?" That was his department that had all these flags, see. And my boss said, "That's something they've been doing ever since I've been here, and before I came." The superintendent said, "Well, they all better be gone by the close of the workday today. If not they're fired." And for fear that my boss would not tell them, the superintendent went right to his office, wrote a memo, and sent it directly back to both departments, one downstairs and one upstairs in the building. It said, "Anybody who is a supervisor and has a Confederate flag in his office after five o'clock today will be fired." They never liked him anymore after that!

But that was an experience. And that was my first experience with the school system where I suffered such outrageous treatment as a Black woman. I'd never been treated like that, in the way I was then. And I never forgot it.

When you were a kid growing up, did you have any negative experiences like this?

I really didn't. My mom, at one time, worked for two white families. And one of them were deaf and mute. And my mother—I told you she was always a forward-thinking person—she taught herself sign language so she could communicate with him. And this family did not have any little children. The other family didn't either. So, my experience as a child with white people had been wonderful, because each one of those families looked out for me, in a sense. For every special occasion, Christmas, Easter, whatever the children celebrated, they made sure that I had all those things that they would have given to a grandchild. So I had gifts from three different sets of people, and I just thought the world was a wonderful place. I just didn't have no idea; my first rude awakening was when I went to work at plan services. I didn't know white people treated Black people so badly! I'd heard of incidents, and a lot of rules that were given to us, in our youth during segregation, were just the way of life.

One perfect example was: you had to be in the house by 10 o'clock. And if you didn't, of course, you were going to be punished. But the way they made sure that rule was kept, they would tell us how white people would go out at night with the trucks and kidnap people and kill them. Just to show you some of the things that went on. And whatever an adult would tell you back then, it was gospel. And we didn't question it. And growing up, they made sure that we were never in their presence when they were discussing things like violence and things like that. When company came to your house, if there were no children with them, you were sent somewhere else so they could have their conversations. And so a lot of things that we might should have heard or should have known, well, I always say we lived in a bubble. And I didn't realize it until I became an adult.

So when you were going to the beaches and stuff and you knew that there was a Black beach and there was a white beach, did you wonder why you couldn't go? Or you just didn't think about that?

We didn't think about it, because it was something we had always done, and we had never done any differently. And not until they integrated these places did we show any interest. Because we felt like, well, what's so unique about them? We really didn't want to associate with them because we had everything we wanted right where we were. So, we didn't need to go over there or want to be with them.

Did you ever feel that your safety may be in danger because you were Black?

I can't remember any incident like that. Because although Richmond had segregation, I did not see a lot of open violence towards Black people. The only thing that we always used to say—and maybe that's what kept us cautious—was that white people made the rules, but they didn't make them for themselves. They made them for us. Because if they broke a rule, there was always some reason why it was alright for them to have done that. But if you broke that rule, you were arrested and put in jail. So we were aware of it. But we felt that, you know, because they were in charge, they were doing it to suit themselves, and to just stay out of their way. That was your best bet. It was that kind of attitude with most of us. But I'm glad the present generation doesn't feel that way.

Did you ever know of anybody being lynched?

I have heard of people being lynched. But I've never heard of them being lynched in the larger cities. We didn't hear about people being lynched in Virginia. But in North

Carolina, and South Carolina, yes, we have heard terrible stories about people being lynched.

I just knew of them from hearing about it. Like they may have had an article in the paper, or by way of the grapevine—someone would pass that on to that one, and tell it, because people were even afraid to talk about it, even if they knew it. Because the Ku Klux Klan . . . everybody Black was afraid of the Ku Klux Klan. And they didn't know who or where they were. Because see, they were dressed in hoods when they paraded and stuff, and you didn't see the faces. And then when they were right in the public, you never saw any evidence of who they were. So you didn't know who you were dealing with.

But I did have an experience once. Telephones at one time, they had two different systems. You could have a party line or you could have a non-party line. And when I moved from Richmond proper to the county, I picked up my telephone one day. I wasn't supposed to have a party line. But I heard these people talking. So I decided to listen to see who they were. And the Ku Klux Klan had tapped into my line and were using it for free. And they were talking back and forth with each other, what they were doing, what they planned to do. But I reported the fact that somebody was on my line. And of course, it was taken off.

Cross burnings, yeah, we even have them now. Sometimes in the area, especially in Chesterfield. We have it. But when the crosses were burning, I never heard anybody say they feared them. It was: "If you come to my house, you will die." You know, that type of attitude [from us]. So you stay away from my house, we're not going to accept this. And then even if they had white neighbors—sometimes they had them because the neighborhood hadn't completely changed over from Black to white. That has been my knowledge of it. But Black people growing up, I had never heard of white people killing Black people violently, people that I knew or knew of. I've heard more of it in these last years than I have heard of it in all my lifetime. When I was growing up, we had boundaries, and most of the people stayed within those boundaries.

Going back to how you were talking about how the KKK had tapped your phone line, what were they talking about when you were listening in on the conversation?

Well, one thing—a word that they liked to use was "niggers." And we don't use that anymore in public. But they were saying, "If those niggers don't do such and such. . . ." Whatever it was. I can't remember now, because I wanted to forget. It was such a shock to know that this was going on . . . this had to be 1985. I thought by then it would have stopped, you know. But it's still going on now. They still got a lot of racism going on.

The Black community lost a lot when it came to integration. And I want to know what your thoughts about integration are today, now that we can look back and see what has happened since then.

Well, when it first happened, I was skeptical about it. And then some of the things that happened to our kids during integration I do not feel helped us as much as they should have benefited. Because it's the negative things, to me, that we glorify. And the things that we could have benefited from, we were not able to develop them as much as we should have. My first experience with integration was with shopping, and the big, main stores in Richmond at the time—the department store was Thalhimers, and Miller & Rhoads, and then another secondary one was Kaufmann's. Now, when you would go to those stores, you could buy things, but you could not try them on. And when they found out that their profits were falling, then they changed the rules. For instance, they would let you try a hat on, but you had to put something on your head before you could put it on. You know, things like that . . . which to me was an insult. And we never thought about it when it was just segregation because we weren't able to ever experience that in the first place. Thalhimers had a basement store, we called it, where they had the things that they did not necessarily want to have upstairs—above. They put it in the basement; you could go there and buy it. And you could try it on down there, but you couldn't try on anything up above.

When we integrated, I don't think the teachers had enough support. And I was working at Whitcomb Court School at the time, which is in a Black community; it was a housing project called Whitcomb Court, and then we had another section where people owned their houses. Before integration, everybody was like one big family, and anybody could discipline a child. Once we integrated, they did not want the Black teachers to discipline the white kids. So, they changed the rule of discipline.

To me, the key to why we succeeded before integration was because our Black teachers loved us and we knew it. They corrected us. We expected it. And we respected them for the way that they treated us. But all of that was taken from out of their hands doing integration because basically white people did not want them to discipline their kids. Some of those things, our kids will never recuperate from. We lost a generation of people because of it.

When my hometown integrated, my mom was in the race riots and one of the first Black classes at the public school and all of that. Do you have any experiences or memories from when the city integrated?

They integrated the schools during the time that my kids were in school. And my kids were extremely smart, not bragging or anything. And so, the teachers wanted them to try the integrated schools, because they felt they would do a great job there. I was one of those parents that didn't want to integrate, because I felt my kids would not be treated fairly. And I did not want them to experience that at that age. So, I did not allow them to go to integrated schools.

One perfect example of that: we have a neighborhood called Oregon Hill. And it was out where the penitentiary was. And it was the poorest class of white people. And they were always causing problems, and they went to the school that my kids would have normally been assigned to. So I did not want my kids to go, because I didn't want them to mingle with those children. And as a result, they stayed in the Black school, and they excelled. They excelled. And the teachers really looked out for them, because we were very supportive of our teachers.

But in this particular case, their school eventually had to take a whole grade—like all sixth grade students, four or five classes—and send them to the school where I didn't want my kids to go to, which was formerly all white, because the Black school was overcrowded. Okay. And so the incident that happened involved my daughter, who is the middle child, and her class, who went to that school. And they had this little girl from Oregon Hill, and she would intimidate all the Black kids. If they didn't do what she said, she pushed them up against the wall. They were afraid of her. But when they would tell the teachers, they would ignore it. They were trying to keep the peace. I didn't care anything about the peace when it came to my kids, okay?

So one day, she decided she was going to hit my daughter. Well, that was the last straw. I called the principal who was in charge at the time, and told him, "I've always taught my kids not to fight. I think there's a better way to settle an argument. So they were taught to talk things out. But she is never to hit my child again." And we never had any more problems after that. Because sometimes, you have to speak up. I taught my kids to respect all adults. You may not like what they are telling you to do, but you're not supposed to have adult discussions as a child. Tell *me* what's going on. And you know, I'm going to see to it that you are treated fair.

Ms. Sandra, Ms. Phyllis's daughter steps in here:

I had to say, hearing my mom when she was talking about it is so true, with regard to our education. And you know, having gone through Richmond Public Schools, and for my entire time it was in what was then the segregated schools. . . . And when I look back and see the difference with my sister and her experience, I really wish, if we could turn back the hands of time, that when they talked about having separate but equal, that we had just had *separate but equal*. If they had kept everybody segregated, as far as I'm concerned, unless you wanted to go—but given the Black schools, the same money, the same equipment, the same books. . . . We didn't need better teachers. Our teachers were much better than the white teachers, because for many of them, their opportunity was teaching. We had teachers with PhDs, but they couldn't teach at the college level. So, we were blessed. I look at my graduating class. And there were 400 and some odd of us. We had people who went to Harvard, Yale, all the prestigious schools, and did well. I don't know if the kids who went to the white schools had the same experience, because facing the racism that some of my friends faced, those that did go, traumatized them at an early age. I faced it in college, but by then, my self-esteem was established. So yeah, I wish we could turn back the hands of time.

I look at the way that schools are, and then you have the school-to-prison pipeline these days. And to me, that is a direct product of integration. And even now, students that graduate from HBCUs do better than Black students that graduate from white colleges. So we need ways that we can bring some of that back to our community. So I agree with you. And on that same note, do you think Dr. King's dream is possible in this country?

Back to Ms. Phyllis:

Oh, yes, I do. I really think it's possible. I would like to say before I get to that point that I think what we need to do is to write our own stories. The white man has been writing it for so long and telling it the way he wanted to. And for important things that we should get credit for, we are not getting credit for, because they are telling the story instead of you. And so I always encourage my kids to keep copies and records of rewards, honors, anything that they think will be part of that future legacy. Give future generations something on which to build their future. And these things that you have kept, you can share with them. And you need to keep a daily diary, because you forget. Write your stories so they will be accurate in history. And also, you should collect any items that you think that your family was a part of, in making history what it is today.

I always say keep the faith. And give true meaning to "Black lives matter." We have to value our own lives. Take pictures. I think that we should not forget that King said that he had a dream. But I believe we have a reality. Because we have seen things happen that we've never seen before. Richmond had its first Black mayor. Then you had the first Black governor elected in the country [author's note: Henry Leander Marsh III and L. Douglas Wilder, respectively]. And then to top it all, Obama was elected the president! How many of us thought it could happen? I know, in my lifetime, I thought it would never happen. And I refused to believe it when they told me, because it just seemed impossible in our society. But I believe the dream is possible. I believe, even if I don't see it, we will see it in due time.

Is there anything else you want to share?

The only thing that I can think of is to let you know how . . . what happened to change Richmond into electing these different people I was talking about, like the mayor and the governor. There was a resident by the name of Curtis Holt, and he felt that Richmond Blacks were not getting a fair shake. So, he sued for a chance to have our voices heard, and he won the case. When he won the case, they had to go by the federal guidelines for all elections. And as a result, Blacks in Richmond became part of certain districts. Redistricting. And we got nine districts, and when Blacks were counted in the voting, five or more of those districts were won by Black people. And that's how we began the journey to become an integrated government here.

Look for the Crusade for Voters organization, which was started by Mr. Brooks, Dr. Reid, and Dr. Thornton—that has a lot of wonderful history that will help you to understand how far we have come.

INTERVIEW NO. 8

REV. JOHN KENNARD

My first name is John, last name is Kennard. I was born in a little town in the Black Belt of Alabama called Forkland, Alabama, in Greene County. It is in the Black Belt of Alabama. And it is surrounded by waters, and it just so happened that the Tombigbee is on the west, and the Warrior River is on the east of the county, and they come together on the south end of the county at a fork. So they named the little town Forkland, and that is where I was born.

First of all, I want to say that if I was born 100 years earlier, I would have been born in slavery. I was actually born in 1952 in the midst of Mr. Jim Crow, and this is the irony of it all: I was one of 12 living children, with my mother and father, and the childhood that I had, I would not trade it for anything in the world. Though segregated, it was the best thing at that time. I could not ever think of another way in which I would want to grow up, because the values we were taught . . . the community was so strong. When one family picked cotton and when that field was over, the endeavor was not over until the neighbors' field was picked. When someone needed a barn built, everybody had a chore. It didn't matter what it was, it may have been straightening out old nails or whatever. There was community in that segregated environment, and that was something else. It was literally better than gold. It was called respect. We were taught to respect the elders. We were taught to respect our church. We were taught to respect each other. It was second to none, and I don't think I could have grown up in a better environment though segregated.

Grade 1 through 12 was an entirely segregated Black school. At that time, teachers cared about the students. So that prepared me for going from a totally segregated environment into an all-white University of Alabama. I had self respect, I had everything that I had been taught as a child, and really another aspect of it is this:

my grandfather, born in 1890, died 1983 . . . my grandfather's father spent his first 20 years as a slave in this county. My grandfather taught me that we were not only equal to any white man, but in fact, we were better. Not genetically better, but better because we earned everything we got in his life, while everything was given to the white man on a silver spoon. So, if given the opportunity, we must take advantage of it. So I have the positive aspect of segregation.

We grew up on a farm. We grew up on the Milton Long Plantation. Though slavery ended in 1865, Black people, because we had nowhere else to go, we actually remained on the plantations on which we were slaves. So I grew up on the Milton Long Plantation now. That was quite an experience. He would come by every now and then. I vaguely remember him. I don't know when he passed on, but he would come along and I always resented the fact that he would call my daddy "Uncle" and my mother "Auntie." And I said to him one time as a little boy, "Oh, you have so many relatives." So just because you are segregated, which was designed by society, it does not mean that you are inferior. That's what our community taught us, and I'm so glad of that. Growing up in that environment with that large family of brothers and sisters and neighborhood, all African American, all respecting one another, all understanding that, come Sunday, whether you wanted to or not, you're going to church to worship the Lord, and then working on the farm . . . it was second to none.

Every now and then, we would get on a wagon, and we would to go to a little town called Demopolis, Alabama. In Demopolis, Alabama, is where I first saw visible signs of segregation—Jim Crow. Colored water fountains and colored bathrooms. I wanted to go to movies, as does every other young child. I never shall forget, I wanted to go and see James Brown and the Famous Flames and something in some movies in the early '60s. And movie theaters were segregated with the whites downstairs and the Blacks upstairs. We promptly got our tickets and went downstairs, only to be ushered back upstairs.

They sent somebody downstairs and told us, "Look, if you want to see the movie, you got to go upstairs." We said, "Why?" They asked, "Do you want to see the movie?"

and I said, "Yes." And they said, "If you do, you must go upstairs." I asked the question, "Could I get a refund back?" He said, "No." So I said, "I will go upstairs, but I'll do it in protest." That was my experience.

I have 12 siblings, including me. We were on land that was owned by the white man, in what was called sharecropping. That was the word that they used. We were basic tenants at the mercy of the owner, and that lasted the first 10 years of my life. I was born in '52. In 1962, my oldest brother wanted to better himself by going to college, at which time Mr. Milton Long did not want Blacks on his plantation to go to college, so he put us off of his land.

Since we were on his land, he knew how many of us there were. The whole idea was to make him rich. And there was always somebody who was going to proudly tell somebody that we had somebody in the family, or in this community, that's going to college. And when he found out, he came over and asked my dad and mother, "Is it true that you have a boy that wants to go to college?" They said, "Yeah." And he said, "Well, we don't allow this on the plantation."

You have to understand segregation. Jim Crow wasn't nothing but slavery, wrapped up in a nice little gift card. That's all it was, no difference. But what Mr. Milton Long did not know was that my great-grandfather was born in slavery. Slavery ended in 1865. Two years later, my great-grandfather teamed up with another former slave by the name of Jerry Graves, and they bought over 160 acres of land. It was in our family. We stayed on that plantation sharecropping because of the fact that it was a means for us to provide for the family, with the decision that we would stay there. When we got put off in 1962, we had somewhere to go.

Sharecropping was another form of slavery. And all the white community owned everything, including the stores and all, and what Black people had to do was if you lived on a man's place, you had to go to his store and do what is called "take up." You had to take up the necessities for you to survive, to plant your crop and everything, and hopefully during the fall, you would have enough to pay off what you have "taken up," or put on your bill. So it was just another way in which to keep you behind the eight ball.

Of course, we were raising cotton, and Milton Long would always say something to the effect of, "If you had made one more bale, you would have been in better shape than ever." So, what we decided to do the next time around was hold back one bale of cotton. And he came up with the same line, and we just happened to have another one. That offended Mr. Milton. He was not used to what we did. And, of course, we didn't raise the voice or nothing like that. We just brought that bale of cotton in late. He would always say, "You could get a bill paid in full if you had produced more and more bales of cotton." So we held that one back so it would be even, then brought him that final bale after he fed us that line. He turned pale-faced.

You were always supposed to be in debt. You couldn't go anywhere because you owed the man. That was the whole premise. It's . . . it was nothing but a new form of slavery, covered up by, as Martin King would say, "certain niceties of complexities." That's all it was. And when my brother . . . by the way, he graduated from Stillman College in Tuscaloosa, Alabama, and he actually taught in the school system in Greene County, for over 40 years. But we were put off of that property and it was a blessing in disguise. I never shall forget. We first moved off the man's place in a wagon . . . and pulled up to something that was our own. And I remember to this day, my father and my grandfather, building the house that we were to move into on our own property. There was nothing like it on the planet.

Were there ever any harsh words exchanged between Milton Long and your parents?

No, not between Milton Long and my parents. They knew. They were not going to make it difficult for us. They would not do that. They knew what the rules were, so they were just, "Yes suh," and this type thing, because my parents wanted us to succeed in life. They subjugated themselves in order for us to survive. They knew the viciousness of white people. They remembered Emmett Till in 1955 in Money,

Mississippi. They knew what white people would do. And, in order to protect us, they would always tell us that you're going have a better life than we have. We're sacrificing for you. So, they took abuses and stuff for us to have a chance in life. And so they wouldn't do that. When it came to the fact that my brother was going to go to college, my daddy was not going to say to Milton Long, "No."

I never heard Milton Long yell at them. He would come over to the property, and he had to cross the Warrior River and come physically over to the property. That meant he was in the Black neighborhood, even though it was his property. He didn't make it a habit of yelling at people. No.

The Westins, who were our neighbors, and the Umsteads, who were our neighbors, I could hear the children saying that they were tired of hearing Mr. Milton saying that if they made just one more bale, it would change things—so it was really the young children's idea to tell the parents that. We did that. Of course he was angry, but we had him. So he couldn't do anything except look down his long nose with them glasses on and do what he had to do. Which was telling us to go ahead and get out of there.

We also raised vegetables on the farm, and my daddy was what you would call a peddler. He had one leg. My father had that since I was born. He was involved in an accident at a mill and lost his leg. He was a peddler. We raised vegetables so that we would have clothes and stuff to go to school with. We would sell them. My daddy and I would get up when I was very young, and I would go with him. We would go to Demopolis, that's where the white people were, and we would go from door to door and ask them did they want to buy butter beans that day?

I'll never forget. We went to one house, and when we got to the gate, a dog came out and raised sand. The man said, "What do you want?" My dad said, "I want to find out if you want to buy some butter beans." The man said, "I might do that if you can get in here." I said to my daddy, "Dad, you need to do something about that dog." He said, "No, don't worry about it." And my daddy opened the gate, and stepped that peg leg in that gate. That dog bit the peg leg, and my dad knocked that dog almost all the way up on the porch. He asked the man, "Can I come in now?" That man didn't know what to do!

So my daddy taught me, don't ever fear anybody. We were entirely . . . it was almost like there was nobody in the community but us. I mean, you know, different families. But we were all Black, all on the plantation, and we got along and respected one another.

Milton Long would come over to check on his land, so whenever we went to Demopolis to buy the goods and stuff, it was like a whole new world for us. Because now we are in an area where Milton Long doesn't come to see you. This time, you're in his element. There is where I saw the white and colored water fountains and signs, and all that foolishness.

The first thing that my dad always told us when we got ready to get on the wagon to go over there when I was young child was, "Okay, look, you're going into a different world. Number one, you all stick together. And number two, don't be arrogant or nothing like that. You don't have to take nothing if somebody says something to you. But don't find yourself in any trouble." And, you know, during that era, if you met a white person, you were supposed to get off the street and let them pass by, and all kinds of stuff like that. We were kids and we stuck together. We'd go into the five and dime stores and stuff like that. And it was really a different feeling to go there. You always got the feeling that somebody was watching you. I didn't like that very well. But we always paid particular attention to what Daddy had told us, which was don't do anything to draw attention to yourself.

But we didn't go often. Just about everything that we needed for survival was produced on the farm. Didn't need to go buy milk because you had cows. Didn't need to get bacon because everybody killed hogs, and when you did that, the whole community benefited. The thing about that kind of living was that nothing belonged to us. It belonged to him.

It was sad to leave the community when he put us off, very sad to be honest with you. Because that was all that I had known, and that was all that we had known. But we knew the reason why we're moving, because we had a brother who wanted to better himself. And whatever sacrifice and wherever we're going . . . it's going to be worth it. When my brother Abraham went to college in 1962, our family was so poor we could barely support ourselves. He couldn't make it on his own. My brother James, who passed away last year, dropped out of school and got him a job to help send my brother to school. Somebody had to sacrifice. He never finished the 12th grade. He got him a job and sent my brother to school.

He worked at what was called Craigers Bakery in Demopolis. He worked there, then later on, he went to what was called a veneer mill, where they made lumber. He stayed down South as long as he could. When my brother graduated, he [James] and my other brother Judge became a part of the Great Migration. They went to the Mecca, the great city of Detroit, and they worked for Ford Motor Company until both of them retired some years ago. He left to better himself. There was literally nothing to do for a young man, except farming. But during that time, all of the farm subsidies—everything, every aspect of farming—went to the white man. You could not go to the Farm Service Agency in your county and request a loan for beginning farmers, because you were Black. That's why they ultimately had to have that suit. My brother literally had no shot. You could work for the man down here for pennies a day, or you could go up and take a shot in another place where you might be able to earn a living. So they went up and made a home in Michigan.

Everybody cried when they left. We were close. But the tears turned into joy when they got hired at Ford Motor Company and called us. I remember every year during the changeover, they would come down South in those brand-new automobiles, and all of a sudden for at least a week or two, we were the baddest family on the block! These boys got these brand-new cars, and man, that was Heaven on earth. I mean, now I could show them off to the kids at school! This was the most awesome thing on the planet. Yes, yes, yes. And then that was always the tearfulness when they got ready to go. But then, there was always the anticipation that they will be coming back down the next year. And they traded cars every three years because they didn't cost that much. So I knew I was going to see my brothers and another car.

After my brother Abe graduated from college, and my brother James and brother Judge moved to Michigan, I had an older brother Alfred who had already left and gone up to Ohio, and he was working for Ford Motor Company also, and so they would then send money back to the family to help us out. Of course, we still farmed, and this time, it was different. Our cow was our own cow because we raised on our own land. Everything that we had then belonged to us. There was no more share-cropping. And my grandfather would always tell us, y'all need to stay out of the stores and keep some of your own money. And so that's what we did. And we were able to survive. After then, the aspirations of the family began to change because everybody then decided that they were going to go to college. And that was good because we could better our lives by going to college. When I graduated, I knew I wanted to go to college because I didn't want to farm. All of those that were my age and onward went to college, and most of us graduated.

When we were growing up, my dad always taught the boys how to hunt. And then we could get together with the girls and we could go fishing on Warrior River. That was so much fun. And then we would always get together and have community picnics. The entire community would get together and have picnics and they would be sitting around telling all the great stories and joking. . . . It was just great fun.

The food was second to none. But we didn't eat anything unless everybody said a Bible verse. And you couldn't say, "Jesus wept!" We would go around and everybody in the whole community was saying a Bible verse, if they wanted to eat. It was a three-day event.

And we would walk home at nighttime. Just walking home in the evening time, and this is after you have gathered your crops, you know. During the spring you planted, then of course four months later you would gather the harvest. And right after you gathered the harvest is when you were going to have your festival. It was kind of like finishing the season in a way.

There were games. Horseshoes, and old men played checkers. But nobody played cards. You couldn't do that. That was somehow off limits. And the music. John Lee Hooker. There was always somebody in the community who could play a guitar. And man, they could sing . . . and we just had a ball.

And on Sundays, you'd have to go to church. Your confession was at church. There was no baptism at the church. You went to the river for baptism. You went to what was called the Backbone Creek, down, down between all of the churches. And the preacher had the waders on, and he walked out there real careful because you didn't want to go out too far. You might not come back!

My grandfather was a deacon. My dad was never a deacon. My mother was on the Mother's Board. Oh, my grandfather was a deacon. I literally idolized my grand-father. I could never do what I've done without the aid of my grandfather. About him telling me what his daddy told him about what life was like in slavery, and the lessons he taught me. He did not like white folks because his daddy went through 20 years—the first 20 years of his life—as a slave. His daddy told him of all of the stuff that they did to his people, and my granddaddy did not like that. And I don't like it either. See, he got it firsthand from his dad. My grandfather always told us to have something on your own. He demanded that you have something on your own, and not just an automobile.

During slavery, it was illegal to teach a Black person to read and write. My great-grandfather could read and write as a slave, because my great-grandfather had an occupation that required him to go from one plantation to another—because nobody could do what he did, the way he did. My great-grandfather was a chim-ney builder, and he perfected the art of building a chimney so that, on the planta-tion he would build it on, and the fireplace, when somebody visited a master, they wanted one like he had. And so my great-grandfather, though he was a slave, he was in demand. And so, when they gave him a pass to go from one plantation to the other, that was good. Except for one thing: they did not realize that my great-grandfather had a white child to teach him his ABCs.

And so he learned how to read and write. He also knew the value of land. By the way, my great-grandfather was half white. His father was a white man, and he resented that growing up.

Basically, as a child, he knew who his daddy was. But then, sooner or later, he's got to be calling the little white boys "Mister" and stuff, and he resented that. I'm sure his father was the master. That's something that they never talked about. But he knew who he was.

My granddad told me many stories of how they would treat Black people . . . make them eat out of troughs and give them clothes to wear once per year. It was just an intolerable existence. It literally existed entirely for the white man. My grandfather told me that his daddy told him that the worst fear that you ever had was when the master died. Or when there was some particular occasion. You had to worry about being sold away from your family, and that was the worst of it all. And he had seen it happen on more than one occasion. Goodness.

My great-grandfather, who was born into slavery, taught my grandfather the same trade he had. And with pride, to this day, I go into what is called the Warrior Swamp. My grandfather built every chimney that's there, down there. With pride, I look up on that, and I am so thankful that I know who built that chimney. It is unbelievable what Black people can do!

When we were put off of the Milton Long plantation in 1962. . . . My grandfather always lived on his own land that his father gave him. So we would go and visit my grandfather. But I had no idea that my grandfather owned that land. When we got put off the plantation, then I found out. And then he told me the story of his dad buying the land with the other slave and dividing it, and my grandfather lived on the land that his daddy gave him deed to.

I actually have recordings of my grandfather. When I was first elected to public office in 1978, I actually went down to record my grandfather. We sat and we talked immensely about many things. Just the communication with him. . . . He told me that, no matter what happens, to develop my mind. You need to make sure that you, number one, stay grounded. Number two, never let the man take advantage of you, because he will if you let him. But if your mind is developed, he can never take advantage of you. And then, he taught me to always look out for the rest of my family.

Did you know any of your other grandparents?

Oh, yeah, sure. My mother's mother passed on in 1967. Her name was Emma Westin. She passed on in 1967, and her mother was actually a slave. Yeah. She passed down most of her stories to my sisters. My grandfather passed down most of his stories to the brothers. That is just the way it worked out, I guess.

My first interaction with young white boys was when I went to college. On June 11, 1963, when I was 11 years old, George Corley Wallace stood in the schoolhouse door at Foster's Auditorium to keep Black people out. I was 11 years old. That was the day that I made up my mind about which school I was going to. Eight years later, I got in there.

I decided to go because of the unmitigated gall of one human being to say to me that I cannot go there and excel in a school, a public institution in the state founded in 1831. My granddaddy could have graduated from up there, given the opportunity, and you're telling me that you don't want me up there because of the color of my skin? I had already been taught that I'm equal to you or better. That is when I knew that was the place for me to be.

That was in 1963, same year Martin King marched on Washington. I was 11 years old, and from that day forward, I made preparations. And when I got there, there were 13,800 white folks and 149 Blacks, and I was number 149. And I made up my mind. Since I wasn't the first Black student to enter, I'll be the first to make the Dean's List.

Did your family watch the March on Washington?

On our Sylvania black and white TV! Yes, yes, yes. Our neighbors were there. We were the first ones in the community to have a TV. You know, the one with the

*One of the fireplaces built by John's great-grandfather,
a talented chimney-builder.*

antenna on the outside. Man! Martin King was the last speaker to get up, and he started speaking in that bass baritone voice, and it was some shouting in the house!

When Martin started talking about I have a dream, and about that dream being deeply rooted in the American dream, and then he started talking about the red hills of Georgia and all of that, man, people were shouting and embracing each other. And literally, a thought pattern that went across where we were listening from, was that, in fact, this stuff was going to end soon. That was in 1963. We thought, really, that segregation was going to end soon. We thought that America was going to move to that point where justice was going to roll down like waters and righteousness as a mighty stream, because that's what Martin made people feel. He had a unique ability to make people see and perceive that. So we thought, "Oh, man, here it comes!" It was a euphoric feeling.

At 11 years old, I could recite Martin King. I could do it all the way through because it was such an impact in my life. It was the most fascinating thing I've ever seen a person do. Here I am listening to John Kennedy saying, "Ask not what your country can do for you, but what you can do for your country," and I mean, that's good. But it wasn't Martin!

The atmosphere was one of complete hopefulness: that the stuff that we have had to endure, we will not have to endure it anymore. And that, pretty soon in this nation, justice *is* going to roll down like waters and righteousness as a mighty spring. That, pretty soon, freedom *is* going to ring in every hill and molehill in Mississippi. I mean, it was there. And he said it in such a dramatic fashion. At that time, we were optimistic about America . . . that perhaps this nation can rise up and live out the true meaning of its creed. Because that's what Martin said.

I was 16 years old when Martin King was assassinated at 6:02 p.m. in room 306 of the Lorraine Motel. I was at home. And I just could not believe it. At that particular point in time, I must tell you, I hated white America. Because I could not understand how they could kill a man who has a dream like this? How could you do that? How could anybody have that much hatred in them for another human being to do what they have done to Martin? And he was, at that time, our only hope. It was devastating.

On that day, everybody that was white stayed somewhere undercover. They stayed everywhere away from us at that time. Because what they had done in the murder of Martin was they had extinguished our only hope. There was nothing left. I remember that. I was 16 years of age. Won't ever forget that.

My parents were involved in the Civil Rights Movement, but they were not in the forefront. They never discouraged us from participating. They always told us to be careful and watch our backs because they knew we were going to do it anyway. But they wanted us to be careful. My parents loved their children, and they wanted to see us alive, and they knew the viciousness of white people firsthand. And they did not want us to become an Emmett Till or a Medgar Evers.

I've heard about how, in various places across the South, sharecroppers came together and formed a union. Did your family or anybody in your neighborhood ever try that?

No, they never tried that. They were aware of the situation. White people set the rules, and we were literally at their mercy. At the end of slavery, we were promised 40 acres and a mule, and we got nothing. So Black people had nothing except a piece of paper called the Emancipation Proclamation, and thrust into a capitalistic society without any capital. So we were at the mercy of the man, and the federal government bears the blame for this.

I remember as a child, the KKK rode through this county once. I saw the Confederate flags and all this stuff. I saw that with my own eyes. But our county was 86 percent Black, and they weren't that fond about that many Black folks in one place. So, we didn't have that much of a problem. They would go to my neighboring county to the west. They would go to Pickens County. You had the majority white there. They would have the big rallies there.

My county, Greene County, was the first county since Reconstruction to have a total Black government. July 29, 1969, they had a special election. And in '78, I became the first Black tax assessor in the state's history. My cousin John Gilmore became the first Black sheriff in this state's history, and my teacher became the first Black probate judge in the nation. So the Klan didn't want to really mess around in Greene County.

Heading to the University of Alabama, what was that experience like?

I had no idea what it was going to be like, and when I went in, I went in with my head high. I found out that there were a lot of adjustments I had to make. First of all, I went into my dormitory, Palmer Hall, which no longer exists. And back then when I went there in '71, in order to prove that the University of Alabama course was not racist, they allowed the computer to choose your roommate. Naturally, with 13,800 white folks and 149 Blacks, would you like to guess what my roommate was going to be? White, okay. Now. How long do you think that white people at that time was going to allow their child to stay in a room with a Black person at the University of Alabama? Not even one night.

Yeah, they got mad, but guess what that taught me? When my roommate left, I had a room to myself! We got to the point where we would actually run them out and encourage them to get the hell out so we could have our own rooms!

I never shall forget the rude awakening I had with the University of Alabama. I was taking religious classes at the university, and you know, I was going to these little churches on campus, and it was my first time going to white folks' churches and all this stuff. I said to the professor, "Let's take this show on the road. Let's go to church outside of the university campus here in Tuscaloosa." So, we went to First Baptist Church in Alberta City . . . the pastor was Reverend Joe Bob Mizell. I remember it like it was yesterday. The year was either '73 or '74. And when we got there, their deacons were on the outside, and they would not let us in, and we wouldn't leave. And we stayed until the Tuscaloosa news picked it up. And finally, *Jet* magazine picked it up. I made the statement that God is not God in America; money is God. That was quite an experience.

We wanted to go in and they wouldn't let us in. So we just stayed there. The police were circling, but they didn't bother us. But the deacons were interviewed, and they said that they didn't let Blacks into their church. At that time, the local newspapers ate that up. And by the way, I had no intention of joining the white church. I just wanted to prove to the professor that the superficiality that you're going through doesn't matter. Some white people can go to church and they're still not going to change. The local papers condemned the church. But, in retrospect, I think I know why. You got to remember, we were University of Alabama students. And just eight years earlier, they had stood in the schoolhouse door to keep us from coming. Now all of a sudden, we can't get into a church. They didn't want that. So they didn't really have a choice.

I've never felt unsafe on campus. I had specific goals when I went there. I remember one of my professors said to me that I was not going to pass her class because she didn't like Black people. I remember that. That kind of sticks in your psyche. And when that happened, I decided okay, you said it, now let me see what I can do. I doubled down, and in the process of trying to get me, she made the ultimate mistake. Some of the rich white people's kids were in the class and in order to try and get me with a low grade, she caught some of them up in the curve, and they kicked her out.

I interacted with my classmates as little as possible, until I met Bruce Wayne Johnston. He's deceased now. He's one of the most congenial people I have met in my life. He came down to Forkland to meet my mother and father. All of my sisters and brothers knew him, too. Bruce was like one of the family. It was a unique experience. It changed a lot of my views as far as setting the entirety of a race in one class or another.

How did your parents feel about you being at the University of Alabama?

They knew that they had done the best that they could. They knew that they had instilled in me the values that were necessary for me to achieve purpose in whatever I chose to do. And after we had our family prayer and I left, they left me in the hands of the Lord, and they didn't worry about it. When I came home, they would tell me always to keep the Lord in front. They had third- and fourth-grade educations, and they would have been perfectly happy if I had just finished high school. When I went there, after I graduated, my next sister Rosie went there and graduated, then my baby sister went and graduated, so we started a tradition. My nephew has been a practicing physician for 20 years, and he's a graduate of the University of Alabama. We restarted a tradition.

I enjoyed my experience there. Growing up going to totally Black schools was the best thing that ever happened to me, and then to go to basically a totally white institution was the next best thing. Because I found out I could excel in either. And I was indeed the first Black student to make the Dean's List at the university, so I knew I could excel in either world.

When I was at the university, the professors didn't really want to make waves. But there were always undercurrents. But the TAs would exhibit that prejudice toward you. Asking us, "Don't you know anything?" and all kinds of crazy stuff like that. But the best thing that happened was when I knew that I could excel in that world; I think that was what really made me feel good. Because in my environment when I grew up, our teachers did the best they could. But because historically, because of segregation and everything before it, we did not get the kind of education in all of those fields that we should have had in prep for a college like the University of Alabama. So when I got there, these kids, with all of their little prep schools, with all of that money that their mom and dad had, and all this other stuff that they had. . . . I mean, I knew I had work to do. But I stayed up until I caught up, and when I caught up, I wanted to get ahead. That's the way it was.

We had the Afro-American Association. Yes, yes, yes. We were tight. We were all we had. White people were not really used to Black people being at the University of Alabama. So when we got to have concerts—and nobody was ever there but white folks—we told them we wanted to see some Black folks. And at Coleman Coliseum, the first one that we went and got was Mr. Al Green. And we didn't realize then how much money this institution had. You mean to tell me we can afford Al Green? And we went and picked him up in a limo? And that started on us petitioning for Black musicians. The next were the O'Jays.

After graduating college, I came back. In 1978, I ran for public office in this county, and I became the first Black tax assessor. I served there until 1989, when I accepted my calling into the ministry. Then I went and got a master's degree, and then I went and got a PhD in systematic theology.

Tell me more about your experience as the first Black tax assessor?

Well, it was what I wanted to do. It gave me an opportunity to do something meaningful. I was over all the land in Greene County where I was born. Once upon a time, Black people could not even own land, but now I'm over all of it. So, it gave me the opportunity to help out my people in Greene County, Alabama. Black people have to be taught the laws of land ownership, and the exemptions you're eligible for. And I enjoyed telling my people that if you reached the grand old age of 65, you are eligible for what is called an Over 65 Homestead Exemption up to 160 acres of land, provided that it is contiguous, and then I would explain to them what that meant.

And I took joy in writing and calling our people. You have to sign up for the exemption every year. And I remember the auditors telling me that I could not write our people and call our people to get them to come in and sign up for the exemption. Because when you go and sign your homestead exemption, you actually sign it for the following year. If you don't sign it, you're going to be taxed, and I would not let that happen while I was in public office. And I remember the auditors telling me, "You can't write these people just to have them sign an exemption because then, we don't get any taxes from them." I kept doing it anyway, because I knew the laws. What he was really saying was that you can't let Black folks know—most of the people that didn't sign the exemption were Black folks.

There was another thing I would not do: the entire time I was in office, there was never one sale. Black folks would lose land in my county for not paying the property taxes. I would not let it happen. I knew it was valuable, and I knew there had to be a line somewhere. If Black people didn't pay the taxes, then it goes up for public auction. If it goes for public auction, who's got the money. So I would not let it happen. They didn't like that.

I butted heads with a slew of them. Butted heads with some of the big boys. I'm sure you've heard of Bear Bryant, legendary coach at the University of Alabama. Well, his son, Paul Bryant, Jr., opened the first dog track in my county after I became tax assessor, and at that time, there were only two dog tracks in the state of Alabama. That thing opened September 22, 1977, and was the fastest growing money-making thing in the state of Alabama. It was in my county, so it was my job to appraise it. He knew what its worth was, but for tax purposes, he wanted to say it was worth $3 million instead of $8 million. His calculations were off. I went down to the only other dog track in the state of Alabama, which was in Mobile, and I got their appraised value.

And I knew the dimensions of it and everything, and I told him we would appraise it at $8 million. And he said, "I'll see you in court." I said, "That's fine. I live in court!"

The day of that court date, he didn't even show up, but his attorneys did. And just before we got ready to go in, they said, "Well, we reconsidered this thing, and it *is* worth $8 million." I said, "I know." I mean, if you want to dare test my intelligence on what I've been doing since I've been here, go ahead. Because I knew what I was doing. And since that time, by the way, he and I have become the best of friends. He just didn't realize back then that he had run into a buzzsaw! I didn't care whether they liked it or not. And ultimately, I gained the respect of all because I treated all fairly.

Do you believe that Dr. King's dream is possible in this country?

Regrettably, sadly, no. When we look at Martin's dream, the last book that Martin wrote was in 1967, when he said, "Where do we go from here, chaos or community," and the very last chapter in that book is called The World House. And in that particular chapter, he just talked about the fact that we live in a world house, and we can either live together as brothers or perish together as fools. And it really ends with a question mark. Which way will we go? How do we fulfill the American dream with a Marjorie Taylor Greene in Washington? With a Ted Cruz in Washington?

I'm afraid you're not going to put the genie back in the bottle.

So, I'm not optimistic. I wish I could tell you differently. But I'm not. I hate to sound like a pessimist. There's always optimism. We have to put God first and have the determination that we're going to make it. And we have to develop our minds.

What are your thoughts on integration?

Well, I should quote what Martin King said about integration to Harry Belafonte in 1967. Just before he died, he said, "We have integrated a house that's on fire."

Integration . . . first of all, there should be no signs that say Black and white or colored and white, those things of segregation. But integration means that I have to subjugate my culture for yours. I am not an African and I am not an American. I am a true hybrid. I cannot totally subjugate my heritage and become what you want me to become. I can't do that. I can't do Clarence Thomas. I cannot do that. And so, even when it comes to raising our children, we literally can't do what the man says in raising them. You're not going to come up with a genuine American kid. Black folk have to raise their children in the Black folk way.

So, with integration, the signs should be down. But when it comes to controlling our destiny, the destiny of our children, we would be better off. . . . When I was in a totally segregated environment, though unequal, the teachers cared. The community cared. I was in a place where I felt like I belonged. And now, you're going put me in a situation. . . . If I am mentally capable I can achieve in that environment. But it's not the same. I mean, look at what they are telling you that you can have in your school system and what you can't.

I'm not optimistic. I'm optimistic of the fact that this is our home, and home is where you make it. Black lives do matter. And, in America, a Black life is a cheap life in the eyes of some. We've got to get to a point where we say right is right, and wrong is wrong. We've got to understand that *every* Black life matters. And it has to matter to everybody, to Black folks included.

The lone voice in the wilderness is what we need. My sadness is that we're not going to get a civil rights bill. We're not gonna get a voting rights bill passed. And that means these morons in these states are going to do what they can to curtail the Black vote. Remember what Malcolm X said. We want to talk about North and South, but he said to Black America that "South" is everything south of the Canadian border.

What message would you send to young Black people?

The fact that this book exists is because somebody chose to be different. You, as a young Black person, need to understand that you are created by God to achieve your destiny, and you cannot do that by being in the boat with others. If you're in the boat with others, you will get no further than the others do on this boat.

The only reason that what you are reading now is available to you is because some-one stepped outside of the boat, and decided that, with God's help, they're going to give you a true authentic view of what Jim Crow was like. Now, that task has already been done. Your task is to ask God what your assignment is while you are on this planet, and go and do likewise.

Spoken like a true Black preacher!

INTERVIEW NO. 9

TREVOR CHAVIS

My full name is Trevor Jolan Summey Chavis. I was a Summey before I married, and I was born in Hendersonville, North Carolina.

I lived in two neighborhoods growing up. When my parents came over from Hendersonville, they moved here to Asheville when I was two. I lived on South Side. There was a South Side of town. And I went to Livingston Street School. It was all-Black—well, all-colored, was what it was called. And after I lived on South Side, we moved to the east side of town. I was living on Pine Street, and that's when I got familiar with Eagle Street, the YMI Cultural Center, the drugstore. I was a little girl at the time, but at that time, we could walk around all over Asheville. We weren't afraid to go places. The schools were all-Black. And I'm thinking about the good teachers that we had. That's what I remember about, you know, being in those neighborhoods, going to those schools. And neighbors were close. We could go to the neighbors' houses. They were just like our parents. And our churches were the gathering place on Sundays. And we walked everyplace because we didn't have a car at that time. So I was walking as a little girl all over Asheville. I wasn't afraid that time. No one bothered you.

My mother didn't work when I was a little girl. She didn't start working until I got to be almost a teenager. But my daddy worked for the Trailways Bus Company. At that time they had Black men as porters, like Pullman porters, at the train station. Porters at the bus station handled baggage. All of that. I remember at that time, my father would sometimes call the buses. You know, when people would come in, they didn't know which bus to catch. And he would get on a microphone and call the buses. He worked so long there.

The stations were wonderful. One was on Wall Street and the other one was on Coxe Avenue. We had nice bus stations at that time for buses. People traveled on the bus and train mostly. My mother didn't work at that time, but later on, she worked at the school. She worked in the cafeteria. She graduated from high school, but my mother was a professional. That's why she worked so hard making sure that my brother and I got our education, because she didn't want us to be laborers in the white people's kitchen. Because that's the way, you know, that's the way it was.

I think my mother was saving for our education even then. When I was very young, like in the first or second grade, she didn't work. My mother started working to help my father out when I was around the seventh or eighth grade. And when she did go to work, my aunt would come up and take care of me. She didn't want to leave me by myself. I have one brother. I was 11 when he was born.

We made our own fun. We had a good time. When it was snow, we would ride on sleds. And if we didn't have sleds, we would take boxes and tear them apart. We would play touch football . . . I played touch football even with the fellas sometimes. We would make our own fun. And at our schools, our teachers would arrange plays. Every year, we would have plays. I always liked music. And every year, we would have a play to close the school year out. An operetta. And that took a lot of my time. And I took piano lessons. I started when I was in the third grade, and that also took a lot of my time. I had a few friends that would be with me, and we would take piano lessons together. And we made our own fun. But most of the time I was on the piano practicing my music.

My music teacher was named Ms. Bowman, and she lived on Albemarle Road. And her daughter was one of the teachers here in the Asheville school system, but she taught in Shiloh. She was a public school teacher. And we would go out every morning to take our piano lessons. It was in North Asheville where she taught piano. Ms. Bowman taught me music lessons. Piano lessons. They cost 50 cents. If we had a dollar then, that was big money!

We would go Christmas caroling and we were in church plays, you know, things of that sort. We'd climb apple trees. And we'd have weenie roasts. We'd get hot dogs, make a little pit in the yard, build a little fire, and roast our franks. We were doing that as little kids.

The fires were mostly made up the street at one of my friend's house. Policeman Fleming. I played with his children a lot. He was one of the first Black officers here. And his children—the boys mostly—would make the fire. But we would take a coat hanger . . . see, I'm going way back now. We didn't have a grill and stuff. We would take a coat hanger and stick it through the hot dog, and roast it. We didn't call them hot dogs then. We called them weenies. And it was fun and pleasant, you know?

Tell me more about the play that you did at the end of every school year.

End of every school year, and most of the time, I would be the person that would take the lead because I could sing. I'll never forget, we had one play, and I wasn't Cinderella, but I was a fairy in *Cinderella*. And then we had one called *The Gypsy Princess*. She was a princess who got lost in the forest, and she ended up in a gypsy campground. I have some of those books right now downstairs. Those operatic books. They're old. They're yellow and everything with age. But I even remember some of the songs from those plays.

I always gravitated towards teachers that can play the piano. At Mountain Street School, it was Ms. Daly, and at Livingston Street School, it was Ms. Kennedy. And, before I started taking piano lessons, I would tap out a music beat on the dresser and pretend I was playing the piano. And my aunt said, "Please get this child a piano!" That's right.

Did y'all have to have auditions and everything?

Well, the teachers would know who could sing, because at that time, we would have devotions every day. That's where I learned most of the hymns that I know. Before I could play real well, I could sing those hymns, because Cathy Evans was my first grade teacher. And she had us in plays. "Just a Little Talk With Jesus" was one of the songs she taught me when I was a little girl, and we'd go sometimes to other churches on Sunday. She would have us to come and sing, you know. And so when it was time for the end of school play, they knew who could sing. Because we had devotions, and the teachers could hear us singing in the class. So, that's how they knew that. I'm glad for the background that I had. We always say what we got from our high school teachers at Stephens-Lee, but our elementary teachers were strong, too.

In the mornings, a teacher sometimes would start a song. And sometimes, they would ask us, "Do you have a song that you would like to sing?" Sometimes, we'd have a Bible verse. And this was every day. Each teacher had their own way of doing things. And that went on through high school. In high school, we would have devotions in homeroom.

See, at that time, we could do it because all of our teachers were Christian. You know, we just went to Baptist, Presbyterian, Methodist, and things like that, but that was the only difference. There was nothing else. No one cared about what song you sang. We didn't have all that. We were doing our own Black thing; we weren't integrated. So, we didn't have to worry about that. It was the good old days. But it did have its drawbacks. And I'll get down to that later.

We had a junior high school. It was Ashton Avenue Junior High. After I left Mountain Street School. . . . As I said, I started off at Livingston Street. My mother moved to the east side, so I had to go to Mountain Street. When we were in junior high, we went to Ashton Avenue. My cousin was the principal. Her name was Rita Lee. Ashton had the seventh and eighth grade. Now, the year that I was in the seventh grade there, the school was condemned. So we had to go to Stephens-Lee in the eighth grade. Our class, the class of '54, was the first class not to graduate junior high from Ashton, because we had to go to Stephens-Lee. And we were on the third floor over at the high school.

One of my friends said, "You know, I always resented you all coming over there in the eighth grade, because it took attention away from us!" She was in the ninth grade, and she said that all of us eighth graders took their attention. And we did!

Asheville's Black high school, Stephens-Lee High School; photo courtesy of Buncombe County Special Collections, Pack Memorial Public Library, Asheville, North Carolina.

Because we had a lot of talent in our class. At Stephens-Lee, I was in the band, and the Glee Club, we called it, under Ms. Ollie Reynolds. And that's why I'm a music teacher today, because of Ollie Reynolds. And that's one reason why I'm a Delta too, because of Ollie Reynolds. I wanted to do everything that she did. I just loved her so much. She influenced my life a lot. Music was just in my bones, I guess. And I've always loved music. I loved going to movies that had musicals and stuff.

Our days at Stephens-Lee were beautiful. Our teachers exposed us to things—our elementary teachers, high school teachers. All the Black teachers here in Asheville were wonderful. I graduated in 1954. There are a lot of teachers that came after I graduated also, that taught at Stephens-Lee.

Why was Ashton condemned?

Because the building was falling apart. The building was old, and we had to get out of there. In fact, they tore it down. But anyway, I graduated high school in '54. After that, I went to Morgan State. It was called Morgan State College then. But it's Morgan State University now. I wanted to go to North Carolina Central at first. And then, one of my boyfriends transferred to North Carolina Central, so I knew I couldn't go where he was! And I tell you who he was. The nephew of Reverend E. W. Dixon. His name was Billy Thomas. And he was ahead of me, and he had gone to Dillard University. And before I know, he's gone and transferred. And I had already been accepted at that time. And he come from Dillard and transferred to North Carolina Central. And I was just recently telling one of my good friends, "I was supposed to be on the train with you all going to Durham every holiday and every school year." I wasn't going to Morgan at first. But after he transferred there, I said, well, I'm going to Morgan. Because I had applied to two places. And two of my friends had already gone to Morgan. And he told me to come on up to Morgan. At that time, you didn't have to go through what you do now for college admission. You'd get in quickly.

Four of us from Asheville went to Morgan at that time. Shirley English, Betty Cullers, and Betty Dunn. And there was some more Asheville people there, too. Morgan had a lot of Asheville people there. Some who had graduated from Stephens-Lee, class of '51 were there. William Buford. He's one of the athletes that played football up there. Betty Ann Scott. Betty Collette. Dr. John Holt was a Morganite, also. He was so happy that I chose Morgan.

And we had to pay that out-of-state fee. But my mother used to tell me, "Trevor, your education didn't cost near as much as your brother's." He went to Morehouse, and he's 11 years behind me, so everything was going up, up up, up up. And a private school too, like Morehouse? My mother and father sacrificed everything for us to go. They built our home in 1953. My uncles built our home. Because my mother's people laid brick and all that stuff like that. So they built our house. My mother and father's house. My granddaddy laid the floors, my one uncle did the plastering, and my two uncles laid the bricks. That's right.

My parents paid for me to go to school. There were no scholarships.

There was a group of us that did the minuet for the Zetas when they would have their debutante ball [in high school]. They would get some of us from the high school you know. So, we had a lot to do. Our teachers made sure we had things to do. I mean, the debutantes in those days, that was really something!

After I graduated from Morgan, I taught school in Edenton, North Carolina. I taught there for years, got married, came here to Asheville, then moved to New York. I wasn't here in the '60s and '70s, but ASCORE was the group that fought for our rights here in Asheville.

Your granddaddy was the one that did our Senior Festival Service when we graduated [high school]. Ms. Reynolds said, "There's a new minister in town, and I think we're going to have him do the festival service." That's a Sunday service before you graduate. We did all of our stuff at Stephens-Lee in the auditorium. And it was big enough for us then. And Reverend Avery was the one that did our service. And he would always say, "That was my first job when I came to Asheville, was to do Trevor and Vernelle's service."

So, honey, we were exposed to the best! Now, I wasn't much of a dancer, but one of our teachers had danced with Katherine Dunham—Catherine Chappelle—and she would go away in the summer. Most of the teachers go away in the summers working on their doctorate and master's degrees. Then, they would come back and give us some of the things that they'd seen in New York. And we would give productions over there at Stephens-Lee. That's right. They were fantastic. She was the best choreographer I think I've ever seen. And then, we had one art teacher, Mr. Lewis . . . that man could take a box and make anything out of it. We had some excellent teachers. We had a preparatory school and didn't even know it!

Now, one time in junior high, I had stayed late to practice a play, and I was by myself catching the bus. Because we had to take the bus down there to junior high school. And this car came along from Asheville High, which was called Lee Edwards then, all-white, and these boys stumped a cigarette on my skirt. I have never forgotten it. That frightened me to death. Because even though we were segregated, I had never had any real bad experiences until then.

Nothing happened, because I didn't tell it. And even if I had told it, they wouldn't have done anything, anyway. But I wouldn't have said anything. Scared me to death. And from then on, I would never go down that way to catch the bus. The bus stop to sit down is where it happened. And after that, I would never go there. Sometimes, I'd walk to town to come home. I was in seventh grade. I was 12 years old.

And I've never forgotten that. I say, if I were to ever see them now, I would. . . . But they're probably dead now!

We couldn't go in the front door. You know that . . . that was every place. Restaurants downtown, restrooms. We knew what we couldn't do, but it didn't really bother us when I was younger because we were used to it. And also, we had so much else to do. We'd just go on to Eagle Street into the drugstore and have fun. We knew we couldn't go into these white places.

I would overhear my parents' grown-up talk about lynching elsewhere, but I don't remember any real bad violence here. We would hear it on the radio, too. We were never afraid because we knew to stay in our own space, and to enjoy what we did have. And we had more of an appreciation, it seemed like at that time, for each other. I don't hate other races, but I was happy to be close to my own people.

Sometimes, we'd come through town at night, and we'd sneak and drink out of the white water fountain. All of us did that. And one white doctor here, Dr. Mary Francis Shubert, her office was never segregated. She was doctor to almost every Black person in Asheville, and she was a good doctor. Her office was down near the courthouse. Those buildings are gone now. And white and Black sat in her office. She didn't segregate. We couldn't go in the hospital at that time, because the hospitals were segregated.

When I moved to Edenton, North Carolina, I participated in some movements under Golden Frinks. He was one of Dr. King's men, and he helped to integrate things in Edenton. In fact, that's when I first heard Dr. King speak in person. In Edenton. He came to Edenton and gave a beautiful speech—oh God, it was something! It was in the armory, that's what they used. Edenton was a pretty little country town, but I didn't like it. I couldn't stand it, but that's where I had to work. And now, every time I look at a North Carolina magazine, guess what's in there? Edenton.

When I started driving, I'd drive through Raleigh going to Edenton. And I would drop people in Raleigh coming back from Edenton, and I'd drop them in Raleigh and drive on to Asheville. I started driving in 1961. I bought me a little '61 Falcon. I said I was going to learn how to drive because I was tired of sitting in the back of the bus. We had to do all that: sit in the back of the bus, go in the back doors of theaters, and one theater, we couldn't go in at all here in Asheville. But everywhere, we had to go in the back door. Everything that happened in the South happened here in Asheville. But seemingly, the white people weren't as mean as they were in the deep, deep South, like Mississippi and places like that. Because even when my brother and ASCORE and all of them. . . . A lot of places wouldn't let them come in. But they kept protesting and marching.

This one thing about my great-grandmother. My father's grandmother and my father's grandfather helped build the AME church in Asheville. I think this was during slavery. And they were free for 50 years after. But they were both enslaved from birth. And my great-grandmother, her name was Margaret, she was forced to become a wet nurse. A wet nurse was when a Black woman would have a baby and she had a lot of milk in her breasts. And she would go around and feed, from her breasts, the white people's babies. My great-grandmother Margaret was one. Life for Black people was like that during that time.

My grandparents on my father's side are Christopher Summey, Sr., and Francis Fortune Summey. I knew them real well. I used to go to Hendersonville to see them all the time. Then, my mother's people were Howard Dixon and my grandmother is Daisy Hamilton Dixon. They were from Spindale. See, my mother met my father when the ladies would come to work on these guesthouses from different parts of North Carolina—they would come to Hendersonville. Because Hendersonville was a tourist town, like Asheville. And my mother worked in a guesthouse. That's where she met my father.

All of our Black businesses were on Eagle Street, or most of them, anyway. Florists, dentists, doctors, beauticians. . . . I have a list of that, too. And the clubs also!

I used to go down to see my grandparents in Spindale every summer. They had a farm. Most families had a lot of land, and my mother's people held on to theirs. My daddy's people didn't hold onto theirs too much, and they didn't have as much, because Hendersonville is more of a city than Spindale is. I would go there every summer. Feed and horses and stuff. And at that time, we had lamps. No electricity out there at that time. Lamps, going to the outhouse, and all of that. I remember all of that. And when I would go over to see my mother's people, they lived more in the city. But they still had a garden, and my granddaddy had a little hog pen in the backyard. People raised their own meat, gardens, and a lot at that time. That's right.

I was the second grandchild on my mother's side, and on my daddy's side, I was the third grandchild. I was born in 1936. I have younger cousins now, and some of them, I don't even know who they are because they're much younger than me. And when you come from big families, you just can't keep up.

And my husband Sam was a Chavis. They have a book about them, but I'm not gonna discuss all that because that's not my side. But those Chavises had that park in Raleigh [author's note: John Chavis Memorial Park]. That's what they tell me. And there's a book that his brother sent. And there's one cousin who lived in Salisbury. Her daddy was the first Black mayor of Salisbury. But this is not my side.

Mayor Lash. That was his name. First Black mayor of Salisbury.

How did you get involved with the Civil Rights Movement?

When I was in Edenton, I would go to the meetings. They would have meetings at the church. Sometimes they would ask us to walk down to the theater. At Morgan, we tried to integrate the movie theater and stuff. But I knew that wasn't for me. That's for stronger people, and that time, I wasn't very strong. I knew what our people wanted, and I wanted it too. So, I'd participate in the boycotts, but the marching . . . that was for stronger people.

Golden Frinks was one of King's fighters. He would leave Edenton and go where Dr. King was all the time. And he invited Dr. King there to speak. They had just started the bus boycott in Alabama. Rev. LeGard used to come back and talk about Bull Connor, about how mean he was. This was in the early '60s. So that's how I got to hear Dr. King. He was very dynamic.

I left Edenton in '63 and came back to Asheville. Stayed here—my son was born. I'd been married two months and got pregnant. So I stayed here. My husband had gone to New York to take this new job. His brother had gotten him a job. See, I couldn't find a job. And I knew I had to work. There were no teaching jobs for Black folks that time. My mother asked me, "What about the white schools?" But they weren't hiring Black teachers.

I couldn't go to Stephens-Lee because Ms. Reynolds had Stephens-Lee sewed up, and Mamie Howell had Hill Street sewed up with the music. And when I came here, they gave me a lot of substitute work to do. So, until my son was born, I did substitute work. But then after my son was born, I went to New York and thank God I was employed up there. I started off like a regular substitute way. You don't have your permanent license to have a license fully, but then, after my daughter was born, I got my permanent license. I was hired at a school called IS-59 in Queens, and I was there 20-something years.

I wasn't excited to move to New York. I didn't want to leave Asheville. But there were no jobs for Black teachers. But God moves in mysterious ways. Because without the benefits that I got in New York, I couldn't have made it. Thank God we were covered. We had very good insurance and we were paid very well way up there. New York pays very well. But I earned because you work hard. You don't sleep, now. You have to work. And I taught music classes, classes like choir class. It was called a major music class. I taught fifth and seventh grade major music vocal. And my class assistant would be there, but most of the time, she wasn't there. This other guy came, and things were better. And one year we went to Rome for a major music festival. So as I said, God knew what to do. God sent me to New York. And I didn't want to go, but He knew what he wanted.

Did you have culture shock when you got up there?

No, because I lived in Queens. I don't live right in the city. And even then, I enjoyed going to the city. Because when I was in Edenton, we would go to Norfolk, which was a pretty big city at that time. That's when we did our shopping, in Norfolk. Because Edenton was near Norfolk. And before I got my car, my landlady's daughter, after we got paid, we'd head to Norfolk to shop!

But things were pretty good. And then I wasn't too far from Virginia where I had relatives. In fact, I went to Hampton's homecoming more than I went to Morgan's. I had a cousin there. And I would drive to Hampton and have a good time in Hampton.

So back to Queens, we found that Northerners were racist too, as far as I was concerned. They didn't want to stay in a neighborhood with you. But their racism is a little bit more subdued than Southerners' is. But I don't have major problems because I didn't go there to be nobody's friend. I went there to work. So, I would go to work. I was there for the children. But, you could work with them every day, but they didn't want to live beside you. They didn't want you to buy a house close to them.

I found that out because one of the teachers overheard something. One of my friends, who was a friend to some of them, was looking for a house. And a guy told me that after she had left the room, they said, "Why did you tell her about that house?" So that kind of stuff. But some white people are sweet and genuine, just like there are some in the South. So you just forget about the bad ones and focus on the people who are real genuine, you know.

I had to raise my children and work. Then, I went back to graduate school. I got my master's at Queens College. My husband and I would get invited to go out by different groups And then at that time, we would have our own things, like bar-becues and stuff like that. And some people would invite us to weddings and Bar Mitzvahs, some of the Jewish people would invite us there, you know, things like that. As far as going out to clubs and stuff, we wouldn't do too much. But if we were invited, we would go out.

And then, when Atlantic City opened up, I would go with people. But I was never one to gamble too much. I'd go to Atlantic City and go in the jewelry store and buy gold chains, shoes, and just have a good time shopping. And I'd eat all the good food! I've found that, in life, you have to make your own fun.

My daughter went to Alvin Ailey dance school. And my son was an artist, and he graduated from the High School for Art and Design. They were both in special schools. My daughter started taking dance lessons when she was young, and I enrolled her in Ailey. That's how she got there. After she got in, my husband and I would go to every performance—even the out-of-town ones. It was beautiful, you know. We did our best for our children, and they excelled. It made us very proud.

What are your thoughts on integration as a whole?

I'll say it like this. Seemingly, our people were better off and we had our own. In some instances, we seemed to be better as a group. We were better in some instances before we integrated. I'm going back to our Black teachers. Our Black teachers seem to be more concerned. And when they integrated, you had white teachers teaching Black children. And a lot of them don't work for our kids. In a way, it's good, and in a way, it's not. They took all of our schools away from us, and our children had to go to their school. And I don't know why they would not keep LS Herring school open, and let the white children come in the Black neighborhood, just like the Black children went in the white ones.

Integration wasn't as good as I thought it would be. Because now I don't see Black faces in places I should see them. I went to Asheville High for a performance one year, and I didn't see any Black kids. I know good and damn well they had talented Black students. And when a lot of places have Teacher of the Year, I don't see a Black face too much. It's always white teachers as Teacher of the Year. And I know that we have excellent Black teachers. But that's not only in the South, that's every place. Even going back to some of the things I told you before, about up in New York, because sometimes, things get messy up there, too.

Do you think that Dr. King's dream is possible in this country?

Before the last two years came into existence, I felt that Dr. King's dream was possible. But after Trump and his mean, arrogant, dumb, jackass presidency, and his influence on so many in Congress . . . I'm praying that they will be voted out. The voting rights bill that Dr. King and so many others died for was struck out. That has made me angry. It just made me kind of disgusted, what's happening.

And my message to our young people, young Black people. . . . You need to go as far as you can in pursuing your education. I believe education is really the key. And know your Black history. You need to know from whence you came, from Africa, to slavery, to now. And above all, stay with God.

I thought Dr. King's dream was possible for so long, even down through segregation. And by us going to Morgan, so close to DC, we were invited to DC many times to sing for the Young Republicans. It just shows how people were able to get along better. And those Capitol buildings that were held in such high esteem, you know how you feel when you would go past the Capitol? And to see what they did on January 6th almost makes you sick. So, even if we've lost faith in some things, like the people and the dream, we have to have faith in God and keep on going. That's the best way that I know how to say it.

INTERVIEW NO. 10

WALT CARR

I'm Walter Robert Carr, Jr., and I was born in Baltimore, Maryland. We lived with my grandparents early on, my father's mother and father, but then we moved into the Gilmore Homes, a housing project in Baltimore. They're actually in the process of tearing it down now, because that was 1940 or 1943, something like that. And the neighborhood, a Black neighborhood, of course . . . stable and clean. It epitomized that mantra that it takes a village. That's how tight the Black community was. And they were all two-parent families. They did not move into the projects with the mindset of staying two, three, and four decades. Everybody wanted to move out; save some money and move out and get a home, which everybody I knew did, including us. As matter of fact, we moved to Philadelphia. My father was working for a Black newspaper, the *Afro-American* newspaper, and he got a job transfer to Philadelphia. So we moved to Philly. My upbringing in Baltimore was stable. I lucked out on some great parents, and I lucked out on their outlook on life and dealing with the struggle. They both got arrested in 1941 on a sound truck for protesting police brutality. And this is 2022 and we are still dealing with it. I got my DNA, my activist DNA, from my parents, particularly my father.

He worked for the *Afro-American* newspaper. He was a circulation manager, and he was also a writer. He had a couple of short stories published years ago when I was a kid, but the job in Philadelphia when he got transferred was circulation management.

My mom never worked until after I was in college. She was always a housewife and stay-at-home mother. She was really the enforcer as far as it came to discipline and whatnot. I used to call her Hard-Hearted Hannah. And Hannah didn't play! And I didn't know she had a great sense of humor until I got about 19 or 20. I didn't see a damn thing funny about Hannah when I was a kid. But she was a disciplinarian. I always joke with the guys that I think she helped me be the dancer that I became, because when she'd hold my wrist with one hand, and be whipping my behind with that strap with the other, I would bust a move!

One time, my sister said, "Yeah, hit him again, I wanna see, yeah, that's the move!" She had a sense of humor that I may have developed over the years. My old man was a little more stoic. Loved music, loved jazz. Played a little piano. I was just blessed with two great parents. I really was.

I have a sister and a brother. My sister is 85. And she's currently living in Ohio. She just moved into a senior development. I understand it's really nice. She's only been there about a year. I have a brother who lives in Baltimore, and he's retired. He was the stage manager for Peabody Institute of Music—John Hopkins Peabody School of Music. And my sister is a retired schoolteacher. And those, those grand-parents that I mentioned briefly? I don't go to college without my grandfather. Neither does my sister. He paid for everything. I got one year of financial aid when I walked on the football team in my sophomore year, but my grandfather paid everything for my sister and I. Books, tuition, the whole nine yards. And I love to bring it up because I'm so grateful, but it's also funny. He was the manager of a Black movie theater—because I lived in segregated Baltimore, of course, in the '40s and '50s and '60s. He managed two Black movie theaters in East Baltimore. As a matter of fact, the Dunbar Theatre was actually built by my great-grandfather, Josiah Diggs. And he sold it to a Jewish concern some years later, with the stipula-tion that his son-in-law, my grandfather, be the manager. And I lived with them. I didn't live on campus—I didn't live in the dorm on campus. I lived with my grand-parents in Baltimore when I attended Morgan State. And I used to . . . they would leave their bedroom door ajar, and I would reach up on the chifforobe and get my coffee money and lunch money. And there would be mounds of quarters and dollar bills and 10s and 20s. For four and a half years, I thought they were movie receipts from the two movie theaters. I didn't find out until almost four or five years after I graduated that my grandfather was one of the biggest numbers backers in East

Baltimore. That was all policy money, street numbers. But like I said, I don't see college or getting my degree without the largesse of my grandparents, my grandfather in particular.

My grandfather was from Eastern Shore Maryland. And, you know, when he came up, I mean. . . . Eastern Shore was like being in Alabama or Mississippi. In fact, any rural area in Maryland at that time. And I did get to know my great-grandfather: very stoic, always suit and tie, he was a businessman. But I don't know where Papa was born, to be honest. My grandmother on my father's side was born in Baltimore. My mother's people, they were all from Virginia.

My great-grandfather Josiah actually started out selling coal and ice. And from the stories that I can recall, he was hustling. I don't mean street hustling, you know, nothing illegal, but it was just honest hard work. Peddling and selling coal and firewood, and then he started buying property. I just found out in a book that he was engaged in politics. A friend of mine wrote a book recently. And when I went to the index and looked in the back, I saw Josiah Diggs. Seemingly, he was very prominent in Black politics when he was coming up in Baltimore. But he got his money through the very limited things that he was able to do being a Negro at that time. Selling firewood, coal, ice, that kind of stuff. And probably some other things that I'm not aware of, but his business acumen was on the money. He was saving and buying property and whatnot. And he did extremely well.

In fact, he wanted to send my father to mortuary school. But my father didn't want to be a mortician. And he was doing so well that he even offered to give my mother and father a house. But my grandmother didn't want us living on Etting Street. Etting Street was the next street over from the street that we lived on. But it was about that class thing that so many Blacks got so caught up in, you know. But they were all working class in that neighborhood. So there really wasn't much of a difference. But on Druid Hill Avenue, McCulloh, Madison, you had, you know, the upside of segregation. Because the Bethlehem Steel worker lived in the same neighborhood as the Black doctor or dentist. But she didn't want us living on Etting Street, and we didn't get that house. But my grandfather did very well as a businessman, and he was the first Black to build a movie house in Baltimore City.

I think the second movie house was the Radio. It was around the corner from the Dunbar.

You talked about Baltimore being segregated to the core. Can you speak more about that?

Actually, it was something that was accepted. You knew the rules, you knew where to go, where not to go. The restaurants were all segregated. You know, we had our own restaurants. Of course, the movie houses were segregated. Schools were definitely segregated. I didn't go to school with white kids until we moved to Philadelphia. That was a whole new experience for me. But schools are originally segregated, as were the neighborhoods, the redlining, the whole nine yards. When I spoke about living in a housing project, a lot of people don't know that housing projects during World War II were built principally initially for whites. But of course, because of segregation, they had to build housing projects for Blacks as well. And whites, when they moved into the housing projects, their goals were the same. To have a place to get them on their feet, save some money, and buy a house. Same with Blacks.

The only thing is, when we decided to move and buy a house, we had the restrictions and the redlining. I've always credited white folks as the ones who started the hood—the ghetto—because of segregation.

The first time I ever experienced racism was as a kid going to Eastern Shore, Maryland, with my grandparents. We had to cross the Chesapeake Bay. And there was no bridge like the double bridge they have now. So you had to go on a ferry boat, you know, drive the car up on the ferry boat, much like you do in Martha's Vineyard. You get on the ferry and go across to Eastern Shore. And that was the first time I'd seen segregated water fountains and segregated restrooms. And there was a long refreshment stand where you could buy refreshments. But the front of the stand was reserved for whites. Negroes, we had to go around on the side to get our Coke or Babe Ruth, Hershey bar or whatever.

Young Walt, pictured in 1945.

And then, on family vacation when I was about eight years old, in Virginia, I remember being puzzled. I didn't question it, but I was puzzled because, once we [went further past] the Mason-Dixon Line, we had to move to the back of the bus. Once we left Baltimore and hit Virginia, we had to move our seats. Of course, at eight years old, I wasn't aware of why, and my father didn't want to explain that to me.

But when I first realized what was really going on, even though at 11, I still couldn't fully grasp it, I found out why my father was upset. We were on our way over to his mother's house, leaving the housing projects. And he was upset, and when we hit Baker Street coming down the steps, he said, "Junior, when you grow up, you're gonna find out you're gonna have to be 10 times better than the white man." But he didn't elaborate. And we just walked on.

But I found out a short time later. This was World War II. My father had learned how to weld. And so he taught a welding class at this war plant. And he taught white guys as well as Negroes how to weld. He found out two months later that the white guys he had taught how to weld, their hourly wage was higher than his. And that was the first time that I was aware that something was wrong with this world . . . but of course, I couldn't grasp it at the time at 11 years old.

So those situations were my first encounters. I didn't run into anything really blatant in Philadelphia. In fact, we even had two or three white families on our block in West Philadelphia. And, you know, played sports in high school. But a buddy of mine in Philly, Johnny Gross, Dr. Johnny Gross, didn't make the varsity baseball team. And he told me he thought that West Philly, or our school, our coaches, had a quota system. All the coaches were white. Matter fact, I didn't have any Black teachers in high school. But he thought there was a quota. And I had never thought about it, but when he said that, I believed it. Because I didn't get moved up to the varsity football team until the end of the season. And right now, and I've been hanging onto this for years, I can name six or seven guys that I knew couldn't so much as hold my jockstrap, okay? And one guy, Gene Toll, I even remember his name, he couldn't even come close to being on my level. But for some reason, I didn't make the final cut at the beginning of that last season.

I didn't really find out until after I graduated that I was going to college. Because I wanted to go to the Air Force. But I didn't know my mother and father had talked to my grandfather, and he had agreed that I could stay with him and that he would pay for all my expenses. So I was really blessed, no question.

I left Baltimore when I was about 12. I never tried to drink out of the whites-only fountains or anything because it's almost like, and I hate to use this term, but it was about knowing your place. You didn't even try to do anything like that. You didn't even try.

When they had the segregated tennis courts, a bunch of Black people protested and picketed these white tennis courts. Swimming pools . . . everything was segregated in Baltimore. Matter of fact, my uncle was a lifeguard and my father was well known as a diver. My mother worked at the colored swimming pool the entire summer and there was no daycare. So my sister and I, we walked from the projects to the pool. And we were in the water six days a week. She had one day off. But that was segregated. Plus, they put the colored pool out there where they kept sheep. They used to have sheep in Druid Hill Park to keep the grass levels down. They put the colored pool out there near where they kept the sheep. But she worked on the women's side one complete summer. We went to work with her every day for an entire summer.

Often, when I think about it, I wonder if my father had some Communist leanings. Because anytime Blacks stood up in the '20s and '30s, you had to be harboring some kind of Communist tendencies or admiration for their stance. I remember my parents' arrest being reported in the Black newspaper that he later worked for, the *Afro-American* newspaper. It was in the headlines. It was he, my mother, and a driver. And I asked him what happened?

Because of segregation and redlining, Blacks only lived in two areas at that time. You either lived in East Baltimore or West Baltimore. We lived in West Baltimore. My father rented a truck with a sound system, with those old-fashioned big speakers on the top. But he was inside the truck, and my mother sat with the driver in the cab. And my father was on the mic. So they started in East Baltimore, because they knew they had to return the truck in West Baltimore. So they went to East Baltimore and he's on the mic talking about how Black folks had to come together and demonstrate. I mean, the brutality among police in most metropolitan areas and cities was unreal in the '30s, '40s, and '50s. So he was trying to organize in the name of fighting police brutality.

Anyway, he said that when he got back to West Baltimore, they were driving on Robert Street, and when they crossed Division Street there, they saw a white cop. They had a reputation for brutalizing Blacks, and my father told the driver to follow the guy. You see, cops were walking their beats back then. The driver followed his orders and followed the cop. And my father was giving his spiel on the mic. The white cop took it for about two and a half blocks. Finally, he just stepped out into the street and started beating his night stick on the asphalt and telling them to pull over. He called a paddy wagon and they locked all three of them up. And the next day, it was all dismissed because my father had a permit and the whole nine yards. But they were arrested for protesting police brutality.

My grandfather, who was still in the numbers business then, he bailed him out. So my mother and father didn't spend a night in jail. They were bailed out.

My father wrote short stories when he worked at the *Afro-American* newspaper. He wrote a newsletter in Baltimore called the *Nitelifer*. And it was a newsletter that you could read on the spot in the bar when you went out, in the barbershop, in the beauty parlor, or wherever. And my father lived to write that editorial.

I can pull down a *Nitelifer* from 1963, '68, '74, '77. And the things he was talking about with regard to Black folks staying unified and demonstrating would still apply today. It was called the *Nitelifer*, and he was called a nightlifer. And it was convenient in size because if you were out socializing, you could just roll up, put in your pocket, and read it later. But any activist DNA I have, I got from my father.

He also was successful in a boycott. You know Black folks, we drink the best liquor. But the distributors never had any Black salesmen during the '60s. So my father used the *Nitelifer* to start a boycott. And he was largely responsible for them hiring a Black liquor salesman. Same thing with Black cigarette salesmen, because there weren't Black cigarette salesmen either. He was a bar guy, and he was a nightlifer. He ran that boycott, and it was very successful. But he lived to write that editorial every week. And every once in a while, I would furnish him with some cartoons to appear in the *Nitelifer*.

I've been drawing ever since I ever picked up a pencil. As a matter of fact, my mother saved everything, so I've got report cards from elementary school where, in the teacher's comments section, it says, "Walter spends too much time drawing and doodling in his notebook." I've always been drawing, ever since I was a kid. And then of course, back then, particularly in the '40s, comic books were big among kids, Black and white. And trading comics was big. You would trade comics with your friends. And you would try to emulate styles. I don't know if they still exist, and I know that art teachers didn't like kids to use them, but there is something called a tracing book, where they actually had professionally-drawn line illustrations, and then a tracing sheet over top of it. And then you would come over with your pencil, pen, or whatever. My parents were very supportive of my drawing, and they always kept me supplied with tracing books.

In school, I wasn't encouraged that much by my teachers. But I was eventually recommended to take Saturday art classes at the Philadelphia Museum of Art. But the classes were on Saturday, and I did not want to go because I wanted to be in the schoolyard hooping. Playing ball with my friends. But my mother and father made me go, and I'm so glad they did. I learned so much during those two summers. And so I had parents who encouraged me.

The last conversation I had with my mother in Cleveland was.... Well, when we lived in the projects, my bedroom was right next to the kitchen. And whenever I brought home a bad report card, which was often, my comic books went to the trash. I mean, I could be a rich man today. She had no idea and I had no idea that they could be collector's items one day. I mean, I had all the prominent comic heroes. And she told me in that conversation that after I had been sent to my room for whatever I had done, as punishment, that she would crack the door and look in on me, and she said, "You were just laying across the bed drawing in your notebook. And I wanted to take that pencil and paper from you because you weren't suffering enough!" But she said she was glad she didn't. And I'm glad she didn't either.

My major at Morgan State was art education, but not because it was truly my first choice. I was an art education major for one reason: I played sports—football and track. There was an old building at Morgan called the Dust Bowl. This was one of the original buildings. It was actually the gym. But it wasn't the contemporary gyms you see today with stands on both sides, spectators for games, but it was a gym where they had PE classes. And at one end was a stage where the drama group would hold their plays and whatnot. But it was also a favorite spot for guys to drop in when they were finished with classes to play some pickup basketball games.

I went into the Dust Bowl one day, and there was a guy standing to my left, I can remember it like was yesterday. Up on the stage was a football coach checking his watch and telling this young man in these gym shorts and T-shirt, "Come on. Come on son, I don't have all day!" The guy on stage had to run to the end of the stage and do a no-hand flip off the stage down onto the gym floor on top of these mats. There were three or four spotters on each side, but he was scared to death. This happened in 1950. And I turned to the guy and asked, "Is this a tumbling club?" And he said, "No, this is tumbling 101." I said, "This is a physical education class?" He said yes. I immediately walked out of the Dust Bowl, walked over to the main administration building, Holmes Hall, where the clock and everything is, went downstairs, pulled my file, and changed my major from physical education to art education. Because I was looking at an F. I know I wasn't coming off that stage and doing a no-hand flip down to the gym floor. And that's got to be an art education major!

Striking the Heisman pose!

What was your college experience like at Morgan?

It was great. It was like family, because it wasn't that many students. The teachers were really dedicated, fine professors who really looked out for you. They kept telling you that you didn't know what was waiting for you out there. This is 1950, and you had to be prepared. My only problem was, I wasn't a great student in high school, and it took me a couple of years at Morgan. . . . I didn't flunk out. I did what I had been doing all through school, which was I did just enough to get by. But I finally began to wake up probably in my junior year, and I would look at other students because I noticed that, even if they were athletes, they were serious about the business of education. Failure was not an option for them. And thankfully, I was beginning to mature and realize why I was in college. I managed to get the degree.

But after practice teaching, which I did very well, I realized that I really wasn't sold on being a teacher. But I wound up getting a job. They were hiring college grads at the Aberdeen Proving Grounds, a military installation in Maryland, and I was an ordnance instructor. I wound up interviewing and getting that job. But the job blew up on me. Instead of getting promoted from a GS-5 3670 to a GS-7, they closed the base in Alabama—the Redstone Arsenal—and the people with seniority came to Aberdeen, and they could bump you with their seniority in grade or experience. And instead of me going from a GS-5 to a GS-7, I wound up being a GS-1 at $3200. And I had just moved into my first apartment. My wife was still in school, and we had a kid.

So I left there after about eight, nine months, and I worked in recreation in Baltimore City for four years as a recreation leader. I loved working with kids doing arts and crafts classes. But I used to go to the post office from time to time and look at job announcements, and I saw a job opening at the Social Security Administration as an illustrator. I didn't know beans about Social Security. All I knew was that it was something that everybody wanted to get. But I didn't know anything about survivor's benefits and insurance and the whole nine yards. But essentially, they had an art department—visual graphics—because they had to disseminate all the material and information out to the general public about the administration and its services.

They did that with leaflets and brochures, booklets, training films. We did all the training aids that the agency required. In-house publications, table model exhibits. The whole business of doing layout and design for publications was a whole new experience for me. I got the job based on my portfolio from Morgan. My drawings and illustrations, and a little bit of cartooning. But I didn't know beans about layout design, typography, or dealing with printed matter. And I used to tell people that it was like getting paid to eat ice cream. I was learning something every day, and I stayed there for 29 years. I wound up being the Chief of Graphics when I left.

In 1960, working at any federal agency, for Blacks, was abominable. It was no chance for advancement. You weren't in management, upper levels, not even lower levels of supervision. In fact, people used to call the Social Security Administration—which the headquarters is in Baltimore . . . in Woodlawn, Maryland, a suburb of Baltimore—they used to call it "the plantation." But for me, because I had that experience at Aberdeen . . . and then I was an oddity, I wasn't in on the claims divisions and anywhere that you're dealing directly with the public, I was in the art department, you know. So when I got to meet people, they didn't have any problem. I'm in this art capacity job. They would ask for your grade, and when I said, "I'm GS-5," they would look at one another and whisper, "He's a 5? Him over there?" Meanwhile, they had 5s, 7s, 9s, 11s, 13s . . . but all Blacks were 2s and 3s. It wasn't until the '60s or the late '50s, when they really started pressing to get equal opportunity boards and bureaus, that Blacks began to move into management.

But overall, it was a great experience. I learned an awful lot, and I started doing actual cartoons on the job. And also, that's when I really started hitting the magazines as a freelance cartoonist. Of course, we had magazines that don't even exist now. *Collier's, Saturday Evening Post,* for example. They all ran cartoons. You would send a batch of cartoons out and they would send you a nicely worded rejection slip in the self-addressed stamped envelope that you furnished. I did sell a couple cartoons to *Playboy,* but when I hit *Ebony,* that was a comfort zone for me. I'm probably in most of the magazines you have because I was a regular on *Ebony's* Strictly for Laughs page.

I don't know if you've ever heard of a guy named Ray Billingsley. He's a Black cartoonist, and he's had a strip now in the mainstream press for 32 years. It's called *Curtis* and he's a little Black kid with his baseball cap backwards. He just won, I call it the Academy Award of cartoonists; the National Cartoonist Society awarded him the Reuben. In their 75-year existence, they never had a Black cartoonist win the Reuben Award, and Ray won it just recently.

I never had aspirations for wanting to do a strip because I had a nine-to-five. I didn't have that needed hustle in me because I had a really good job. It was just a sideline hustle. You know, I could keep my hands in the pie, and do cartoons and send them out. And then, *Players Magazine* came out. That was like the Black version of *Playboy,* even though it wasn't Black-owned. And I just stayed with that. I didn't think seriously about doing a strip until I retired in 1990. And it really scared the devil out of me because I sent this cartoon strip idea to a syndicate out in LA called Creators Syndicate. And they actually responded and told me to send them some more.

And that's what really scared me, because you've got to be really funny in the mainstream press, 365 days a year. I was scared to get it. And I finally heard from them, and they told me that it had nothing to do with the quality of the artwork, the penmanship, or the story ideas. They said they just didn't feel like they could market it at that time, because their salespeople have to go out and sell it to the newspapers. And so that didn't take off.

It dawned on me that you never saw the Black perspective or a Black point of view, a Black spin on global and national issues that impact the Black condition in America, in the mainstream press. On the editorial pages of mainstream press, the only time you saw Blacks in editorial cartoons, it was something negative or catastrophic. And I've been very critical of some of the cartoons I've seen even in Black newspapers. And that's when I came up with the idea of attempting to provide that service for Black newspapers. I've been doing it since '93 now.

There was never any conflict when I was working at the SSA and doing my illustrations on the side because that was on my own time, even though I was using their materials. I didn't have to buy any ink or brushes, but no, there was never any conflict. Matter of fact, they wrote me up in the in-house paper a couple of times. They wrote about my work. Johnson Publishing, who published *Ebony*, not only did they do *Jet*, but years ago they had something called *Negro Digest*. It was a spin off from *Reader's Digest*. Same size, same kind of format, but later that became *Black World*. Between *Black World* and *Ebony*, a couple of sales here and there, I was cool. Handling a strip at that time would have been difficult because that's a time-consuming job. And I liked to hang out in the clubs and the bars, and in the cabaret parties to socialize, you know? But essentially, that's how I evolved with regard to cartooning.

What was it like when you saw a magazine that had your cartoon in it for the first time?

Oh, that was sheer euphoria. Yeah, I'm pretty certain that was the first illustration that I did for *Ebony*.

There was a strip that was almost like a Black version of *Peanuts*, but it was called *Wee Pals*. *Wee Pals* by Morrie Turner. And it was an integrated group of kids. Black, Hispanic, Asian. And it took me a while to realize it, but after Morrie broke that ceiling with *Wee Pals*, a couple more strips came along. One was called *Luther*, and one was called *Quincy*. But it never dawned on me until years later that, while the syndication had opened up to Black cartoonists—because the door had been shut for years—they were reluctant to deal with adult scenarios. All these three strips I just named: *Quincy, Wee Pals*, and *Luther*, they were all for kids. They were all about children. And like I said, they paved the way. And you didn't have another break-through until years later with a guy named Aaron McGruder. He did a strip called *Boondocks*.

He lived in Columbia, Maryland. And he really was the first one to come hard with a narrative regarding social justice, racism, and the like. In fact he had, at that time, one of the biggest intros into the cartoon market of anybody. I think he came in with, like, I don't know how many hundred newspapers. But he was so controversial given certain areas, that sometimes they wouldn't print some of his cartoons given the subject matter that he had chosen for that particular day. But that's a big gap between McGruder and those earlier people that I mentioned.

Black cartoonists have been in that box for years with regard to mainstream press. And the irony of it is that one of the all-time greats in cartooning was a Black man, even though he passed as a white man. George Herriman. He did *Krazy Kat* back in 1910. He was from New Orleans, where that's not uncommon, you know. Mixed heritage of Blacks and whites, and people who can pass. But his name was George Herriman. And William Randolph Hearst, who owned just about every paper in the country, was a big fan. And Herriman just took off with

Krazy Kat. But he was a brother, though, even though he didn't live as a brother. He passed as a white man.

When I was coming along, all my cartoon heroes were white. My first two major heroes were Milton Caniff, who drew *Terry and the Pirates* and *Steve Canyon*, and then Will Eisner, who drew the *Spirit*. And he had a little Black sidekick kid called Ebony. But when I moved to Philadelphia, I saw every Black paper in Philadelphia. The *Philadelphia Afro-American*. Saw the *Pittsburgh Courier*, which is one of my clients now. They started with me in '93. And the *Philadelphia Tribune*. And it was in the *Courier* that I discovered my first Black cartoon heroes. Jackie Ormes, not only Black but a female, and then a guy named Ollie Harrington, who did a single panel strip called *Bootsie*. And, in fact, Harrington left his whole collection to Ohio State's comic archive. So I've been a cartoon buff forever, it seems.

Going back to some of the other cartoonists' work, you said that it seemed to be more of a market for kids, but not adults. Why do you think that was?

I think they didn't want to deal with anything that heavy. With the focus on young people, little kids and whatnot, it's more frolic and joy and fun. It's full of all kinds of crazy things kids are known to do, and, you know, parents, kids, relationships, sports, and all that. But when you get into adults, I always figured that they were scared of a cartoonist like Aaron McGruder. Somebody who brought it right down to the wire and exposed all the hypocrisy. And I don't think they were ready for it years ago, I really don't. Even today, I get the *Baltimore Sun* and the *Washington Post*. There are 43 or 44 comic strips in the *Washington Post*. Only two of them are Black. The *Baltimore Sun* has 22 comic strips. Only one of them is Black.

So we've been knocking. We've cracked the door, but we still trying to make ourselves known. And right now is not the best time because so many papers are failing. And the Black press has always been struggling from day one. I mean, Black or white, it's never about paper sales. It's about the advertising dollars. You know what I mean? And Black papers have always been struggling. But there's almost I think 185 or 190 Black newspapers that still exist—even though a lot of them are online now. And in better days, all Black papers used to come out at least twice a week, Tuesdays and Fridays. Generally, I know the Baltimore *Afro* used to come out twice a week, and the Philadelphia *Afro* came out twice a week. But now all Black papers, all my papers, they can only come out once a week.

It's a tough time now to aspire, perhaps, to be a comic strip artist in print. But there are certain other platforms that you can probably go to. I'm so far behind on what's going on there. I'm still technologically challenged. But there's a lot of stuff going on online with cartoons. There's a woman named Barbara Brandon. You remember some years ago there was a Black female cartoonist in mainstream press, and it was just talking heads where they were all Black women?

Where I'm Coming From, I think it was called, by Barbara Brandon. Her father was one of the creators of one of those children's strips that I mentioned earlier. Brumsic Brandon was the creator of *Luther*. And a guy named Ted Shearer was the creator of the strip called *Quincy*. Yeah. And, of course, Ray Billingsley did *Curtis*. But Barbara Brandon was exposed to cartooning all her young life because she used to help her dad with his strip *Luther*. And then she had some drawing skills. And for a while, for years, she was in mainstream press with these talking heads, all Black women, called *Where I'm Coming From*.

Right now, I'm thinking about giving it up. My eyesight is not what it used to be. Hand–eye coordination is pretty good. But I don't know whether I'm burnt out or what, but I'm really getting pissed off more than I used to. Because at 89, I'm just sick of trickle-down citizenship. We've been doing this stuff ever since I've been on this earth. Dealing with the establishment, and the oppression that we've received over the years, and the indignities that we've suffered in life.

I have a problem with the N word. I don't use it anymore. Like everybody else, I used to use it. And I stopped using it years ago, when my oldest son told me that he didn't use it. And I'd never thought about it before. But he got me to thinking about it. And it finally dawned on me not too long after that conversation. Something I read had to do

One of Walt's recent political cartoons, "Pipeline." Or as he calls them, "CARRtoons"!

with lynching. And then I really thought about it. What do you think was one of the last words a Black man, woman, or child heard ringing in their ears just before their lives were snuffed out by a lynching party? By some crazy white folks? It was that word.

So to call somebody that you love that word . . . that's not a term of endearment to me. It really isn't. Several people I know say they stopped using it. Thinking about before you're getting held off that bridge, or getting hung from that tree, those are the last words you hear, that you'll be taking to your Maker, and it's ringing in your ear, the N word. So that's my take on it. I don't use it.

It will occasionally get dropped among my buddies. And when the occasion presents itself, I'll take the lead and say something about why I stopped, hoping that I'm leaving something on their mind to think about as they actually digest what I've just said. And then white folks will invariably say, "Well, they use it. Why can't we use it?" You know, we shouldn't be using it. They definitely can't use it, but we shouldn't be using it either. That's not for me. My son was the first one to pull me up, and I'm glad he did. Glad he did.

I've been a cartoonist for over six decades. That's another reason why I'm tired right now! I'm reading newspapers diligently, and I'm always trying to come up with ideas. What I do is I send two or more cartoons out every week because I want to get them out of my mind, out of my head, and onto paper. And then I give them the option. Except for this one paper in Wilmington, North Carolina, whose editorial is laid out for two cartoons. And every week, they've got two. But most papers only want one.

Every once in a while, the *Pittsburgh Courier* will want them a sports cartoon. Because the *Courier* has always been big in sports coverage. The *Pittsburgh Courier* will run the editorial cartoon on the editorial page, and they might, if they have space, run something they particularly like, usually on the sports page, particularly if it's sports subject matter. And that is the paper who I'm close to now. I used to sell it as a kid in Philadelphia. And a lot of people don't know that prior to the elaborate draft programs they have now in the NFL, with all the coverage on ESPN and all the major networks, every year from the '40s up through perhaps the early '60s the *Pittsburgh Courier* used to feature an all-American HBCU team at the end of the season. The outstanding all-Americans from Black colleges. As a matter of fact, my only claim to fame when it comes to football is that I played with a guy named Roosevelt Brown from Charlottesville, Virginia. He was inducted to the NFL Hall of Fame. He was a starting left tackle for the New York Giants about 12 or 13 seasons. I love to tell this story because, like I said, the draft was not as sophisticated as today, with all the TV coverage and hoopla. The franchises used to meet when they were going to draft and they would have film, tapes, scouting reports, telegrams, newspaper clippings, what have you. And on the table one day back in 1953 or '54, there was a *Pittsburgh Courier* lying on the table. And Roosevelt Brown was all-CIAA. He'd been all-CIAA two years in a row, and 6⊠ 4⊠, 240 max. And they took a flyer on him and they drafted him. And as raw as he was, they realized once he got to camp that they had a jewel. And he was a star on that line through all their glory years, from that point until he retired. But it was in a Black newspaper, the *Pittsburgh Courier.* Yeah.

How did you deal with critics of your work throughout the years?

Actually, because of my subject matter and my audience, I haven't read any real critics. I'm usually applauded or people appreciate the things that I'm displaying in my illustrations, my visual images and whatnot, and any themes and ideas that align with it. Though something happened recently. Somehow some white guy got my email address and I forgot what he said. But it was disparaging. Either he had run across some of my stuff, or it might have been after that article appeared where I was interviewed. I think it happened after that. And I'm just wondering how he got to see some of my cartoons, because the only way you see my cartoons now is in a Black newspaper. And they were all political. Whereas my cartoons with *Ebony, Jet,* and *Black World* were all gag cartoons, you know, just general gag cartoons.

But I didn't start doing the editorial or political cartoons until '93. But he must have seen something that I did somewhere. I've actually had one cartoon published in the *Washington Post.* A guy named Courtland Milloy was writing for the *Washington Post* for years. Every Wednesday, he has a column in the *Washington Post.* He did a really nice interview with me, and it appeared in the *Washington Post.* And shortly after that, I got a cartoon published in the *Post,* because their staff cartoonists had just recently retired. Today, they are still running different cartoonists, although there is one guy who appears there quite a bit.

They are probably going to keep it this way because a lot of papers have gotten rid of their staff cartoonists and they mine from a consortium of cartoonists because it's cheaper to hire freelancers. And since this guy Toles retired, they have been taking freelance work coming in. And I haven't sold anything since that one that appeared after my article appeared in the *Post*. But today, I sent out cartoons about HBCUs, you know, being threatened with bomb threats this week.

I borrowed something that my president, President Wilson at Morgan, said in an email he sent out to everybody. He just simply said, "Stay strong, and remain resilient." So I had that on a sign and a comment with a kid saying, "Black Minds Matter." And I had about eight or nine different colleges, you know, kids from Spelman, Howard, Morgan, and so on. And they were talking to people who were obviously extremists on the right: Ku Klux Klan, skinheads. And these kids were letting them know that we're standing tall and we will not be moved. I just sent that in today.

So most of my audience is Black, and everybody has been in tune. I've been doing this for 29 years, the political cartooning. Now, Black papers only come out once a week, so I've only got 52 shots. And so, some time ago, even before he left office, I said, you know, I can't spend a lot of time fooling with Trump when we got so many issues in the Black community to deal with. And so I'm trying not to get caught up in that, and focus on stuff that we need to talk about.

Sometimes, I have to put the brakes on myself with regard to how harsh I can be because of the audience, the viewership.

I'm also one of the founding members of the 100 Black Men of America, the Maryland chapter. I was one of the charter members for the Maryland chapter. And we try to reach out. And that's what I liked about working in recreation. We couldn't save everybody. But we saved a lot of kids through recreation. I mean, Baltimore's recreation centers are a third of what they used to be. And I think that's one of the biggest pitfalls in most cities: they don't invest in our young people. They can find money for a new youth detention center, but they can't find money for a recreation center?

One of my biggest complaints all over the country is we don't invest in our youth. The cover of my book says it all. *Just Us*. I used the term "the storm continues." That's a term taken from Frederick Douglass. But *Just Us* is a play on the word justice. But also, Richard Pryor in one of his LPs years ago, when he got locked up and went to jail, he said, "That's all that was in there behind bars. Just *us*." Where's the justice in that?

But right now I'm just trying to come up with how I can end this whole thing in a dignified manner, let these people know ahead of time if I have any leads who can take my place. But I'm still wedded to doing it as best I can for as long as I can. I get ahead of myself sometimes to the point where, something that was hot last week and I did a cartoon, something else came up . . . and you only got that one shot, because they only come up once a week. And I've had cartoons back up on me to the point where the relevancy of them has passed, because it happened two weeks ago.

Right now, I'm also wrestling with the idea of a second book, because I had over 1200 cartoons to select from when I did this two years ago. I've been talking about a second book, and I use a local printer, the printer who printed my father's *Nitelifer*. I have a great relationship with Time Printers in Baltimore—it's a family, the Maddox family. In fact, Alby, the CEO and president, he just retired and went with a publishing company in Baltimore. He said he wanted to try some new things.

The title will be *Ain't Jingling My Keys No More*. Years ago, whenever I was leaving a strip mall or commercial mall in the evening, and I was going to the parking lot to my car, and a white woman happened to be near me going to her car, I could see that apprehension on her face. I would see that apprehension and clutching at the purse tightly and whatnot. And I used to just jingle my keys, just to put her at ease. I'm not worried about you or your pocketbook or whatever it is. But then, and I think this whole Karen thing had something to do with it, I realized that it's not my responsibility to make you feel comfortable.

So I came up with a name that was catchy: *Ain't Jingling My Keys No More*. And of course, I have an illustration of, you know, a Black guy with keys, and a white woman, both heading to their cars in the parking lot. I've got cartoons up the ying-yang. It consumes you. When I go to bed at night, I'm usually looking at the news and trying to think of something. Then, I read two newspapers every day. And when I wake up in the morning, I'm laying there for another half hour or 40 minutes trying to think of a cartoon idea or something I'm trying to tie together.

I've got these pads all over the place, and the other day, I just grabbed a bunch of them and sat down and just weeded them out. Got very critical of them. Some of them, I toss. I'm pretty certain that I'm going to stop some time this year. I'm going to stop. I always kid that doing political cartoons has kept me from going upside some white man's head with an alley apple—a brick. I can always vent out my frustrations with racists and racism with visual images.

Did you ever experience any racially motivated violence?

My grandparents were from Eastern Shore Maryland, like I said, and that's like, being in Jackson, Mississippi, or Montgomery, Alabama, back in the day. My Uncle Frank had done some work for a white man, and there was a dispute over his pay. And while he and the guy were arguing about the pay, the guy's son showed up. And him being a Black man at Eastern Shore—now Uncle Frank wasn't that big, but he didn't take no guff. And the guy put his hands on him and pushed Uncle Frank or something, and he wound up beating both of them up. And of course, when my relatives found out, they had to hide him. Because they had heard about what happened and found out that white folks were looking for him. And that ferryboat that I mentioned, they couldn't put him on a ferry to get into Baltimore. So they had to drive him through Delaware, up from the Eastern Shore, up through Delaware to come down to Maryland. And he moved to Baltimore permanently. They had to get him out of the Eastern Shore.

I'm not sure what type of work he was doing, but I'm sure it was some type of labor. I don't know, farm work, might have been involved with the waterfront, you know, crabs and seafood, whatnot. I don't know. It was in the '20s . . . '28 or '29. I was born in '32. They just knew they had to get him out of that area. But that was a very volatile situation for him to be in. For a Black man to be beating up a white man, two of them, at that time.

What was it like when Baltimore was actually integrated?

It was slow. I remember . . . having lived in Philadelphia, I knew what a real amusement park looked like. There's an amusement park called Woodside Park. Had all the major rides, roller coasters, you name it. It was integrated, of course. But there was an amusement park in Baltimore that, in the '60s, CORE and some activists from Social Security—they had some activist groups—they picketed this amusement park. A friend of mine, Mason, he actually got hit in the head with a brick. He worked for Social Security, and I remember he had a patch over one eye. It had turned into a brawl this one particular day. And there were demonstrations because of the restaurants and hotels and the whole nine yards. But the reason I bring up the amusement park is, having been exposed to a real honest-to-God amusement park, like you would you see at Coney Island or somewhere else, when we were finally allowed into this amusement park, it was a dump! I mean, we couldn't believe it. I kept on thinking about Mason getting hit in the head, what he and the others went through to get us permission to come to this amusement park. And it was a dump.

We had a dance, and we decided to have it at this amusement park. And we rented their ballroom, which was called the Dixie Ballroom. And I think that's the first time I really got a chance to see the place. And it really just ticked me off that they wanted to keep us out of this raggedy, rundown place because we were Black. And it wasn't even a first-rate amusement park. And eventually, a big flood came through here one time and the body of water that bordered the amusement park flooded. So they actually ended up tearing it down.

But the restaurants, you know, I remember you couldn't go into the restaurants. I know there was a delicatessen called Nate's, Jewish-owned, on the main drag in Baltimore. And that was a big deal when they started letting us go in. Then, the movie houses opened up downtown. But one of the biggest catastrophes as far as Baltimore is concerned with recreation. . . . So there's the Apollo in Harlem, right? There's the Howard Theatre in DC. Well, in Baltimore, it was the Royal Theatre. And they really dropped the ball and they let them tear down the Royal Theatre. Because the theater was a part of that Chitlin' Circuit. Motortown Revue, and all the Black acts that used to come through the Howard Theatre in DC, the Regal in Chicago, the Apollo in New York, and Earl Theatre when I was in high school in Philadelphia. But they tore that place down, and they tried to placate the Black community by erecting a big statue of Billie Holiday. But that should have never happened.

There's another old theater in Baltimore called Hippodrome, which was segregated, of course. It was for whites only for a long time. Well, guess what? They didn't tear the Hippodrome down. But they tore down the Royal. That should have never happened in Baltimore.

Being a bachelor for a while, when I went to the movies, going to the Black movies, I knew I could get my dinner in there because they sold hot dogs. When things integrated, and my girlfriend at the time wanted to go to the Hippodrome, my only problem with going into this previously all-white theater was that I didn't know whether they sold hot dogs or not! But when we went, it was a Black ticket-seller and Black ticket-takers, and they sold hot dogs.

But there wasn't a lot of controversy about admissions to the restaurant and the movie houses once integration did come, back in the '60s. But you still deal with those situations where racism is so deeply embedded that even things that have been halted on a large scale, in a more subtle way, you still see it.

That's the way I've seen it since I've been in Baltimore. I didn't go back to Philadelphia when I graduated from Morgan State. I was born and raised here—I only really had a straight five-year window in Philly from the 7th grade to the 12th grade. So, I stayed in Baltimore, and I've seen the growth and the change, and the resistance. The community I live in now is one of those planned communities in Columbia, Maryland. The whole mindset of the developer was inclusion. That's what Columbia is all about, and I've been here since '44. I've been here practically half my life. Here in Columbia, Maryland. It's about an 18-minute drive to Baltimore. 15 minutes if you're riding with my wife!

What are your thoughts on integration as a whole?

Well, actually, integration had its pluses and minuses. Now, when it came to business, once we could live anywhere, or go anywhere, stay in hotels anywhere, and all that, Black businesses took a hit. No question about that. I'm also an aficionado of tap dancing. My uncle was a tap dancer, and I tap. There was a tap dancer named Peg Leg Bates, and he had a resort up in New York, upstate New York, and you couldn't get in there to save your life. I mean, the place stayed packed! Buses from all over the East Coast—from New York in particular. But once we discovered Atlantic City and other outlets where we could go, it went under.

And that's happened to a lot of businesses in the Black community. Once integration happened, we abandoned a lot of places. And that did hurt. If separate but equal had really worked, there wouldn't have been a need for integration really. When I was living in Baltimore, all up through high school, every textbook I ever saw came from the all white schools. I didn't notice it until I was in junior high school. We got hand-me-downs—everything was hand-me-downs. And so, it affected every aspect of Black life. Social, education, and even today, one of the biggest problems in most Black communities is healthcare access. And access to high quality food. You know, you have food deserts. Black people when they go to supermarket, if they don't have a car, they got to take a streetcar to go to a supermarket, because there are no big giant supermarkets in most Black areas.

The inequity and sentencing—harsh sentences get dealt out to Black defendants as opposed to white defendants, for the same crime. There's no addressing reentry into society after you've served your time. And your penalties for having been to jail. I mean, you've served your time, paid your debt, and you may have gotten your associate degree while in college, or taken some college courses. You've seen the light, so to speak—you had to rehabilitate yourself. And when you get out, you may think, I'm gonna go to school, I'm gonna take some courses. But guess what? When they get out, they're a convicted felon. They cannot get a student loan. And when you go to get that job, and you fill out those boxes on an application, you have to answer whether you have ever been convicted of a felony? You can lie and say no, get the job, and they find out. So you get fired. Or you can be honest and say yes. And that means you're definitely not gonna get the job.

You can't get housing, public housing. There are just so many things stacked against us. And with regard to police, this whole business about police reform, the left really mishandled that when they first started talking about it. Because early on, when they were talking about defunding the police, what should have appeared in the article was not necessarily defunding the police, but transferring those funds towards some responsibilities that police shouldn't even be dealing with. And that got lost somewhere. For instance, the police shouldn't be dealing with the homeless, they should not be dealing with mental health situations, and things like that. You should not send a gun to a domestic situation. It's going to escalate it.

I mean, there are so many things, and we *all* got to take steps, including Black folks. I did a cartoon that had something to do with this guy. You know, he was making money, and he said he was tired of selling balloons, candles, and teddy bears. Because every time you turn around, we're attending vigils, one after the other, each week, for people getting shot. Kids getting mistakenly killed, and what have you.

And then the police. Why can't there be a committed effort to have a national database so that an officer can't kill somebody in one town, and go get a job in another town? You can have an officer who's been on the force for 19 years, and has got like 14 civil complaints about him overstepping the boundaries when engaging with the public, brutality and whatnot. And they assess the situation. And they make the determination that this guy is unfit to be on the force. And they rightfully fire him. Good. That's good leadership. But the same cat shouldn't be able to drive 26 miles down the road to the next township and get a job as a cop! He couldn't do that if they had a national database.

Do you believe that Dr. King's dream is actually possible in this country?

Well, you know, that's why I'm ticked off so much right now. I'm so tired. And we done prayed on it, we've done every march. I guess it gets better over spans, but

we keep going back to sleep. I mentioned something about trickle-down citizenship early on. It seems that it's always going to be something catastrophic, Emmett Till or George Floyd, and then we have riots afterwards. And then you get a lot of hoopla and cries from leadership, and something is passed, another bill, and then we go back to sleep. That's why I love that term "woke." Because you got to be woke. They want you to go back to sleep.

And the thing that really ticks me off is . . . because I do editorial cartoons now, I have to watch Fox News. I've got to dial in once a while and see what those fools are saying on One America News and Newsmax, because they all vying for the same viewership. And I call it the race to the bottom, because they're all lies, all conspiracies. And I'm at a point now where there's anger whenever I hear something, or see something, or something is revealed to me. And I don't like that idea of dealing with it. It's because I've been dealing with it for so long. I've seen it for so long. And you can legislate all you want, but won't do any good until you change some hearts. That's what's got to be changed. Some hearts.

And this whole business about critical race theory. My take on it, first of all, is it's not being taught in school. It is not being taught. But what they also don't want is for you to go too deep into history. Pure and simple. They're afraid that white kids are going to feel guilty. I don't want white kids to feel guilty. That's not the goal, I don't think. It's actually to make you a critical thinker, and to make you critical of history. What they're afraid of is that white kids will come to realize what their forefathers—their grandfathers, and great-grandfathers—were capable of. All the evil, heinous things that they did. That's what they're trying to shield from these white kids.

I don't want these kids to feel guilty. I do want them to understand that they are the beneficiaries of white supremacy and white entitlement. This one guy that sits next to me in the gym is from Missouri. He's Jewish. He said he didn't know any Black people until he mentioned a guy named George Lyle or something [author's note: Garry Lyle], who went to George Washington University, where he went. And I remember the guy's name because he played safety for the Chicago Bears. He didn't know any Black people. He sits next to me on a bike in the gym quite often. In fact, sometimes I get a little tired of talking at length to him about anything dealing with politics. But I told him, "You might not be aware of it, but you live in an all-white Jewish community, right? Well, that was orchestrated by the housing situation, you know, redlining of prospective Black buyers." He was not going to be steered into your community by a realtor. That's just what it is. Well, he nodded. I mean, he knew I was telling the truth. There was no chance that a Black family was going to be able to buy in that area. We were all shoved into one area.

Even now, when it comes to urban renewal, it actually is urban removal. And wherever there are landfills, you better believe that the first community nearest that landfill is a Black community. When they decide to cut a swath of land to build a freeway or something, it's going to border a Black community. That's another reason why we got to vote. Not only do you vote, but once your candidate is fortunate enough to win, you gotta hold their feet to the fire. Because without it, we will stay marginalized. We gotta step up and take charge and control.

And the sisters, I've got the utmost confidence in them. The sisters are on the front lines for the Black community every day. A lot of brothers out there today have to do better. What happened in Georgia, with Warnock's win, wouldn't have never happened without Black women. They grab it by the throat, and they're committed. Nothing but respect for Black women. Love them to death, they're solid.

But Black men scare me when it comes to politics. They really do. Your vote is important. Essential. That's the word to use for it. If you can find a reason to do everything else in the world, you need to drag yourself to the registration, get to the polls, and vote. When it comes to Martin Luther King's dream, I'm like Fannie Lou Hamer. I'm sick and tired of being sick and tired. And it's beginning to weigh on me. I've been dealing with this now for a long time. I'm just exhausted, I guess, is the best way to put it.

But I'm going to stop the political cartoons. And I don't know what I'm gonna do. I said I'm gonna get back to some other work. I have got several unfinished paintings and maybe I'll find some other artistic outlets, like dealing with pastels.

I'm still doodling now sitting watching TV. Got pads around the house. On the nightstand, on the coffee table, I've got a pad everywhere that I can use to write down some ideas. I sent out three cartoons today. The one about historically Black colleges, I sent that to the *Post*. So maybe I'll get a shot at getting that one published. I just did a podcast with Richard Prince, a podcast featuring cartoonists of color. It was very, very interesting and well done. And it's the first time I've been able to sit down with other cartoonists since 2020. I put together a little symposium about Black cartoonists at the Baltimore Museum of Art. And I had Ray Billingsley there and other talented people. So I still enjoy it. But I think I'm going to slow down soon.

ACKNOWLEDGMENTS

I would like to thank each person who entrusted me with their story for inclusion in this collection. The lessons, vulnerability, humor, and truths that you all shared will touch many, and I'm so grateful for your openness. I will always treasure the time I've spent with each of you, and I look forward to many years of blessed fellowship to come!

To my family, the Averys, the Watsons, and the Moores, and to my extended family, those from Hill Street Baptist Church and the Black Asheville community, I thank God for your love and support. To my friends who have become family, and my Sorors in Delta Sigma Theta Sorority, Inc., I am endlessly grateful for you.

Special thanks to Terrell, Kyla, Skylar, and Andrea for so often being my first readers. Thank you for always being willing to carve out time to examine my work with a critical, loving eye. It means more than you know!

Much gratitude to my editor, Nick Thomas. From our very first conversation, we built a rapport over our shared love of African American history and uplifting marginalized voices. Your thoughtful guidance and expertise helped bring this book to life in ways that I never imagined. Thank you for seeing the vision from the beginning.

Thanks to everyone at Levine Querido for putting beautiful, thoughtful books out into the world. It's an honor to have *Those Who Saw the Sun* be part of such an amazing catalog.

Finally, thanks to Dr. Alfred Brophy, a great professor and mentor, for always seeing the potential in my writing, and helping me to grow as an author and historian.

APPENDIX

100 Black Men of America—an African American men's civic organization and service club, founded in 1963, whose stated goal is to educate and empower African American children and teens; their motto is, "What They See Is What They'll Be."

1921 Tulsa Race Massacre—a two-day-long attack on the Greenwood District in Tulsa, OK, a community known at that time as the "Black Wall Street" and one of the wealthiest African American communities in America.

40 Acres and a Mule—a wartime order proclaimed by Union General William Tecumseh Sherman during the Civil War promising land to freed families, which created the widespread expectation they would have the right to own the land they had been forced to work as enslaved people; under President Andrew Jackson the government reneged on this promise and others.

Aaron McGruder (b. 1974)—writer, cartoonist, and producer best known for creating *The Boondocks*, a comic strip and TV series.

Abraham Lincoln (1809-1865)—16th U.S. president from 1861-1865; leader of the Union during the Civil War.

Absalom Jones (1746-1818)—a prominent abolitionist and clergyman in Philadelphia, PA; founder of the first Black Episcopal congregation and the first African American to be ordained as a priest in the Episcopal Church.

Adam Clayton Powell, Jr. (1908-1972)—pastor, activist, and U.S. Representative for Harlem, NY, from 1945-1971; the first African American to be elected to Congress from New York, as well as the first from a Northeast state.

Affordable Care Act (2010)—an overhaul and expansion of the U.S. healthcare system, designed to provide coverage to more people, lower costs, and improve quality; colloquially known as Obamacare.

African Methodist Episcopal Church (AME)—a predominantly African American Methodist denomination, and the first independent Protestant denomination to be founded (led by Richard Allen in 1816) by Black people; to this day remains one of the largest Methodist denominations in the world.

The Afro-American—a newspaper group founded in 1892 by John H. Murphy, Sr., a formerly enslaved man, which at one time published in 13 different editions across the country (including Baltimore, Washington, DC, Philadelphia, Richmond, and Newark) and continues to this day.

Afro-American Association—an organization founded in 1962 at UC Berkeley, originally as a study group, which was hugely influential for the Black Power movement; Huey P. Newton and Bobby Seale were both members.

Al Green (b. 1946)—singer, songwriter, pastor, and record producer.

Alamo Theatre—a theatre in the Farish Street District in Jackson, MS, which was a neighborhood known as the Black Mecca of Mississippi before desegregation.

Alice Walker (b. 1944)—Pulitzer Prize-winning writer and social activist; author of *The Color Purple*.

Alvin Ailey (1931-1989)—dancer, director, choreographer, and activist who, together with a group of young African American modern dancers, founded the Alvin Ailey American Dance Theater and later School in New York City; one of the most influential figures in 20th-century modern dance.

Amsterdam News—a weekly Black-owned newspaper based in Harlem and serving New York City, founded in 1909 by James H. Anderson.

Andrew Jackson (1767-1845)—7th U.S. President from 1829-1837; slaveholder.

Anita Hill (b. 1956)—lawyer, educator, and author, and professor at Brandeis University; she became a national figure in 1991 when she accused then-U.S. Supreme Court nominee Clarence Thomas, her former boss at the U.S. Department of Education's Office for Civil Rights, of sexual harassment.

Apollo Theater—music hall and performance venue for African American performers in Harlem, NY; first opened in 1913.

ASCORE (Ashville Student Commission on Racial Equality)—an organization founded by Civil Rights leaders in Asheville, in 1960, to push for the integration of public spaces and better jobs for Black people in Western NC. [Author's note: My grandfather, Rev. Nilous Avery, was an advisor and mentor for ASCORE, opening the doors of Hill Street Baptist Church for the students to meet.]

Atlanta Daily World—the oldest Black newspaper in Atlanta, GA and the first Black daily newspaper; founded in 1928.

Baptist—one of the most prominent branches of Protestant Christianity; characterized by only baptizing professing believers, with complete immersion, as well as a broad diversity of belief between churches.

Barbara Brandon-Croft (b. 1958)—cartoonist best known for *Where I'm Coming From*, the first national syndicated strip from an African American female cartoonist; daughter of Brumsic Brandon, Jr.

Billie Holiday (1915-1959)—jazz and swing singer.

Billy Graham (1918-2018)—white evangelist and Southern Baptist minister; he insisted on racial integration for his revivals and crusades starting in 1953.

The Birth of a Nation—a 1915 silent film about the Civil War and Reconstruction, noted for its technical innovations, historical inaccuracies, and racist depictions of Black people; enormously popular with white audiences upon release, it is credited with inspiring the rebirth of the Ku Klux Klan.

Black Belt—a region of dark, fertile soil in the South, mostly Alabama and Mississippi; has also been used to describe areas of the South with a majority Black population.

Black Church—the faith and body of Christian congregations and denominations, primarily Protestant, which minister predominantly to African Americans. There are various denominations, including Baptist, African Methodist Episcopal, and Pentecostal, but most Black churches follow Black Liberation Theology doctrine. Rooted in activism, Black Liberation Theology aims to empower churchgoers, and make the gospel relevant to the struggles of African Americans.

Black Codes—restrictive laws which governed the conduct of African Americans both before and after the Civil War.

Black Greek letter organizations—historical African American fraternities and sororities, known collectively as the Divine Nine, and the National Pan-Hellenic Council; the Nine consist of Alpha Phi Alpha Fraternity (founded 1906, Cornell University); Alpha Kappa Alpha Sorority (1908, Howard University); Kappa Alpha Psi Fraternity (1911, Indiana University); Omega Psi Phi (1911, Howard University); Delta Sigma Theta Sorority (1913, Howard University); Phi Beta Sigma Fraternity (1914, Howard University); Zeta Phi Beta Sorority (1920, Howard University); Sigma Gamma Rho Sorority (1922, Butler University); and Iota Phi Theta Fraternity (1963, Morgan State University)

Black Panther Party—a widely popular and influential Black Power political organization in the late 1960s and early 70s, founded by Huey P. Newton and Bobby Seale in Oakland, CA in 1966.

Black Power—a movement that began in the early 1960s and which advocated for Black pride, economic independence, and new social and cultural institutions for Black people, which did not necessarily seek to integrate with white society.

Bloody Sunday—the first of three Civil Rights marches in 1965 along the highway from Selma, AL, to the state capital of Montgomery, with the aim of demonstrating the desire of African American citizens to exercise their constitutional right to vote; the march was assaulted by Alabama state police officers, drawing national attention and outrage, and helping lead to the passage of the Voting Rights Act later that year.

Booker T. Washington (1856-1915)—educator, author, speaker, and advisor to several U.S. presidents; born into slavery, he became a leading intellectual of his time, and founded the Tuskegee Normal and Industrial Institute (now Tuskegee University) and the National Negro Business League; in contrast to W.E.B. Du Bois, he advocated for agricultural and technical education and self-help, racial solidarity, and relative accommodation with the white majority.

Brown v. Board of Education of Topeka (1954)— U.S. Supreme Court decision that ruled racial segregation of children in public schools was unconstitutional; helped establish the precedent of the illegality of the "separate but equal" doctrine.

Brumsic Brandon, Jr. (1927-2014)—educator, artist, essayist, and civil rights activist who created comic strips for over six decades, most famously *Luther*, one of the earliest mainstream comics to star an African American character; father of Barbara Brandon-Croft.

Bud Biliken Parade—an annual public procession in Chicago, IL, at the end of summer, begun in 1929 by Robert S. Abbot, founder of the *Chicago Defender*; the largest African American parade in the U.S.

Bull Connor (1897-1973)—politician and white supremacist who served as Commissioner of Public Safety for Birmingham, AL, for more than two decades; most infamous for using fire hoses and attack dogs against civil rights activists.

Cain and Abel—in the Book of Genesis in the Bible, the first two sons of Adam and Eve; when God favors Abel instead of Cain, Cain murders Abel, and God condemns Cain to a life of exile.

Carnegie Hall—concert venue in Midtown Manhattan, opened in 1891.

Charlottesville Unite the Right rally—a white supremacist rally that took place in Charlottesville, VA, in August 2017.

Chattel slavery—the form of slavery where enslaved people are the personal property of their owners and may be bought, sold, and owned forever; the form of slavery practiced on Black people in America.

Chicago Defender—an African American newspaper founded in 1905; from 1956-2003 published daily as the *Chicago Daily Defender*.

Chitlin' Circuit—a group of performance venues in the East, South, and Midwest for African American musicians, comedians, and other performers during the era of racial segregation; venues included the Regal in Chicago, the Royal in Baltimore, the Howard in DC, the Apollo in Harlem, and others.

Civil Rights Act (1964)—a civil rights and labor law which outlawed discrimination based on race, color, religion, sex, national origin, and later sexual orientation and gender identity; one of the primary achievements of the Civil Rights Movement.

Civil Rights Movement—the movement in the 1950s and 60s, preceded by similar campaigns in previous decades, by African Americans and allies to end legalized racial discrimination, disenfranchisement, and racial segregation in the U.S.

Civil War—the war fought from 1861-1865 between the Union (the North) and the Confederacy (the South); the central cause of the war was slavery, and the dispute of its expansion into new western states, leading to more slave states, or its prevention from doing so, which was widely believed would eventually extinguish slavery.

Clarence Thomas (b. 1948)—longest-serving current Supreme Court justice and the second African American to serve on the Court; an originalist and considered to be the Court's most conservative member.

Clark Atlanta University—an HBCU in Atlanta, GA, formed with the consolidation of Atlanta University (founded in 1865 by the American Missionary Association, and the nation's first institution to award graduate degrees to African Americans) and Clark College (founded in 1869, and the

nation's first four-year liberal arts college to serve a primarily African American
student population).

Clinton, Mississippi Riot (1875)—a riot started during a political rally for Charles Caldwell, a formerly enslaved person and Republican state
senator, which resulted in the deaths of at least four white people and five Black
people but which was followed by vigilante violence against more Black people
in the ensuing days, resulting in the deaths of at least 50 African Americans; the
riot served as a pretext for the end of Reconstruction in Mississippi.

Colored—racial descriptor used in the U.S. during the Jim Crow era to refer
to an African American.

Communism—a form of socialism whose goal is a society with common
ownership of the means of production and the absence of social classes, money,
and state.

Community Reinvestment Act (CRA)—a federal law
enacted in 1977 that requires the Federal Reserve and other federal banking
regulators to encourage commercial banks and savings associations to help
meet the credit needs of all segments of their communities, including low- and
moderate-income neighborhoods; was designed to curb redlining.

Congress of Racial Equality (CORE)—a civil rights organization founded in 1942 by an interracial group of students in Chicago, IL;
pioneered the use of nonviolent direct action and played a pivotal role in the
Civil Rights Movement.

Cross burning—a practice associated with the Ku Klux Klan, designed
to intimidate and threaten Black and other non-white people; was most likely
inspired by a scene in *The Birth of a Nation.*

Crusade for Voters—an organization founded in 1956 to increase
voter registration and political awareness, provide candidate recommendations,
and push for equal political job opportunities for the Black Richmond
community.

Curse of Ham—a reference to Genesis 9 in the Bible, which describes an instance of Noah cursing his son Ham's descendants to be slaves; in later centuries, the narrative was incorrectly interpreted by some as an explanation for dark skin, as well as a justification for slavery of Black people.

Curtis J. Holt, Sr. (1920-unknown)—a social activist in Richmond, VA, who led campaigns on issues of both race and class.

David and Goliath—the battle between the Philistine giant, Goliath, and a young David, as described in the Book of Samuel in the Bible.

Diane Nash (b. 1938)—Civil Rights activist whose work included co-founding the SNCC, leading the 1960 Nashville sit-ins, and helping guide the Freedom Riders; was awarded the Presidential Medal of Freedom in 2022.

Dillard University—an HBCU in New Orleans, LA, founded in 1930 and incorporating earlier institutions of higher learning founded as early as 1869.

"Dixie" (song)—first made in 1859, a song about the South that became the unofficial anthem of the Confederacy; has remained popular with some white Southerners into modern times; "Dixie" has also since become a nickname for the South.

Douglas Wilder (b. 1931)—a lawyer and politician who served as Governor of Virginia from 1990-1994; the first African American to serve as governor of a U.S. state since Reconstruction.

Dunbar Theatre—first opened in 1916, the first African American-owned theatre to operate in Baltimore; closed in 1958.

Earl Theatre—first built in 1924, a prominent theatre in Philadelphia, PA for big band jazz music in the 1930s and 40s; closed in 1953.

Ebony—a monthly magazine founded in 1945 by John H. Johnson (also the founder of *Jet* magazine and *Negro Digest/Black World*), focused on news, culture, and entertainment for a Black audience.

Emancipation Proclamation (1863)—a proclamation and executive order by President Abraham Lincoln on January 1st, 1863, during the Civil War, that declared all enslaved persons in the secessionist states to be free;

also allowed for formerly enslaved people to be received into the armed services of the United States; its issuance redefined the Civil War for the North as a fight for freedom.

Emmett Till (1941–1955)—a 14-year-old African American boy who was abducted, tortured, and lynched in Mississippi in 1955; his murder and the fact that his killers were acquitted drew nationwide attention to the racial violence and injustice prevalent in the South and galvanized many African Americans to join the Civil Rights Movement.

Episcopal—a mainline Protestant denomination, first organized after the American Revolution, and part of the worldwide Anglican Communion.

Equal Employment Opportunity Commission (EEOC)—a federal agency established via the Civil Rights Act of 1964 to administer and enforce federal civil rights laws against workplace discrimination.

Ernie Green (b. 1941)—a member of the Little Rock Nine.

Fair Housing Act (1968)—a federal law, signed by Lyndon B. Johnson during the Martin Luther King, Jr. assassination riots, that prohibited discrimination concerning the sale, rental, and financing of housing based on race, religion, national origin, or sex; considered the final great legislative achievement of the Civil Rights Movement.

Fannie Lou Hamer (1917–1977)—a civil rights activist at the forefront of the Movement in Mississippi; worked with SNCC to organize the 1964 Freedom Summer voter registration drive in the state; at the 1964 Democratic National Convention, was vice-chair of the Mississippi Freedom Democratic Party, who openly challenged the legality of the state's all-white, segregated delegation.

Farm Service Agency—an agency of the U.S. Department of Agriculture that supports farms and farming communities.

Federal Deposit Insurance Corporation (FDIC)—an independent agency created by Congress during the Great Depression to maintain stability and public trust in the nation's financial system (by insuring deposits, examining and supervising financial institutions, etc).

Federal Home Loan Bank Board—a board created in 1932 that governed the Federal Home Loan Banks, the Federal Savings and Loan Insurance Corporation, and nationally-chartered thrifts; it was abolished and superseded by the Federal Housing Finance Board and the Office of Thrift Supervision in 1989.

Fillmore District—historical neighborhood in San Francisco, CA, that was a hub for many different ethnic groups, including African Americans; the center of the music scene in the city, especially jazz; became a target of urban renewal which led to the removal of many Black residents after the 1960s.

Fisk University—an HBCU in Nashville, TN, founded in 1866, shortly after the Civil War; the oldest institution of higher learning in the city.

Florida A&M University—an HBCU in Tallahassee, FL, founded in 1887; the first modern HBCU marching band, the Marching "100", was created here in 1946.

Ford Motor Company—automobile manufacturer founded in 1903 and headquartered in Dearborn, MI (near Detroit); jobs like those at Ford were a major reason many African Americans moved North during the Great Migration.

Fort Valley State University—an HBCU in Fort Valley, GA, founded in 1895.

Fourteenth Amendment (1868)—the Constitutional amendment which granted citizenship to all persons "born or naturalized in the United States," including formerly enslaved people, and provided all citizens with "equal protection under the laws," extending the provisions of the Bill of Rights to the states, among other rulings; also gave Congress the power to enforce this amendment, which eventually led to the passage of the landmark Civil Rights legislation a century later.

Frederick Douglass (1817/1818–1895)—a social reformer, abolitionist, orator, writer, and statesman; after escaping slavery in Maryland, he became one of the principal leaders of the abolitionist movement, and after the Civil War continued to push efforts for racial equality and later women's rights; author of numerous notable autobiographies and speeches.

Freedmen (Native American)—formerly enslaved African Americans of the Five Tribes of Oklahoma in the Southeastern U.S. (the Choctaw, Chickasaw, Cherokee, Muskogee, and Seminole Nations); citizenship status within these tribes has been largely denied to Freedmen ever since; the term also applies to their descendants.

Freedom Riders—groups of white and African American civil rights activists who participated in bus trips (Freedom Rides) through the American South in 1961 to protest segregated buses and bus terminals.

G.I. Bill (1944)—colloquial name for the Servicemen's Readjustment Act, passed to provide benefits to WWII veterans including low-cost mortgages, low-interest loans, and educational benefits; Black veterans experienced discrimination in the distribution of these benefits, but nonetheless the bill helped expand the population of African Americans attending college and graduate school.

George Herriman (1880-1944)—cartoonist of mixed-race Creole descent, best known for the comic strip *Krazy Kat*.

George Wallace (1919-1998)—politician who served as governor of Alabama for four terms in the 1960s-80s; staunch supporter of Jim Crow laws.

Golden Frinks (1920-2004)—civil rights activist and field secretary of the SCLC; the principal organizer in North Carolina during the 1960s, known as "The Great Agitator."

Gone With the Wind—a 1939 film, based on the 1936 novel by Margaret Mitchell, that is the highest-grossing (adjusting for inflation) in history; it has been criticized for glorifying slavery and the mythology of the Lost Cause of the Confederacy.

Great Debaters of Wiley College—the debate team of Wiley College, founded and coached by Melvin B. Tolson in 1924, which traveled around the country and was a pioneer in interracial collegiate debates; in 1935, they defeated the national champion debate team from the University of Southern California; James Farmer was a prominent team member.

Great Migration—the relocation of more than 6 million African Americans from the rural South to the cities of the North, Midwest, and West from about 1916-1970, driven by Jim Crow and the attraction of jobs.

Gwen Ifill (1955-2016)—journalist, newscaster, and author; the first African American woman to host a nationally televised U.S. public affairs program.

Hampton University—an HBCU in Hampton, VA, founded in 1868 as Hampton Agricultural and Industrial School.

Harlem—neighborhood in Upper Manhattan, NYC; it became a major destination for Black Americans during the Great Migration and has remained a center of Black American cultural life to this day.

Harlem Renaissance—an intellectual and cultural revival of African American arts, politics, and scholarship, centered in Harlem, NY, from roughly the end of WWI (1917) to the onset of the Great Depression and WWII (1930s); also known as the Black Renaissance.

HBCU marching bands—marching bands at HBCU schools, which have formed their own particular styles and traditions since the 1940s and are often centers of school cultural life and ambassadors for schools outside of campus.

Henry Leander Marsh III (b. 1933)—civil rights lawyer and politician; first African American mayor of Richmond, VA.

Henry Louis Gates, Jr. (b. 1950)—literary critic, scholar, professor, historian, and filmmaker.

Hill Street Baptist Church—started in 1915 in Asheville, NC; when led by Reverend E.W. Dixon, published and distributed one of the first black newspapers in Asheville, *The Church Advocate*; was led by Reverend Nilous

McKinley and Mrs. Christine Watson Avery for decades [Author's note: My grandparents!].

Historically Black Colleges and Universities (HBCUs)—institutions of higher learning that were established before the Civil Rights Act (1964) with the intention of primarily serving the African American community; many of these schools were founded in the decades after the Civil War and are located in the South.

Home Mortgage Disclosure Act (1975)—a law requiring many financial institutions to provide mortgage data to the public, to ensure they are serving the housing needs of communities and to shed light on lending patterns that could be discriminatory.

Howard Theatre—a theatre in Washington, DC, founded in 1910 and continuing to this day; billed as the "Theatre for the People," it was known for catering to an African American clientele and featured many top musical acts in its heyday.

Howard University—an HBCU in Washington, DC, founded in 1867.

Huey P. Newton (1942-1989)—co-founder and Minister of Defense for the Black Panther Party.

Integration—the process of leveling barriers to association, creating equal opportunities regardless of race, and the development of a culture that draws on diverse traditions, rather than merely bringing a racial minority into the majority one; includes the process of desegregation, but desegregation is considered largely a legal matter, whereas integration largely a social one.

Jackie Ormes (1911-1985)—cartoonist known for characters such as Torchy Brown, Candy, Patty-Jo, and Ginger, which countered stereotypical images of Black Americans in the mainstream press; the first African American woman to have a regularly published comic strip.

James Brown (1933-2006)—entertainer, record producer, and bandleader.

James Farmer (1920-1999)—leader in the Civil Rights Movement who co-founded CORE and initiated and organized the first Freedom Ride.

Jeanes supervisors—a group of African American teachers who worked in southern rural schools and communities between 1908-1968; established by white Quaker philanthropist Anna T. Jeanes and Booker T. Washington.

Jet—a weekly magazine founded in 1951 by John H. Johnson (also the founder of *Ebony* magazine and *Negro Digest/Black World*) focused on news, culture, and entertainment for a Black audience; the magazine was notable for its coverage of the Civil Rights movement, including the murder of Emmett Till, the Montgomery bus boycott, and the activities of Martin Luther King, Jr.

Jim Crow laws—state and local laws that enforced racial segregation in the South; generally these laws were ended by the Civil Rights Act in 1964 and Voting Rights Act in 1965; the name derives from the song "Jump Jim Crow," performed in blackface by white actor Thomas D. Rice beginning in 1828, which led to the term "Jim Crow" becoming a pejorative term for Black Americans in the 19th century.

John and Jane Doe warrants—a warrant for the arrest of a person whose name is unknown.

John Chavis (1763-1838)—minister, teacher, abolitionist, and the first African American to graduate from a college or university in the U.S.; he founded a school in Raleigh, NC, in 1808 that taught Black and white children.

John F. Kennedy (1917-1963)—35th U.S. president from 1961-1963.

John Lee Hooker (1917-2001)—blues singer, songwriter, and guitarist.

John Lewis (1940-2020)—politician and civil rights activist who was a leader in the Civil Rights Movement—participating in the Nashville sit-ins, the Freedom Rides, the March on Washington, Bloody Sunday, and as chairman of the SNCC—and served as a member of the U.S. House of Representatives for 17 terms.

Johnson Publishing—a media company founded in 1942 by John H. Johnson (1918-2005) in Chicago, IL, that published notable African American magazines like *Ebony, Jet,* and *Negro Digest* (later *Black World*).

Juilliard School—performing arts conservatory in New York City.

Julian Bond (1940-2015)—civil rights activist, politician, professor, and writer who helped establish the SNCC and the Southern Poverty Law Center.

Krystal's—fast food restaurant chain based in the Southeast.

Ku Klux Klan (KKK)—white supremacist, right-wing terrorist, and hate group; has existed in three primary periods (during the Reconstruction Era; in the 1910s-20s; and in the early 1940s-60s).

Langston Hughes (1901-1967)—poet, novelist, and playwright; prominent figure of the Harlem Renaissance.

Langston University—an HBCU in Langston, OK; the only HBCU in the state.

"Lift Every Voice and Sing"—a hymn with lyrics by James Weldon Johnson (1871-1938) and set to music by his brother, J. Rosamond Johnson (1873-1954); after its first recitation in 1900, the hymn was communally sung within African American communities, and in 1917, the NAACP began promoting it as the "Negro National Anthem."

Literacy tests—tests which claimed to create an educated and informed electorate, but in practice, especially in the South, were used to prevent African Americans particularly from registering to vote.

Little Rock Nine—the nine teenagers who were the first African American students to integrate Little Rock's Central High School in 1957 following *Brown v. The Board of Education* in 1954; the resistance of white mobs drew national attention and eventually the U.S. Army and National Guard to protect the students.

Los Angeles Sentinel—Black-owned weekly newspaper established in 1933.

Lynching—the extrajudicial killing of someone by a group; in the U.S., during the period between Reconstruction up until the Civil Rights Era, thousands of African Americans were lynched in a widespread campaign of racial terror designed to enforce subordination and segregation.

Lyndon B. Johnson (1908-1973)—36th U.S. president from 1963-1969; signed many of the principal civil rights legislation, including the Civil Rights Act of 1964, Voting Rights Act of 1965, and the Civil Rights Act of 1968 (which included the Fair Housing Act).

Malcolm X (1925-1965)—a primary leader of the Black Power movement, initially within the Nation of Islam, who advocated for liberation "by any means necessary."

Manpower Development and Training Act (1962)—legislation designed to train and retrain thousands of workers unemployed because of technological change.

March on Washington for Jobs and Freedom (1963)—a massive protest march for Black civil and economic rights involving some 250,000 people; helped lead to the passing of the Civil Rights Act of 1964; the occasion of Martin Luther King, Jr.'s "I Have a Dream" speech.

Margaret Bonds (1913-1972)—composer, pianist, arranger, and teacher; one of the first African American composers to gain recognition in the U.S.; frequently collaborated with Langston Hughes (for ex, the cantata *The Ballad of the Brown King*); daughter of Monroe Alpheus Majors.

Martha's Vineyard—an island off the coast of Massachusetts that is a popular summer destination with a long-standing Black community.

Martin Luther King, Jr. (1929-1968)—minister and activist; the most prominent leader of the Civil Rights Movement and practitioner of nonviolent civil disobedience.

Mary McLeod Bethune (1875-1955)—educator, civil and women's rights leader, government official, and advisor to President Franklin

Delano Roosevelt; founder of the National Council of Negro Women and the school that eventually became Bethune-Cookman University.

Mason-Dixon Line—the demarcation line between the states of Pennsylvania, Maryland, Delaware, and West Virginia; informally the demarcation between the North and South.

Maxine Waters (b. 1938)—politician who has served in the U.S. House of Representatives for 15 terms; the most senior of the 12 Black women serving in Congress.

Medgar Evers (1925-1963)—civil rights activist and the NAACP's first field officer in Mississippi; led an investigation into the murder of Emmett Till; himself murdered by a white supremacist and member of the Ku Klux Klan.

Melvin B. Tolson (1898-1966)—poet, professor, and essayist; coached the Great Debaters of Wiley College.

Melvyn R. Leventhal (b. 1943)—white Jewish lawyer who worked for the NAACP's Legal Defense Fund in Mississippi during the Civil Rights Movement; together with Alice Walker was the first legally married interracial couple in the state.

Methodist—a mainline group of Protestant denominations following the teachings of John Wesley, first begun in the early 18th-century.

Metropolitan Opera House—opera house on the Upper West Side of Manhattan.

Milton Caniff (1907-1988)—white cartoonist famous for the *Terry and the Pirates* and *Steve Canyon* comic strips.

Mississippi Delta—the northwestern portion of the state of Mississippi (and actually the delta of the Yazoo River); some of the most fertile agricultural land in the world.

Mississippi Valley State University—an HBCU in Itta Bena, MS, founded in 1950.

Monroe Alpheus Majors (1864-1960)—physician, civil rights leader, and writer, and the first Black physician to practice medicine west of the Rocky Mountains; author of *Noted Negro Women*, a book of biographies; father of Margaret Bonds.

Morehouse College—an HBCU in Atlanta, GA, founded in 1867; the largest men's liberal arts college in the U.S.

Morgan State University—an HBCU in Baltimore, MD, founded in 1867 as Morgan College.

Morrie Turner (1923-2014)—cartoonist most famous for the creation of *Wee Pals*, the first American syndicated strip with an integrated cast of characters.

Motortown Revue—the package concert tours given by Motown Records musical artists throughout the U.S. in the 1960s.

Mulatto—a person of mixed white and Black ancestry.

Murder of James Chaney, Andrew Goodman, and Michael Schwerner—the murder of three civil rights activists who had been working on the Freedom Summer campaign to register African American voters in Mississippi; the three men—one Black, two white and Jewish—were killed by the Ku Klux Klan.

National Archives—a federal agency charged with the preservation and documentation of government and historical records.

National Association for the Advancement of Colored People (NAACP)—an organization founded in 1909 to address ongoing violence and discrimination against Black people; a prominent group during the Civil Rights Movement through the present.

National Conference of Christians and Jews (NCCJ)—a social justice organization founded in 1927; their name was changed in the 1990s to the National Conference for Community and Justice to better reflect the breadth and depth of its mission.

National Urban League—a civil rights organization founded in 1910 and based in New York City, dedicated to economic empowerment, equality, and social justice for African Americans and other historically underserved groups; the oldest and largest community-based organization of its kind.

Negro Digest—a publication founded in 1942 by John H. Johnson (also the publisher of *Jet* and *Ebony* magazines) seeking to evoke the format of *Reader's Digest* for a Black audience; in its heyday was a major forum for black writers and intellectuals; later known as *Black World*.

Negro Motorist Green Book—a guidebook published from the 1930s-60s, originated and published by Harlem mailman Victor Hugo Green (1892-1960), that provided a list of hotels, boarding houses, taverns, restaurants, service stations, and other establishments throughout the country that served African American patrons; an indispensable resource for the era's successful Black-owned businesses and rising Black middle class.

New Journal and Guide—newspaper based in Norfolk, VA, founded in 1900, focusing on local and national African American news, sports and issues; formerly called the *Journal and Guide* and the *Norfolk Journal and Guide*; at one point during WWII was the largest Black employer in the South.

Nikita Khrushchev (1894-1971)—leader of the Soviet Union from 1953-1964.

Nonviolent civil disobedience—the active, professed refusal of a citizen to obey certain laws or commands in order to effect change; the primary tactic of the Civil Rights Movement.

Normal school—an institution created to train teachers, usually for primary schools.

North Carolina A&T State University—an HBCU in Greensboro, NC, founded in 1891 as the Agricultural and Mechanical College for the Colored Race; the largest HBCU in the U.S.

North Carolina Central University—an HBCU in Durham, NC, founded in 1909.

The O'Jays—R&B group, originally formed in 1958.

Office of the Comptroller of the Currency—an independent bureau in the U.S. Treasury that charters, regulates, and supervises all national banks, federal savings associations, and federal branches and agencies of foreign banks.

Oklahoma Eagle—Black-owned newspaper founded in 1922 and based in Tulsa, OK; successor to the *Tulsa Star*, which burned in the 1921 Tulsa race massacre, and one of the only newspapers to report on the event.

Ollie Harrington (1912-1995)—political cartoonist and advocate for civil rights; his most famous comic strip was *Dark Laughter* (later renamed *Bootsie* after the popular main character), the first Black comic strip to receive national recognition.

Oral tradition—a form of communication that passes knowledge, art, ideas, and cultural material orally from one generation to the other, either without or parallel to a writing system.

Passing—when a member of one racial group is accepted or perceived as a member of another; usually used to describe a Black or brown person passing amongst the white majority.

Paul Laurence Dunbar (1872-1906)—poet, novelist, and short story writer; one of the first African American writers to achieve international renown.

Peg Leg Bates (1907-1998)—dancer and entertainer.

Perry Mason—fictional criminal defense lawyer of books, TV shows, movies, and radio, known for his decency and honesty.

Philadelphia Tribune—oldest continuously published African American newspaper in the U.S.

Pittsburgh Courier— African American weekly newspaper that published from 1907-1966, then re-opened by John H. Sengstacke (1912-1997; also the owner of the *Chicago Defender*) in 1967 as the *New Pittsburgh Courier*.

Players—a magazine from 1973-2005 that aimed to be the "Black *Playboy*."

Plessy v Ferguson (1896)—U.S. Supreme Court decision which upheld racial segregation laws provided that facilities for each race were equal in quality, leading to the "separate but equal" doctrine; the case stemmed from

Homer Plessy, a mixed-race man, deliberately boarding a "whites-only" train car in New Orleans, LA.

Poll tax—a payment required for voting, often used to restrict voting rights; abolished by the 24th Amendment in 1964 and a later decision by the Supreme Court in 1966.

Poor People's Campaign—a 1968 effort, led by Martin Luther King, Jr. and the SCLC, seeking economic justice for poor people in the United States; King embarked upon the campaign after seeing that gains in civil rights had not improved the material conditions of life for many African Americans; after King's assassination, the campaign was led by Ralph Abernathy.

Presbyterian—part of the Reformed tradition within Protestantism, with roots in the 16th-century teachings of John Calvin and John Knox.

Pullman porters—men hired to work as porters—assisting passengers— on railway sleeping cars operated by the Pullman Company; from the late 1860s till the 1960s, Pullman porters were exclusively Black, and helped contribute to the development of an African American middle class; the porters also formed the first all-Black union in 1925.

PWI (predominantly white institution)—an institution of higher learning in which white people account for 50% or greater of the student enrollment.

Ralph Abernathy (1926-1990)—minister and civil rights activist; close friend and mentor of Martin Luther King, Jr.; helped lead the Montgomery bus boycott, co-created the SCLC, and was president of the SCLC and led the Poor People's Campaign after King's assassination.

Raphael Warnock (b. 1969)—pastor and politician; current junior U.S. Senator from Georgia.

Ray Billingsley (b. 1957)—cartoonist and creator of the *Curtis* comic strip.

Reconstruction Era (1865-1877)—the turbulent era following the Civil War that involved the effort to integrate the former Confederate states and the 4 million newly freed African Americans into the U.S.

Red Cross—international non-profit humanitarian organization.

Redistricting—the process of redrawing the lines for voting districts in a given area; when done to favor a particular party or demographic, known as gerrymandering.

Redlining—discriminatory practice in which services (i.e. credit, insurance, healthcare, etc) are withheld from potential customers who reside in neighborhoods classified as "hazardous" to investment; the term originates from government homeownership programs that used color-coded maps to rank the loan worthiness of neighborhoods and discriminated against Black neighborhoods.

Regal Theater—a night club, theater, and music venue in Chicago popular among African Americans from 1928-1968.

Resolution Trust Corporation—a temporary federal agency from 1989-1995 that helped resolve the savings and loan crisis of the 1980s.

Richard Pryor (1940-2005)—stand-up comedian and actor.

Ron Brown (1941-1996)—politician who served as the chairman of the Democratic National Committee (DNC) and the U.S. Secretary of Commerce during Bill Clinton's first term, the first African American to serve in either position; killed in a plane crash in Croatia in 1996.

Rosenwald school building program—a project that led to the construction of over 5,000 schools, shops, and teacher homes to educate African American children in the South; begun in 1913 by Booker T. Washington and Julius Rosenwald (1862-1932), the latter a white Jewish businessman then the head of Sears, Roebuck & Company; by 1928, Rosenwald Schools made up more than one in five Black schools operating throughout the South.

Royal Theatre—theatre and music venue in Baltimore for Black audiences; first opened as the Douglass Theatre in 1922 and closed in 1971.

Samuel Houston (1793-1863)—Texas general and statesman; slaveholder.

Sanford and Son—TV sitcom that ran from 1972-1977.

School-to-prison pipeline—education and public safety
policies that push students into the criminal legal system; also refers to the
disproportionate tendency of minors and young adults from disadvantaged
backgrounds to become incarcerated because of increasingly harsh school and
municipal policies.

Segregation—the systematic separation of people into racial or other
ethnic groups in daily life, in realms such as housing, medical care, education,
employment, and transportation; in the context of the U.S., refers primarily to
the separation between white and Black people.

Separate but equal—the legal doctrine that racial segregation did
not violate the Fourteenth Amendment as long as all facilities provided were equal;
in effect following the Civil War and confirmed by the Supreme Court in *Plessy v.
Ferguson* (1896); in practice, the separate facilities provided to African Americans
were rarely equal, and usually were not even close or did not exist at all.

Sharecropping—a system where the landlord allows a tenant to use the
land in exchange for a share of the crop produced; in the South, implemented
after the Civil War by white landowners to farm crops like cotton and tobacco;
many Black Americans were severely limited by this system.

Shaw University—an HBCU in Raleigh, NC, founded in 1865; the oldest
HBCU to begin offering classes in the South.

Sit-ins—a form of nonviolent direct action that involves one or more people
occupying an area for a protest, often to promote political, social, or economic
change; during the Civil Rights Movement, many sit-ins were performed at
lunch counters and other establishments to protest segregation.

Smithsonian Institution—the world's largest museum, education,
and research complex, based in Washington, DC.

Social Security—social insurance program consisting of retirement,
disability, and survivor benefits.

**Southern Christian Leadership Conference
(SCLC)**—a civil rights organization founded by Martin Luther King, Jr. and

others following the Montgomery bus boycott in 1957 to coordinate nonviolent direct action throughout the South, drawing especially on the support of the Black church.

Southern Regional Council—a reform-oriented organization based in Atlanta, GA, and founded in 1944 which seeks to promote voter registration, political awareness, and racial equality.

Spelman College—a historically women's HBCU in Atlanta, GA, founded in 1881 as the Atlanta Baptist Female Seminary.

Spirituals—genre of Christian music by Black Americans dating back to the era of slavery, combining African musical traditions and European Christian hymns (e.g. "Steal Away" and "Couldn't Hear Nobody Pray"); originally passed down as an oral tradition and brought to a wider audience by groups like the Fisk Jubilee Singers and the Hampton Singers in the late 19th and early 20th centuries; many subsequent genres of music derive from it, i.e. blues, gospel, and jazz, and consequently R&B, rock 'n' roll, hip hop, etc.

Standard Industrial Classification (SIC) codes—a government system for classifying industries.

Stephens-Lee High School—a school for African American students and pillar of the Black community in Asheville, NC; first opened in 1923 and closed in 1965.

Stillman College—an HBCU in Tuscaloosa, AL, founded in 1875 as the Tuscaloosa Institute.

Stokely Carmichael (1941-1998; later known as Kwame Ture)—prominent leader within the Civil Rights and Black Power movements; succeeded John Lewis as the leader of SNCC.

Student Nonviolent Coordinating Committee (SNCC)—the principal group for students participating in the Civil Rights Movement; emerged from student-led sit-ins at segregated lunch counters in Greensboro, NC, and Nashville, TN.

Talented tenth—a term associated with W. E. B. Du Bois, referring to a Black intellectual elite who might acquire education and become directly involved in social change for the entire race.

Ted Shearer (1919-1992)—cartoonist and advertising art director who created the *Quincy* comic strip, one of the first mainstream comics with an African American lead.

Tennessee State University—an HBCU in Nashville, TN, founded in 1912; known earlier as Tennessee A&I State College.

Vernon Jordan (1935-2021)—civil rights attorney and business executive who participated in the Civil Rights Movement and eventually became a close advisor to Bill Clinton.

Virginia State University—an HBCU in Ettrick, VA, founded in 1882.

Virginia Union University—an HBCU in Richmond, VA, founded in 1865 as the Richmond Theological Institute.

Voting Rights Act (1965)—a law enacted in 1965 that prohibited racial discrimination in voting; a major achievement of the Civil Rights Movement.

W. E. B. Du Bois (1868-1963)—sociologist, socialist, historian, and Pan-Africanist civil rights activist; co-founder of the NAACP and the Niagara Movement; author of *The Souls of Black Folk, Dusk of Dawn,* and *Black Reconstruction in America* among other works; in contrast with Booker T. Washington, he advocated for political action, protest, and a civil rights agenda, and the importance of developing a Black intellectual elite.

Watch Night—late-night Christian service held on New Year's Eve; in the Black Church, the tradition stretches back to the night of December 31st, 1862, when congregants awaited the news of the Emancipation Proclamation taking effect.

West Hunter Street Baptist Church—prominent church in Atlanta, GA, founded in 1881.

Wiley College—an HBCU in Marshall, TX, founded in 1873.

Wiley Immanuel Lash (1908-1995)—first Black mayor of Salisbury, NC.

Will Eisner (1917-2005)—white cartoonist who created the series *The Spirit* and pioneered the graphic novel form.

William Randolph Hearst (1863-1951)—white businessman, politician, and newspaper publisher who founded Hearst Communications.

Willie Lynch letter—also known as the "Willie Lynch speech," an address purportedly delivered by a slaveholder named William Lynch in Virginia in 1712, regarding the best means of control of enslaved people within the colony (setting them against each other); since proven to be a hoax.

Woodrow Wilson (1856-1924)—28th U.S. President from 1913-1921, the first Southerner to be elected since Zachary Taylor in 1848; supporter of racial segregation and the Lost Cause mythology.

Woolworth's—chain of retail five-and-dime stores that were among the most successful and prevalent in America in the late 19th and 20th centuries.

Zora Neale Hurston (1891-1960)—author, anthropologist, and filmmaker; central figure in the Harlem Renaissance; author of *Their Eyes Were Watching God*.

ABOUT THE AUTHOR

Jaha Nailah Avery is an African American woman and proud Southerner. Hailing from Asheville, North Carolina, she received her law degree from the University of North Carolina at Chapel Hill, where she studied constitutional and civil rights law. She spent several years in the startup tech space before embarking on her professional writing career, and her work can be found in the *New York Times*, *Rolling Stone*, and *Architectural Digest*. She is a member of Delta Sigma Theta Sorority, Inc. and a Diamond Life member of the NAACP. Her aim is to always document, celebrate, and preserve the stories of Black people, communities, and history.

SOME NOTES ON THIS BOOK'S PRODUCTION

T he case, endpapers, and interiors were designed by Chindo Nkenke-Smith. The text was set by Westchester Publishing Services, in Danbury, CT, in Freight Big Pro, a type family created by American designer Joshua Darden, whose elegant strokes and serifs were designed to "knock someone's socks off but with the touch of a feather." The display was set in Termina, from American designer Mattox Shuler, characterized by its generously wide letterforms. The book was printed on FSC™-certified 90gsm Sappi Magno Natural Paper paper and bound in India.

Production supervised by Freesia Blizard
Editor: Nick Thomas
Assistant Editor: Irene Vázquez

LQ
LEVINE QUERIDO